irreverent guides

San Francisco

other irreverent guides: Amsterdam • Boston • Chicago
London • Manhattan • Miami • New Orleans • Paris
Santa Fe • Virgin Islands • Washington, D.C.

irreverent

San Fr

guides

ancisco

BY

LIZ BARRETT

A BALLIETT & FITZGERALD BOOK

MACMILLAN • USA

Where to eat ethnic...

Embarcadero Farmer's Market, see Getting Outside

Spot the Chili Peppers by the pool...

The Phoenix, see Accommodations

Get an in-room Shiatsu massage...

Miyako Hotel, see Accommodations

Taste the best focaccia in town...

Mario's Bohemian Cigar Store Café, see Dining

Appreciate chocolate as art...

Joseph Schmidt Confections, see Shopping

Horse around...

Golden Gate Park, see Getting Outside

Eat chops with Sam Spade...

John's Grill, see Dining

Shop with drag queens and strippers...

Piedmont Boutique, see Shopping

Dine on venison...

Cypress Club, see Dining

Pose in the trippiest hotel lobby...

The Hotel Triton, see Accommodations

Spend Sunday in the park.

Stow Lake, see Getting Outside

what's so irreverent?

It's up to you.

You can buy a traditional guidebook with its fluff, its promotional hype, its let's-find-something-nice-to-say-about-everything point of view. Or you can buy an Irreverent guide.

What the Irreverents give you is the lowdown, the inside story. They have nothing to sell but the truth, which includes a balance of good and bad. They praise, they trash, they weigh, and leave the final decisions up to you. No tourist board, no chamber of commerce will ever recommend them.

Our writers are insiders, who feel passionate about the cities they live in, and have strong opinions they want to share with you. They take a special pleasure leading you where other guides fear to tread.

How irreverent are they? One of our authors insisted on writing under a pseudonym. "I couldn't show my face in town again if I used my own name," she told me. "My friends would never speak to me." Such is the price of honesty. She, like you, should know she'll always have a friend at Frommer's.

Warm regards,

Michael Spring

Michael Spring
Publisher

a disclaimer

Prices fluctuate in the course of time, and travel information changes under the impact of the varied and volatile factors that influence the travel industry. Neither the author nor the publisher can be held responsible for the experiences of readers while traveling. Readers are invited to write to the publisher with ideas, comments, and suggestions for future editions.

about the authors

Liz Barrett is a lifelong resident of the San Francisco Bay Area who not only attended the first Human Be-In, but actually remembers it. Her articles have appeared in many national publications and have been syndicated by the *New York Times*. She has also been a special guest on National Public Radio.

Carl Corsi, who contributed to the Nightlife and Entertainment chapters, has been researching and writing the *San Francisco Nightlife Guide* (Insight Publications) since 1989.

photo credits

All photographs © 1995 by f-stop Fitzgerald Inc.

Balliett & Fitzgerald, Inc.
Series editor: Holly Hughes / Executive editor: Tom Dyja / Managing editor: Duncan Bock / Production editor: Howard Slatkin / Line editor: Chris Mitchell / Photo editors: Rachel Florman, Sue Canavan / Assistant editor: Maria Fernandez / Editorial assistants: Sam Weinman, Jennifer Leben Macmillan Travel Art director: Michele Laseau

Design by Tsang Seymour Design Studio

All maps © Simon & Schuster, Inc.

Air travel assistance courtesy of Continental Airlines

MACMILLAN TRAVEL
A Simon & Schuster Macmillan Company
1633 Broadway
New York, NY 10019

ISBN 0-02-860655-8
ISSN 1085-4835

special sales

Manufactured in the United States of America

contents

Introduction

San Francisco, so Rudyard Kipling said, "is a mad city inhabited by perfectly insane people whose women are of remarkable beauty." What he didn't say was that half of those women are men.

It is no secret that San Francisco is the gay capital of the world, but that is emphatically not the city's only personality. Olive O'Suddin, the roller-skating nun-in-drag who leads the peripatetic Sisters of Perpetual Indulgence, is a treasured icon here, no doubt about it, but so is Herb Caen, the venerable *Chronicle* gossip columnist who once dubbed the city "Baghdad by the Bay" and can still make or break a new restaurant with one flick of his fork.

That counterpoise is precisely what makes San Francisco such a great city. You can go to the opera in blue jeans or have a hamburger in a tuxedo. Let a snooty doorman in white gloves carry your Louis Vuitton luggage into the Fairmont Hotel on (S)Nob Hill or toss it into a rental car and check into the Phoenix, a funky Tenderloin motel where John F. Kennedy Jr. once got double-booked into a room with ex-Blondie star Debbie Harry. Dress in black from head to toe and squish belly-to-butt with the South of Market hordes at Slim's, a nightclub started by musician Boz Scaggs, or dust off your gold sequins and sip champagne at Bimbo's 365, a swank time-warp supper club where you almost expect to see Lucy and Ricky Ricardo at the next table, especially when Tito Puente is on-stage.

Do anything you want, any way you want, and you'll fit right in. Visitors, in fact, tend to feel so simpatico with San Francisco that they can't resist comparing it to their own hometowns. New Yorkers justify their fondness for the city by saying it's not like the rest of the West, that it is the only city with any real culture west of the Mississippi (or west of the Hudson, for that matter). Europeans insist that San Francisco is much more like Europe than America. Even expatriates of cozy heartland locales have found parts of the city wonderfully familiar.

In truth, San Francisco is not New York at all, nor would it want to be. People don't come here to make the Big Time, they come to have a good time. When you sit down at a bar, fellow drinkers may well strike up a conversation with you, but you probably won't be asked what you do or where you went to school or who your daddy is. Frankly, nobody gives a damn. It's not that San Franciscans are indifferent or without ambition; it's just that they are more focused on a cordial lifestyle than on an impeccable pedigree. Besides, it wouldn't be polite to ask, and San Franciscans are nothing if not polite. (If you've ever attempted to negotiate the streets of New York in an automobile, you'll be relieved to know that Bay Area drivers do not cruise the city with their horns permanently engaged in the honk mode.)

There are also a few flaws in the whole San-Francisco-is-so-much-like-Europe idea. Being considered the Paris of the West is a compliment, one supposes, though it is highly doubtful that all those chain-smoking French existentialists would ever put up with San Francisco's tough no-smoking laws. Nor would the city's vigorous entrepreneurial mentality be likely to appeal to that crowd. It was suggested to one young French waiter, for example, that he was lucky to work for Alain Rondelli, the superb chef whose restaurant on Clement Street is one of the finest in the city. "Lucky?" he asked incredulously. "Lucky to have a job?"

"Ah, you are French," the customer replied.

The waiter smiled proudly. "To the bone," he said. Voilà.

North Beach is supposedly the most European-style neighborhood in the city. It's true that you can drop by Figone Hardware for a set of imported Italian boccie balls, but just down the block in Washington Square, dozens of Asian senior citizens gather on Sunday mornings for group tai-chi. You can observe this hardly European thing from a window seat across the street at Mario's Bohemian Cigar Store, a café with the best focaccia sandwiches in town.

Half-Italian, half-Asian, North Beach is also the very womb from which thoroughly American Beatniks originally sprang. It still houses Lawrence Ferlinghetti's City Lights Bookstore and Vesuvio's on opposite sides of Jack Kerouac Street as well as many other active beat volcanoes. Farther down the Columbus Avenue umbilical cord, psychedelic shops staffed by the progeny of sixties hippies sell original Fillmore concert posters for a small fortune and blast Richie Havens' albums at decibel levels that left their predecessors among the hearing-impaired. Lyle Tuttle, whose tattoo client list included Janis Joplin, has his own mini-museum in celebration of painted flesh. It's a fitting bookend to a neighborhood bordered on the other extreme by strip joints and peep parlors. You make the call; is this Europe?

It's easy to see how exiles from college towns find the Haight and the Mission District so familiar and yet still exotic enough to entice them. Both neighborhoods are constantly reinventing themselves, and each new incarnation includes remnants of past lives, like apartments that have collected eccentric odds and ends left behind by a succession of short-term tenants. The corner of Haight and Ashbury now houses a GAP and a Ben & Jerry's ice cream store, but the sidewalk is still a loitering ground for restless, purple-haired teenagers in tie-dyed T-shirts and leather jackets. The smell of illegal smoking materials is so thick, you can take a single deep breath in passing and get happy for the rest of the day. Within one 3-block stretch is the Piedmont Boutique, a glamorous gewgaw shop that caters to drag queens and strippers; Cha Cha Cha, one of the trendiest and most crowded tapas bars in the city; and Aub Zam Zam, home to a bartender who's famous for mixing what is commonly believed to be the best martini on the planet.

The Mission District is itself another planet, or so it seems. Part Latin Quarter and part New Bohemia, it mixes traditional Mexican and Central American culture with lesbians, beatniks, poets, musicians, artists, hipsters, and assorted pretenders of virtually every urban persuasion. Vivid murals dress the neighborhood (especially 24th Street) like a Diego Rivera fantasy, and virtually every corner taqueria is worth a taste-stop. The sidewalks on Mission Street are trimmed in bright orange-and-blue tiles, and the center of the barrio is lined with palm trees. Yet a block away, cafés, bookstores, restaurants, bars, nightclubs, and a vibrator museum have turned Valencia Street into "the hippest hood in the city," according to Chip Conley, whose lively hotels have lodged everyone from Brenda Lee to Nirvana. Valencia Street is no gentrification project, though. It retains a low-rent, funky feeling and a solid respect for the Latin culture in which it is centered. While punk cha-cha bands play at the Elbo Room, mariachis stroll a few doors down to play a few tunes and pass the hat at La Rondalla, and live jazz may be on the menu at Radio Valencia. It's casual. It's friendly. It's inexpensive. It's like taking a vacation to two completely different and equally festive countries at the same time. There's no place like it anywhere else.

Nor is there any place like San Francisco itself—much to the relief of conservative talk show hosts and other petulant patriots, who often liken the place to Sodom and Gomorrah. Face it, the city has always been a haven for those who are a tad on the weird side by Presbyterian standards. That's why people came out here in the first place—to escape from the oppressive conventions of an East Coast dominated by Old World principles, and that's essentially why they keep on coming. If San Francisco had a Statue of Liberty, she would beckon, "Send us your odd, your bizarre masses, your tired beatniks, ancient hippies, drag queens, poets, and artists, your temperamental opera singers and recalcitrant pastry chefs, your feminist firebugs and immortal quarterbacks, your transsexual tennis players yearning to be free."

Lest you get the idea that the entire city is an alternative universe populated strictly by the cast of *La Cage Aux Folles*, it should be clearly stated for the record that scads of utterly "normal" people reside in San Francisco's many diverse districts, from the breezy bayside Marina to the steep cliffs that bounce crashing waves back out to the Pacific Ocean. The Sunset District seems like a middle-class suburb, cut off from the city's clamor by Twin Peaks and Golden Gate Park. The Marina has a Safeway where singles congregate to squeeze more than the melons, but the neighborhood also houses little old ladies and upwardly mobile lawyers alongside millionaire ballplayers and stately yachtsmen. St. Francis Woods is a hidden, fairy-tale neighborhood with private drives and storybook houses. Pacific Heights renamed Specific Whites by *Betty and Pansy's Severe Queer Review* is a beautifully manicured enclave for San Francisco's richest and most powerful elite. (There is a pit bull inside one of those gigantic Victorian mansions, but the discreet sign merely warns: "Chien bizarre." Apparently they expect their burglars to speak French.) The modern apartment complexes in Twin Peaks could be in Pocatello, Idaho, and no one would know the difference, at least not from an architectural standpoint.

The irresistible beauty of San Francisco lies in its gentle refusal to fit into any mold, beginning with the very ground upon which it is built—steep hills and wide valleys dropping off suddenly at the edge of the continent. It's cold in the summer and warm in the winter, with sudden and notable exceptions, of course. It has been struck by earthquakes that would have destroyed other cities, but merely brought out the best in San Francisco. During the 1989 earthquake, a New York sports writer who happened to be here covering the World Series at Candlestick Park observed, "If this had happened at Yankee Stadium, we all would have been trampled to death in a stampede." Not here. Ordinary citizens jumped out of their cars and directed traffic on the streets. Plumbers, truck drivers, and major league ballplayers climbed into the rubble with rescue workers to try to save people trapped in the collapsed freeway. There was virtually no violent crime on record for nearly three days—no looting, no rioting, not even any hoarding of supplies. When the World Series resumed three weeks later, 64,000 people—some wearing hard hats just in case—joined hands and sang out with homegrown rock icons Jefferson Starship: "We built this city on rock and roll."

That is it. That is why Tony Bennett left his heart here. That is why Betty and Pansy offer visitors the following advice: "Give yourself one year, and then if you don't like San Francisco, you can leave....San Francisco is a wonderful place to change your mind. Nobody holds you to yesterday's decision."

San Francisco Neighborhoods

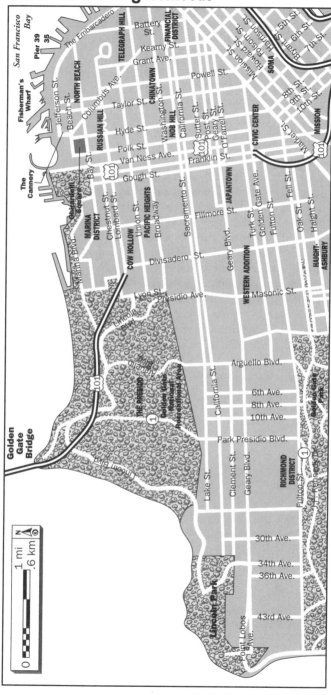

you probably didn't know

Can I call it Frisco?... Most locals would sooner hear fingernails scratching across a chalkboard. "Frisco" sounds too much like "Vegas" or some other honky-tonk town. And it certainly doesn't suggest a place where you'd leave your heart. In any case, it is best to skip the indelicate nickname unless you're willing to accept dirty looks, slow service, and tables by the ladies' room.

Where are the best "vertigo views" of the city?... Standing at the top of some of San Francisco's steeper hills, you may feel a tad trembly and nauseous, like Jimmy Stewart in the Hitchcock film *Vertigo*. To heighten this sensation, take a glass-elevator ride, available for free in several of San Francisco's elegant hotels. The Westin Saint Francis (Union Square) has the fastest elevator in the city, ascending at 1,000 feet per minute. If you can keep your eyelids up and your stomach down, you'll catch panoramic views of downtown, Coit Tower, and the bay. Around the corner from the Saint Francis, the Pan-Pacific Hotel has a 17-story ride, but the cars face the inside of the building, looking onto an atrium that's one of the most elegant in the city. Five blocks away, at the Fairmont Hotel, take the skylift, which zips up at about 100 feet per minute to the Fairmont Crown, 24 floors up, for a leisurely view of Chinatown, Nob Hill, the Financial District, Coit Tower, and the South Bay Peninsula. Beware of small weddings in the elevators—they can seriously cramp your view. Down at the Embarcadero Center, the Hyatt Regency's glass lifts take you to a revolving restaurant/cocktail lounge that offers a great 360-degree view and ridiculously overpriced drinks that invariably include the requisite hardware—paper umbrellas, swizzle sticks, pineapple chunks, you name it. Mel Brooks panicked on the way up here in *High Anxiety*.

Where's the best place to hop on a cable car?... When you catch a ride on a cable car—yes, they do look like the ones in the Rice-A-Roni commercials and, yes, they do ring those bells—don't wait in line with all the tourists at the turnaround stops at the beginning and end of the lines. Walk a few blocks up the line (follow the tracks) and do as the locals do: Hop on when the car stops, hang on to a pole, and have your $2 ready to hand to the driver. He'll take coins or bills, and can even make change. Warning: Don't stand too close behind the gripman or his elbow might smash into your chest when he yanks the brake to stop the car. And whatever you do, don't call them "trolleys"—you'll be branded instantly as a tourist.

How does one dress for fog al fresco?... From June through August—summertime in the rest of the Western world—fog tends to engulf San Francisco from late afternoon until noon the next day. If you are a baseball fan, you'll soon discover that Candlestick (Now 3Com) Park is equipped with one of the bay's 26 foghorns, which comes in handy at chilly night games. Locals don't mind the mist, though. They dress in layers and immerse themselves in it. To make the most of a glorious foggy morning, sip a frothy cappuccino in a cozy neighborhood cafe until around noon, when the fog burns off and you can tie your sweater around your waist, roll up your shirtsleeves, and soak up the sun for a few hours. And no matter what the weather seems like during the day, always bring a coat or jacket along at night.

What is meant by "basic black and perils?"... If you're going to wear black, stay out of the ocean. Sure, thousands of local surfers have worn black wetsuits and survived, but others have found Pacific sharks to be most unreasonable—their vision isn't all that great and they have a fierce appetite for sea lions, a hazardous combination for unidentified black-coated mammals floating around at suppertime. Fortunately wetsuits come in a variety of bright colors.

Where is the best place to park?... That's a question that baffles even the meter maids. A quick survey of the neighborhoods will reveal cars parked and double-parked on sidewalks, in front of fire hydrants, in towaway zones, on corners, in crosswalks and, in the Mission District, right down the middle of the street. The math is fairly simple: There are around 800,000 cars in the city on any given day, and less than 600,000 parking spaces. That adds up to 2.3 million parking tickets a year and unknown numbers of drivers still circling the city in a frenzy. There are some city-run garages that won't require you to mortgage your house in order to park for a few hours, but in most private garages you can pay up to $22.50 for a Friday night in popular areas like North Beach. Avoid the whole mess by using public transportation or cabs.

What's the best way to avoid getting mugged?... Muggers aren't a huge problem in San Francisco, but the city does have its share of pickpockets and other assorted scam artists who tend to prey on tourists. Standard rules of urban behavior apply: Don't keep your wallet in your rear pants pocket, and leave your purse at home or keep your hand on it all the time, especially when you're riding a bus (a favorite haunt of pickpockets). The favorite crime in San Francisco, actually, seems to be car vandalism, especially in the Mission District, where a car parked on the street for more than an hour has at least a 50/50 chance of getting its mirrors smashed. Solution: Take a cab.

What do you say to San Francisco cabbies?... The most-often-asked cabbie question in San Francisco is, "How often do you have to change your brakes?" Believe me, you don't want to know. One driver estimates that the hills are so treacherous he has to change his brakes once a week, while another casually replies, "Oh, a couple times a year, maybe." Either way, most drivers would rather avoid the topic, especially if you're headed down a grade that would rival K–2. Best advice: Forget the slope; look out the side windows instead.

What's the quickest way to get a date?... If you're a heterosexual type (fondly known as "breeders" by the gay community), in town alone and wishing you weren't, you might want to check out the Guardian's singles' events. A mixed bag of singles—shy desirables, curious newcomers, horny Hetero Sapiens, and, yes, some terminally unattractive loners—usually meet at a local watering hole, where some sort of appetizerish food-like substances are served; the Guardian throws in a free looking-for-love ad for attendant mixers and minglers. At least it's not sleazy, and who knows? Call the Guardian's Romance Hot Line (tel 415/552–5222) for information.

What's the best-kept secret about the symphony?... If you're a morning person who loves classical music, the San Francisco Symphony's open rehearsals have a seat with your name written on it. Before most major concerts, the symphony allows the public to attend final rehearsals at Davies Hall for just $15. Aside from the bargain-basement price, many afficionados prefer these rehearsals over the concerts because the music is equally as exquisite and you get to see and hear the performers and conductors in a relaxed, intimate circumstance. Most open rehearsals take place on Wednesday mornings, 9am to noon. They sell out quickly for popular international performers, so call the Symphony box office (tel 415/864–6000) for a schedule while you are still planning your trip, and order tickets in advance if possible.

Who was the last emperor?... Around the time of the Gold Rush, San Francisco was home to California's first monarch—not a butterfly or a drag queen, but a self-coronated royal who called himself Emperor Norton. (He also claimed to be Protector of Mexico.) Still commemorated 150 years later by a town that cherishes its oddballs, the emperor was a real, live person who got invited to all the society affairs, whether or not the city fathers believed his claims to sovereignty. The old codger had a lot of influence on local customs and was apparently quite an impressive figurehead. A century later he gained further immortality, portrayed as a close friend who visited Ben Cartwright at the Ponderosa on the television show "Bonanza." Even Hoss tipped his hat to His Majesty. If that's not proof of authenticity, what is?

How long has San Francisco been a gay capital?... During the Gold Rush, "real" women were so scarce that desperate prospectors gladly paid them 3 ounces of gold for a single kiss. No one knows how many enterprising impostors whipped out the Max Factor and painted their lips red to pick up a few extra nuggets back then, but mascara and falsies have rarely seen a sales slump since. According to Trevor Hailey, the city's premier gay historian, the city became an established haven for the gay lifestyle with the Gold Rush; then the opening of the Panama Canal led countless gay sailors to this port, followed by an influx of gay artists and entertainers during the Bohemian era of the twenties and thirties. World War II brought thousands of Pacific-bound military men—yes, queers in the armed forces, whether General Eisenhower knew it or not—many of whom returned after the war to live where their forbidden lifestyle was accepted. By the time the Beatnik movement bongoed to the cultural forefront in the fifties, there was no question that North Beach was the place for gay "angry young men" to proclaim their sexuality to the world. Every major city has a gay subculture, but there's nothing "sub" about San Francisco's gay culture—it is definitely a predominant and celebrated part of life here.

What does the future hold?... A *Chronicle* poll once estimated that 37 percent of Bay Area residents believe in astrology; virtually every newspaper in the city features a horoscope. The most eccentric is definitely Rob Brezsny's "Real Astrology" in *SF Weekly*. He might tell you that you are "the pothole in the road to ruin" or suggest that you "stroll on over to the oldest tree you know and pour a bottle of mountain spring water over your head while confessing all your sins."

What should you do if you fall in love with the city and decide to stay?... You're going to need a job, and the Westin Saint Francis Hotel just happens to be on a long-term job search for a dedicated coin-washer. Until a couple of years ago, every coin that was tendered at the hotel was put through a sort of tumbler that sterilized those copper pennies and Buffalo nickels so that no customer was ever given a coin in change that wasn't fit for the white glove test. The current manager regrets that the money laundering service, as it were, was indefinitely postponed when the career coinman retired; the hotel's human resource department has yet to find a candidate with the proper experience. Interested?

accomm

1

odations

Think about the
movie *Bullitt* for a
moment. Picture
Steve McQueen
in that manly
green Mustang,
screeching all over

San Francisco's steepest hills at the approximate speed of light. Then remember the two of them (Steve and the 'stang) pulling into a huge, semi-circular driveway in front of a palatial hotel with ultra-dignified doormen and an ornate lobby that seemed to have you-can't-afford-this written all over it. That memorable scene, in case you didn't already know, was filmed at the Fairmont Hotel.

Even the unflappable Gorbachevs, former First Family of the Soviet Union, were visibly dazzled when they saw the Fairmont in 1990. (Mr. G. said San Francisco is so beautiful people should be thankful they don't have to pay extra tax just to live there; Mrs. G. seemed to be fumbling in her purse, presumably for her American Express card.) Most visitors will never see the inside of the opulent $6,000-a-night penthouse suite—a three-bedroom, four-bath mini-mansion with an outdoor terrace, immense drawing room, grand piano, two-story circular library (4,000 volumes), dining room that seats fifty, 24-karat gold fixtures, lapus lazuli fireplace, secret passages, and its own vault. But the rest of the hotel is actually affordable by big-city luxury standards—rooms start at $189 a night. That's a bargain compared to equivalent accommodations in New York, London, Paris, or Tokyo.

The fact is, most of San Francisco's hundreds of lodgings are very reasonably priced, starting as low as $39 a night for adequate rooms at Marina motels; on the other end of the spectrum are overpriced rooms that appeal primarily to extravagant tourists and top out at about $500. But why spend a ton of money on a cookie-cutter room in a tourist-ridden downtown hotel when you could stay in real San Francisco for $69 a night at a place like the Phoenix, a Gilligan's-Island-meets-the-Jetsons motel where the grunge rock band Nirvana hid the eggs for the first annual Easter egg hunt?

When Luciano Pavarotti is in town, he stays at the elegant Inn at the Opera, a tiny, 25-foot-wide Victorian hotel with rooms from $115, where services include complimentary clothes pressing upon arrival and the Act IV restaurant, which is considered one of the most romantic, intimate spots in the city. Allen Ginsberg chose Hotel Bohème ($95 and up), a hip, cozy, and surprisingly quiet haven on Columbus Avenue, just footsteps away from City Lights Bookstore. Europeans love North Beach's hidden San Remo Hotel, a delightful three-story Italianate Victorian where rooms start at $35 and the penthouse, a funky little rooftop cottage with its own sundeck and a stunning panoramic view, is one of the best deals in the city at just $85 a night.

Neighborhood inns, bed-and-breakfast houses, and private rentals are plentiful in San Francisco. Many of them are historical buildings and have wonderful little gardens or afternoon teas to add to their allure. If, however, charm is not a consideration and money definitely is, there are several super-thrifty options, such as the YMCA, AYH hostels, and the infamous Green Tortoise Guest House, which also features cheapo bus tours (they like to call it "adventure travel"). There's even an RV park out by the Cal Trans station where you can hook up your Winnebago if camping in a gigantic parking lot on the edge of a city appeals to you.

Winning the Reservations Game

First of all, forget the major hotels if you're planning to visit in October. Some of them are almost fully booked 20 years in advance during that best-of-all-possible months in San Francisco. Don't let that discourage you, though—the most interesting places to stay, and the best deals, are rarely on the standard list of hotels that appear on travel agents' computer screens, so they don't get booked up so fast. San Francisco's tourist season is year-round, and hotel prices tend to remain fairly fixed throughout the year (some few increase April–October). You're not likely to find an off-season bargain rate around town, but many hotels, especially in tourist areas, offer special rates for multiple-night stays, including meals or discounts on tours and attractions. The deals range from downright pathetic—a free bottle of cheap, plastic-corked champagne and a Gray Line tour through Fisherman's Wharf—to the sumptuous, whimsical "romance packages" offered by the Joie de Vivre Hotels, including the Phoenix, the Commodore, the Nob Hill Lambourne, the Abigail, and the Archbishop's Mansion. Not all packages are advertised, so always ask the hotel or reservation agent if any are available. If you want to stick to the tourist-and-conventioneer circuit, last-minute vacancies and special discounts may be available through reservation services, most of which are computerized, so they know exactly which rooms are available. Many of these services offer 50%–75% discounts. Try **California Reservations** (tel 800/576–0003), **San Francisco Reservations** (tel 800/677–1550), **Central Reservations** (tel 800/548–3311), or **Hotel Reservations Network** (tel 800/964–6835). **Bed and Breakfast International** (tel 800/872–4500) can set you up in more than a hundred private homes, guest houses, and inns in San Francisco, starting at $55 a night (two-night minimum). Their specialty is matching travelers' tastes and

SAN FRANCISCO | ACCOMMODATIONS

budgets to their ideal place to stay, including private sublets of entire homes or apartments (two-week minimum) that often cost less than $45 a day. Owner/director Sharene Klein personally visits each property and can tell you absolutely everything about each place, from the kind of flowers that bloom in the garden to the owner's personality quirks. Tell her what kind of vacation you hope to have, and she'll put you in a place that's likely to make it happen. **American Property Exchange** (tel 800/747–7784) rents luxury apartments at $85–$275 a night; **Best of Nob Hill–United Commercial Brokers** (tel 800/498–3537 within California, 408/279–3747 outside California) handles five Queen Anne Victorian apartments with antique furniture, fireplaces, and laundry service at weekly or monthly rates of $125–$200 per night; and **Executive Suites** (tel 415/567–5151) has 100 luxury condominiums, including maid service, fitness centers, saunas, pools, and laundry, for $65–$145 a night, depending on length of stay (special government and corporate rates are also available). Many other short-term options are outlined in a free lodging guide available through the San Francisco Convention and Visitors Bureau (tel 415/974–6900).

Is There a Right Address?

Most of San Francisco's major hotels are located near the **Financial District, Union Square,** and **Fisherman's Wharf**. The prime spots for world-class luxury hotels are Union Square and **Nob Hill**. There are many small "boutique" hotels and inns mixed among the giant towers and palaces, so the touristy neighborhoods shouldn't scare you off completely—the location is extremely convenient for walking and for access to public transportation. But—and it's a Big But—you can easily be sucked into paying much more money than is necessary for a room with about as much personality as a Holiday Inn in Elko, Nevada. The thing is, you can't tell from the outside of the building or from the lobby what the rooms will be like. Take the Westin Saint Francis, for instance. It is an absolute architectural gem, one of the loveliest hotel exteriors in the Western world, but the rooms in the tower are, well, ordinary. Sure, they're spacious and full of expensive furniture, but they still look like they were punched out of the Universal School of Semi-Fancy Hotel Room Design. The whole thing is just too pastel. The views are spectacular, but you can see those from the elevator, and that's free.

Neither **Chinatown** nor **Japantown** is loaded with hotels, but each is worth considering. Japantown isn't as interesting as it sounds—mostly a bunch of import shops and food stands in a bland mall but it does have the most authentic Japanese hotel in the city, the Miyako, with Zen gardens, futon beds, and in-room Shiatsu massage. Chinatown is crammed with everything: Crammed with people, crammed with fish, crammed with odors, exotic vegetables, cheap souvenirs, great little food joints—but it is not crammed with good places to spend the night. You can, however, find a bed in Chinatown for $30–$40 if you don't mind sharing a bath. You can't beat the location—near downtown, Union Square, North Beach, and (perish the thought) Fisherman's Wharf.

The **Tenderloin**—usually called by other names to divert attention from its reputation as a seedy, whore-and-drug-infested pit—is a block-by-block situation. One minute you can be strolling past a series of charming little shops and neighborhood taverns, and the next you're being accosted by panhandlers in front of a dilapidated homeless shelter or a shop that sells pornography. On the outer edges of the neighborhood are some of the trendiest and most fun lodgings and restaurants in town, but as a rule, the hotels there are either faded old beauties or transient houses best left to guests who rent them by the hour for "professional" purposes.

Van Ness Avenue is a long stretch of wide road that cuts through the city from the Mission District to the Marina. Inch for inch, it probably has more chain hotels and motels in its immediate vicinity than any other street in the city. It also has some beautifully restored old standards, like the Hotel Richelieu, that are close to entertainment and theater but mercifully removed from the constant stream of pickpockets and hustlers that usually hover around theater districts. (The Great American Music Hall puts most of its performing artists up at the Richelieu.) The **Civic Center** area houses the ballet, the opera, the symphony, the main library, and City Hall, along with a number of wonderful boutique hotels such as the Inn at the Opera and the Abigail, and exquisite restaurants that are virtually empty after 8:30pm (San Franciscans tend to eat before performances). Right smack in the middle of it all is a plaza that has been a constant battle site for San Francisco's intractable homeless problem. Some people find that repugnant; others chalk it up as an integral part of urban life. Public transportation is a breeze in this centrally located neighborhood, and parking is very reasonable at the Civic Center garage. (Don't go to any of the private garages near the Opera House or you may have to call home for extra cash.) **Lombard Street**, in Cow Hollow, is Motel Row, and don't count it out if you're looking for a low-profile, inexpensive place to stay. The area stretches from the Marina to the Presidio, and there are plenty of scenic vistas and worthwhile seafood houses that are local favorites. The more residential neighborhoods—the Mission District, the Haight, the Castro, Noe Valley, the Sunset, Pacific Heights—have fewer hotels, but many boast wonderful inns and bed-and-breakfast houses. The **Mission District** is a lot of fun, but has few places to stay; the **Castro**, the **Haight**, and **Pacific Heights** have several beautiful Victorian bed-and-breakfast options; **Noe Valley** is charming but primarily residential. Some of the inns in the outer reaches of the **Sunset District** offer the city's most gorgeous views of the Pacific Ocean.

The Lowdown

Irresistible Deals... Europeans and seasoned travelers love the **San Remo Hotel**, an Italianate Victorian jewel hidden away in a residential area of North Beach. The owners haven't raised their rates for so long that single rooms start at $35 (not a misprint), but the San Remo would be a delight at twice that price. Rooms are small but very cozy, with antique beds and armoires, old-fashioned ceiling fans, and lace-curtained windows that open wide to let in the cool bay breeze and the sounds of San Francisco's lively Italian neighborhood. The atmosphere is friendly, casual, and totally international; bathrooms are shared, and even the water faucets are European—cold on the left, hot on the right. **The Phoenix** is the exact opposite of the San Remo. It is New World all the way, as American as Velveeta and Andy Warhol. Of all the city's lodgings, the Phoenix is the place for deviant minds to meet. Rock stars and other eccentric celebrities relax around the mural-bottomed pool, while a barbecue grills that night's dinner for the adjoining Miss Pearl's Jam House, a scene in its own right (see Dining).

Grande dames worth considering... It almost goes without saying that the **Fairmont Hotel** is synonymous with San Francisco. It sits on top of Nob Hill as though it alone were holding court over the city (never mind that the Mark Hopkins is virtually across the street). The lobby is fancy, fancy, fancy and the velvet furniture is red, red, red, matching the bellhops' uniforms. The overall effect is about a half-degree shy of gaudy, but its history keeps it within the grande dame category.

The Mark Hopkins International is a traditional favorite of San Franciscans who appreciate elegance but don't have much of a stomach for gewgaw. It shares the top of the hill with the Fairmont but is notably less glitzy. It's a few dollars more expensive than its Nob Hill neighbor, too, but by the time you're paying that much, who's counting? The rooms themselves are plush but not extraordinary, unless you want to pop for a large suite with a Jacuzzi and a view. The best part about the hotel is probably the famous Top of the Mark cocktail lounge, still one of the most romantic spots in the city and worth a visit even if you have no intention of staying at the hotel. It has been the traditional spot to kiss a lover good-bye since World War II. The charm of the **Westin Saint Francis** in Union Square decreased considerably when the huge tower was added on, but it still has a few merits. The elegant front entrance, used for the television series "Hotel," remains magnificent, and stepping into the lobby will probably always make you feel like a million bucks (or at least like you might need a million bucks to stay there very long). Afternoon high tea in the Compass Rose is a civilized antidote to the shopping frenzy just outside the door. If you're intent on staying at the Saint Francis, get a room in the older part of the hotel—the tower rooms are big and boring, except for their views, and they cost more.

In search of painted ladies... San Francisco has no shortage of painted ladies, be they the brazen gold-lamé-hot-pants variety or the architectural type (Victorian mansions with elaborate paint jobs). Both are found all over town, but the most famous Victorian painted ladies—the ones featured in the tourism posters—are on Alamo Square, virtually across the street from the **Archbishop's Mansion**, built in 1904 and now a bed-and-breakfast inn. The huge rooms and ornate decor almost make you dizzy, but "Texans love it," says the owner. "It makes them feel like they're in their own castle for a few nights." Most of the rooms have massive canopy beds, working fireplaces, and deep, old-fashioned bathtubs, and all guests are served breakfast in bed.

The Red Victorian Bed and Breakfast Inn in Haight-Ashbury, known affectionately as the Red Vic, is much more eccentric and much less expensive than the Archbishop's Mansion. It's right on Haight Street, and fits in perfectly, if that gives you a clue. Group meditation is offered every morning in the back of the lobby, and owner Sami Sunchild has left her artistic thumbprint all over the inn with poem/paintings that make you want to run right out and stick a flower in your hair. Each room has its own theme, from a Persian-esque suite that looks like a good home for a hookah-smoking caterpillar to a quasi-psychedelic "LOVE" wall that certainly does not appear to be conducive to sleep. Most rooms share baths; be ready for aquariums and other surprises when you go to wash your face. The Red Vic is fun, it's clean, and it's definitely only in San Francisco.

In the same neighborhood but not at all in the same vein is the **Victorian Inn on the Park**, at Lyon and Fell Streets, just across the Panhandle from the house where Janis Joplin once lived. The inn, a registered historic landmark, is a restored Queen Anne Victorian that caters to a more subdued clientele than the Red Vic, though it, too, had its heyday as a hippie crash-pad. It's an outstanding example of Victorian architecture, and the antique furnishings are comfortable and elegant, despite signs of wear.

Over the hill and down past Market Street from the Haight, Noe Valley has many lovely old Victorians, among them a private residence, **Haus Kleebauer**, that makes two two-room suites available for guests. If you ever watched "The Andy Griffith Show" and wished you could take a bite of Aunt Bea's cookies, you must go to Haus Kleebauer—they bake fresh chocolate chip cookies for their guests every day. The beds here have European-style featherbeds on top of the mattresses, for those who are interested in creature comforts.

When money is no object... **The Clift** (formerly the Four Seasons Clift) is just about flawless—a sophisticated, elegant retreat for aristocrats and other travelers with plenty of credit. The large, high-ceilinged rooms have been meticulously restored to their prime 1915 state, with all the modern luxuries added for dessert. Possibly on the theory that rich children grow up to be rich adults, the Clift has a Very Important Kids plan that caters to young aristocrats, with everything from teddy bears to Nintendo games. The topper is the wonderful Redwood Room, a lusciously romantic art deco piano bar. **The Stouffer Renaissance Stanford Court Hotel**, called simply Stanford Court by residents and taxi drivers, is a historic landmark up on Nob Hill that once housed the founder of Stanford University. Many San Franciscans consider this the ultimate landmark hotel, but some people find it a bit difficult to feel at home in a lobby with a stained-glass dome—church pews and a confessional wouldn't seem out of place. The antiques-filled rooms are more welcoming, but if they seem too stuffy, you can always head for the bathroom, where you can flick on the television, pick up the telephone, and lather yourself into a froth with French-milled soap.

When money's too tight to mention... There are lots of safe and comfortable, sometimes even scenic, cheap lodgings in San Francisco, starting as low as $10 a day per person. The best bets for quality and location are the YMCA, hostels, budget Chinatown hotels, and Lombard Street motels. The **Central YMCA** offers private rooms with shared baths from $26 a night, including free coffee and muffins in the morning and use of the health-club facilities and pool. There are also rooms with private baths and a dormitory (for AYH and IYH members only). The hotel is staffed 24 hours a day and there are no curfews; men and women are welcome.

Chinatown's bargains include the **Grant Plaza**, a clean, comfortable hotel that many locals recommend to budget-minded visitors. All rooms have a private bath, and start at $39; a Super Saver package includes breakfast and free parking. Another Chinatown cheap sleep is the **Hotel Astoria**, where rooms with shared bath start at $31 (some rooms also have private bath). Hostels include the **AYH Hostel** at Union Square, a relatively new facility for AYH members only, starting at $14 per night; the **Green Tortoise Guest House**, a North Beach spot that offers a choice of a hostel with dorm facilities ($14) or private rooms with shared bath (starting at $20); the **Inter-Club/Globe Hostel**, South of Market, with dorm and private rooms, a cafe, bar, and sundeck, starting at $10 a night; and the **San Francisco International Hostel** (AYH) at Fort Mason, a dormitory with a view of the Golden Gate Bridge starting at $13. Dozens of inexpensive motels line Lombard Street along the Marina—a prime location for bay views and walking tours—and at least half of them start at less than $50 a night. From here you can easily walk to Fort Mason, Fisherman's Wharf, Aquatic Park, the Marina Green, the Exploratorium and Palace of Fine Arts, the Presidio, and many excellent neighborhood seafood restaurants. Public transportation is a snap, and many of the motels have free parking for guests. The **Bel Aire Travelodge**, a two-story Marina District favorite, has been owned and operated by the same family for three generations; also family-owned, the **Marina Motel** was converted from a California Colonial-style apartment building built before the Golden Gate Bridge—the courtyard has many plants as old as the building itself. The **Holland Motel** is a small lodging (20 rooms) that's not exactly big on charm, but it's clean, comfortable, and proud of the fact that "none of the showers back up" in the renovated bathrooms. The **Sea Captain's Motel** features kitchens, a Jacuzzi, and free doughnuts and coffee on weekends; the **Surf Motel**, a two-story, horseshoe-shaped stucco motel unmistakably built in the Fifties, has several large suites (two bedrooms, living room, and full kitchen) that were home to a substantial assembly from the Russian Consulate last time we checked. The 30-room **Lombard Plaza Motel** has two cathedral-beam ceiling suites that were the setting for a local movie about "some Mafia hit man," according to the amiable desk clerk, who bills himself as "short, fat, and very good looking."

Lavender lodgings... Gay tourists are to San Francisco what Disney World pilgrims are to Orlando, Florida: big business. So surrender, Dorothy. If the idea of seeing men holding hands is a problem for you, you're in the wrong town, especially during Gay Pride festivities in June. Many mainstream hotels offer special Gay Pride discounts (ask when you call for reservations), and some lodgings cater almost entirely to a gay clientele. Many others that are not gay per se are staffed by a predominantly gay workforce, which can turn an otherwise ordinary little spot into a really fun place for gay travelers to stay. For the inside word, one of the best and funniest sources is **Betty & Pansy's Severe Queer Review**, available from A Different Light Bookstore (tel 800/343–4002). Recommended gay-oriented lodgings include the inexpensive **Leland Hotel**, occupying a Victorian at Polk and Bush Streets; the European-style **Pension San Francisco** (Market and Gough Sts.); the Western-themed **Black Stallion Inn** (Castro St. between 19th and 20th Sts.); and two other converted Victorians—the **24 Henry Guesthouse** in the Castro District and the **Inn San Francisco** on South Van Ness Avenue. Lesbian options include **Sappho's Inn** (Fulton and Fillmore Sts.), with its backyard garden; tiny **Bock's Bed and Breakfast**, on Willard Street near Golden Gate Park; and the **House O'Chicks**, in a Castro Victorian on 15th Street near Noe Street.

Turning Japanese... The **Miyako Hotel** is authentic Japanese, even when that means bowing to Americans by including Western-style beds and bathrooms in many rooms. It is so much like an elegant Tokyo hotel, in fact, that most Japanese tourists opt for other, more "American" hotels for their vacations in San Francisco. Here's what's best about the Miyako: the rates (much lower than Hotel Nikko in Union Square), the in-room Shiatsu massages, the deep Japanese soak tubs, the tokonama (alcoves for displaying Japanese art), the down comforters on the futon beds, the Zen gardens inside the traditional rooms, and the sunlight filtered through Shoji (rice paper) screens on every window. Don't confuse this hotel with the Best Western Miyako Inn nearby. One of the most Japanese things about **Hotel Nikko** (Union Square) is the astronomical fee it charges for a Japanese suite—$975 per night. If that doesn't make you feel like you're in Tokyo, nothing will. Those suites are not that much better than the Miyako's, but they do feature a better view of the city and an in-room well for performing the traditional tea ceremony. At the opposite end of the fancy scale is **"Minshuku" Suzume No Oyado**, a Japanese bed-and-breakfast inn in the Richmond District. It has only six rooms—516 fewer rooms than Hotel Nikko—and half of those share a bath. However, complimentary breakfast, dinner, and tea are provided, all for as little as $55 a night. They'll even pick you up and take you back to the airport in their free shuttle. To give you a hint as to the authenticity of the place, Japanese newspapers are one of the amenities.

For writers in search of a muse... If you believe that sleeping in the same bed a famous poet once did will somehow bring you closer to your magnum opus, you have quite a few options in San Francisco. Even the most ardent literary historians haven't been able to establish with certainty the exact number or locations of all the places Allen Ginsberg is rumored to have slept in his beatnik heyday; recently, however, he is known to have stayed at **Hotel Bohème**, a tasty little North Beach hotel just a short walk from Lawrence Ferlinghetti's City Lights Bookstore. A small black awning on Columbus Avenue is the only clue to the hotel's whereabouts (next to Stella Bakery and Cafe); you have to push the doorbell to get buzzed in to the narrow staircase that leads up to the foyer and reception desk. Do it, even if you don't stay there, just to see the foyer's dozens of museum-quality photographs of North Beach in the Forties and Fifties, including many shots of legendary poets and musicians holding forth in local joints. Once you get upstairs, the street noise disappears, and you could easily be in Paris, or better yet, in North Beach. If you're looking for a relaxed yet elegant refuge right in the thick of it all, this is it. It'll take a lot more money to spend a night at the **Sheraton Palace Hotel**, originally known as just the Palace, where only writers who had already become rich and famous could afford to stay. Oscar Wilde stayed here when he was 27 years old and apparently drank the entire town under the table; Rudyard Kipling arrived a few years later, but was rejected by both the *Chronicle* and Ambrose Bierce's *San Francisco Illustrated Wasp*. The Sheraton Palace is still lavish and elegant; modern conveniences have been installed, but the furnishings are restored antiques that will make you wonder if any of Oscar Wilde's molecules could still be floating around in the upholstery somewhere. Meanwhile, as long as you're spending some money, consider the **Huntington Hotel** on Nob Hill, where Eugene O'Neill and his wife moved from the Fairmont after they left Tao House in Danville, some 30 miles away in the country. Today the hotel is still a discreet lodging for the "old money" crowd who want to be left alone, as far as possible from anything resembling flash or celebrity. **The York Hotel** is neither a fancy land-mark nor a charming North Beach haven, but it was home for a while to Ron Kovic, who wrote *Born on the Fourth of July* and *Around the World in Eight Days*. While staying at the York, Kovic wrote eight novels in 38 days, according to Don Herron's *The Literary World of San Francisco* (City Lights Books). Behind on a deadline? The York might be just what you need to churn out those last few chapters. It's also considered to be gay-friendly.

Taking care of business... To the business traveler, happiness is a warm fax machine; ecstasy is one right there in your room. Guests at the **Ritz-Carlton** will find just that, along with a voice mail system in every room, a fully operational business center, complimentary transporta-tion, and every other amenity a generous expense account can buy. The **Nob Hill Lambourne** is a model hotel for health-conscious business execs—every room has its own exercise equipment as well as personal computer, fax set-up, and compact stereo unit, all at rates the same or less than a nondescript room at some of the major hotels in the area. A bit farther from the Financial District, in Japantown, the **Miyako Hotel** caters to a clientele of lots of Japanese business travelers, with fax machines and voice mail in the rooms, as well as translation services. Business travelers seeking offbeat accommodations could try the **Inn at the Opera** or the **Hotel Bohème**, both of which are equipped with in-room voice mail and fax modem hook-ups, yet offer a European-style ambiance quite different from the standard business-travel hotel.

Family values... Oh, to be a kid again. They get all the good stuff and don't ever even think of offering to pay. At the **Clift Hotel**, children are supplied, free of charge, with everything from toys and Nintendo to milk and cookies and smaller versions of the luxurious bathrobes Mom and Dad are wearing. Parents can be provided with a babysit-ter and, if by chance they left the baby bag at home, every item imaginable (bottles, diapers, clothes etc.) needed for an infant. The **Westin Saint Francis**'s Kids Club is another program geared toward pleasing guests 12 and under: Members receive a sports bottle or tippy cup with complimentary refills at the hotel's restaurant, along with free food from a special kids menu, while parents request such necessities as strollers, cribs, bottle-warmers, and stepstools. The Westin Saint Francis's glass-enclosed elevators add an amusement-park thrill to the whole experience. The **Sheraton Fisherman's Wharf**, a four-story hotel just a block from the waterfront, doesn't compare aesthetically to the Westin Saint Francis or the Clift, but it accepts pets and has a heated outdoor pool (a relative rarity in San Francisco), which compensates in kids' hearts quite well. It's also well-located for Fisherman's Wharf and all those tacky kid-pleasing attractions. Or, for kids with a wacky sense of humor, here's a more unorthodox choice: the **Mansions Hotel**, a converted Victorian inn that has magic shows every night, as well as a document museum with papers signed by the likes of George Washington, Abraham Lincoln, and of course, Harry Houdini.

If there's a pet in your entourage... A number of San Francisco hotels make special provisions for pooches, ranging from simply tolerating their presence to greeting them in the lobby with a doggie biscuit. For the lowdown on off-leash parks and beaches, as well as restaurants and cafes that will allow you to bring Rover in with you, get *The Dog Lover's Companion* by Lyle York and Marcia Goodavage (Foghorn Press, tel 415/241–9550). Lodgings that accept pets include some lower-priced motel properties such as the **Best Western Civic Center Motor Inn**, the **Laurel Motor Inn** in Pacific Heights, and the **Rodeway Inn** on Lombard Street's motel row; big mass-market chain properties such as the immense **San Francisco Marriott** and **Sheraton Fisherman's Wharf**; and even, surprisingly, a couple of top-end luxury hotels—the **Westin Saint Francis**, the **Campton Place Hotel** (no dogs over 25 pounds—leave the Rottweiler home), and the **Clift Hotel**, whose Very Important Pet program includes greeting with a biscuit. Some small distinctive properties that are canine-friendly include the tiny **Haus Kleebauer** bed-and-breakfast in Noe Valley, the whimsical **Mansions Hotel**, **Pension San Francisco**, and **Inn San Francisco**, which takes pets on occasion. Always call in advance for pet policies and required deposits.

Luscious love nests... *Town and Country* said a night at the **Archbishop's Mansion** is "like a night in a well-written romance novel," which is ideal if you like romance novels. It's probably the only hotel in the city where you'll find a huge bathroom with a working fireplace and a claw-footed bathtub right in the middle of the room, smelling of perfume and just waiting for a candle-lit soak for two. (Do you hear that mood music yet?) The next morning you can keep the spark alive as long as nature allows—the mansion staff will serve you both breakfast in bed. If that whole Danielle Steel thing bores you, perhaps the passion of the opera will get your motor running. Couples have been known to hold intimate wedding dinners in front of the fire at the Act IV restaurant at **Inn at the Opera**, then walk across the street to pump up the volume with a fervent aria at the Opera House. The Inn at the Opera is the most sumptuous small hotel in the city, and we do mean small—the entire building is only 25 feet wide, which kind of makes you wonder how Luciano Pavarotti keeps from feeling cramped when he stays there. Still, the sense is one of airy coziness, partially because all of the windows open for real fresh air. If you've got that truly, madly, deeply kind of thing going on, and you're willing to prove it with some serious money, take your amour across the bay to the lush, 22-acre **Claremont Resort** and book a telescope suite, where San Francisco's lights will twinkle just for you all night long. It is one of the best views of San Francisco you'll ever find. The picture window is as big as a movie screen and is fitted with a wide, wraparound window seat custom-made for those spontaneous harmonic convergences. And if you pause to look out the window during the day, you'll see acres and acres of beautifully landscaped grounds (irrigated by the resort's own wells). Play tennis, swim, get massages, eat in the superb restaurants, have cocktails in the bar, do it all, but by all means get back to your room in time for a private bottle of California bubbly (the wine list is unbeatable) and the view.

I'm with the band... You don't have to be on assignment for the *National Enquirer* to be curious about rock stars, but you do have to know where they stay at night if you want to sneak a peek. We'll tell you the best spots, but you have to promise to follow the two cardinal rules of stargazing: (1) don't stare; and (2) don't ask. So here goes: **The Phoenix** is the supreme hot spot for rock stars and other nonconformist celebrities. Originally a kind of futuristic, sleek motel in the Fifties, then a hooker hall in the 1970s and 1980s, it was bought in 1987 by Chip Conley, who managed to snag his first celebrity guest, Brenda Lee, when she stopped one day to ask for directions to another hotel. After that came Arlo Guthrie and a few others, and the celebrity guest register mushroomed. Sinead O'Connor, John F. Kennedy Jr., Deborah Harry, Wim Wenders, the Sex Pistols, Nirvana, the Red Hot Chili Peppers, M.C. Hammer, k.d. lang, R.E.M., John Waters, Dr. John, Etta James, River Phoenix, Keanu Reeves, Chubby Checker, David Bowie, Bonnie Raitt, Bo Diddley, and the Cowboy Junkies are just a few of the stars who have lounged by the infamous mural-bottomed swimming pool in the Tenderloin. Offbeat stargazing doesn't get any better, and the rooms start at under $70, so reserve well in advance. **The Hotel Richelieu** puts up a lot of the bands that play at the nearby Great American Music Hall, but the pickings are generally a little slimmer and far tamer than the Phoenix. The celebrity guest register is a bit iffy; your best bet is to find out who's playing at the Great American during your vacation. It might be Etta James and it might be the Bulgarian State Women's Chorus, you never know. The Richelieu has been hosting music stars since it was built in 1908 when the Great American was still just a bordello, and it proudly displays in the lobby the costume of one of its first celebrity guests, Jenny Lind. The staff is young and hip and friendly, and can direct you to all the happening clubs in town. Celebrity guests at the **Inn at the Opera** are more along the lines of opera stars, artists, and dancers—Mikhail Baryshnikov, Twyla Tharp, David Hockney, Placido Domingo, Oscar de la Renta, Robert Rauschenberg, Philip Glass, Herbie Hancock, the Tokyo String Quartet, and the principal dancers of the American Ballet Theatre— but there are a few surprises to round out the list, such as home run king Hank Aaron, and Gaylord Perry, who holds the major-league record for spitballs. This superb hotel is very popular, so reserve well in advance.

That's why they call it modern art... Two hotels worth visiting purely for the *lobbies d'moderne* are the **Hotel Triton** and the **Commodore**. The Triton lobby looks like what would have happened if Kandinsky had gone into business as a hotelier. The furniture and the people who sit upon it are all part of the glorious confetti that make you want to walk right up to the front desk and say, "I don't care how much it costs, I want to join the party." The stylish desk clerks add to the sense of chic, but they often have that deadpan look that docents wear when they think you might be trying to pay less than the standard "donation" to get into a museum. The Commodore is an entirely different flight of fancy: It used to be an ordinary, clean, reasonably priced hotel, until Chip Conley (see The Phoenix, above) got hold of it—where have we heard this before?—and turned it into some sort of modernistic Love Boat. When you first walk in, you're met with a huge relief mural that depicts the hidden treasures of San Francisco. Then, because you're supposed to feel like you're on a cruise ship, there's a gigantic, goofy Wheel of Fortune you're supposed to spin to win a prize—anything from a free cable car token to a $25 gift certificate at Miss Pearl's Jam House. Hang around for happy hour and the ship's social director will tell you what's going on in the city that night—hopefully it's not shuffleboard on the poop deck.

We gotta get outta this place... Fog getting to you? Think you'll scream if you see one more panhandler on Market Street? Here's the cure: Get a car and drive across the Golden Gate Bridge, then another 12 miles to Mill Valley, one of those cozy little towns that forces you to use the word "quaint" to describe it. (It was, however, the setting for the 1970s satire *Serial*, starring Martin Mull, Sally Kellerman, and a flotilla of hot tubs—luckily, most of the Marin County stereotypes that inspired this book and the 1980 movie have gone to spawn elsewhere.) Get yourself a balcony room at the **Mill Valley Inn**, a European-style *pensione* where your free breakfast is served at a popular local espresso cafe. Go ahead, mingle with the locals—half of them are screenwriters and you know how they love to talk. After that, you'll be ready to calm down a bit at **Tea Garden Springs** (see Getting Outside) with a massage and an herbal elixir. And if that still doesn't do it, get back in the car, head farther up the coast to Point Reyes National Seashore, and check into **Manka's Inverness Lodge**, a hunting lodge built in 1917 and later transformed into a romantic inn; the extraordinary restaurant here serves game grilled in the fireplace and local line-caught fish. Try to get one of the private cabins, and whatever you do, don't miss dinner in the restaurant.

The Index

$$$$$	over $200
$$$$	$150–$200
$$$	$80–$150
$$	$50–$80
$	under $50

Abigail Hotel. This hotel is absolutely perfect for travelers who like charm, great food, international company, and an inexpensive bill when they check out (rooms start at $79). You can't beat the location—right in the middle of the Civic Center area—and its trendy Millennium restaurant has the best organic food in the city. (We're not talking mung beans here, we're talking high-style, innovative cuisine.).... *Tel 415/861–9728, 800/243–6510, fax 415/861–5848. 246 McAllister St., San Francisco, CA 94102, Civic Center BART/MUNI Metro stop. 61 rooms. $$$*

Archbishop's Mansion. This bed-and-breakfast inn has been hailed as the most spectacular place to stay in the city, and as the most elegant in-city hotel in the United States. Maybe yes, maybe no. Try a night in the Carmen Suite, soak by candlelight in a claw-footed tub next to a working fireplace, savor a delicious homemade breakfast served to you in bed and make up your own mind.... *Tel 415/563–7872, 800/543–5820, fax 415/885–3193. 1000 Fulton St., San Francisco, CA 94117, 5 MUNI bus. 10 rooms, 5 suites. $$$–$$$$$*

AYH Hostel at Union Square. This hostel for AYH members only is in the heart of Union Square and features several rooms with private baths for families, as well as the normal dormitory facilities, starting at $14 per person. It is wheelchair accessible. Reservations are required.... *Tel 415/ 788–5604, fax 415/788–3023. 312 Mason St., San*

Francisco, CA 94102, Powell/Mason cable car; 7B or 38 MUNI bus. 218 beds, 30 with private bath. $

Bel Aire Travelodge. This modern, two-story chain motel located along the Marina offers free airport pickup and free parking. Rooms are modern and comfortable, but nothing fancy.... *Tel 415/921–5162, 800/280–3242. 3201 Steiner St. (off Lombard St.), San Francisco, CA 94123, 28 or 30 MUNI bus. 32 rooms. $–$$*

Best Western Civic Center Motor Inn. This budget chain motel is nondescript, but clean and convenient. It has a sunny outdoor pool, offers free parking, and allows pets.... *Tel 415/621–2926, 800/444–5829. 364 Ninth St., San Francisco, CA 94103, Civic Center BART/MUNI Metro stop. 57 rooms. $$–$$$*

Black Stallion Inn. The *Severe Queer Review* calls this the city's only "leather-levi-western bed and breakfast." It's right in the Castro District, and has a fireplace and a sundeck in the public rooms—sometimes you need both on the same day in San Francisco. Breakfast is included.... *Tel 415/863–0131. 635 Castro St., San Francisco, CA 94114, Castro St. MUNI Metro stop. 8 rooms. $$$*

Bock's Bed and Breakfast. This tiny, non-smoking bed-and-breakfast near Golden Gate Park and the University of California medical school has sundecks, laundry facilities, and fax service. Continental breakfast is included. There is a two-night minimum stay.... *Tel 415/664–6842, fax 415/664–1109. 1448 Willard St., San Francisco, CA 94117, 5 MUNI bus. 3 rooms. $–$$*

Campton Place Hotel. This small luxury hotel is noted for its elegance (bathrooms have marble floors, brass fixtures, and cushy bathrobes) and comfortable intimacy. Personal service is a hallmark here. Dogs under 25 pounds welcome.... *Tel 415/781–5555, 800/426–3135, fax 415/955–5536. 340 Stockton St., San Francisco, CA 94108; Powell/Hyde and Powell/Mason cable car; 2, 3, 4, 30, or 45 MUNI bus. 116 rooms, 10 suites. $$$$–$$$$$*

Central YMCA. The reliable old standard in cheap lodgings is an especially good deal when you consider that the rooms are private (some with private bath) and include use of the health club and pool as well as free coffee and muffins in the morning. At $26 for a single ($36 for a double), that's a steal. (Rooms with private bath start at $37.50.) Dormitory accommodations are also available to AYH and IYH members for $15, including all the same amenities. Both men and women are welcome.... *Tel 415/885–0460. 220 Golden Gate Ave., San Francisco, CA 94109, Civic Center BART/MUNI Metro stop, 15 MUNI bus. 106 rooms, plus 6-bed dormitory. $*

Claremont Resort Hotel, Spa & Tennis Club. This lush, romantic retreat, just four BART stops away from downtown San Francisco, was voted the best urban spa in the United States, and it's no small wonder. The 22 acres of landscaped grounds are just the backdrop for the landmark Victorian hotel (1915), the Bay Area's premier private tennis club (open to guests), and a $6 million holistic health and beauty spa. The restaurants are among the best in the East Bay and the bar has a panoramic view of the bay.... *Tel 510/843–3000, 800/551–7266, fax 510/543–6239. Ashby and Domingo Aves., Oakland, CA 94623-0363, Rockridge BART stop (plus a cab). 239 rooms. $$$$–$$$$$*

The Clift Hotel. A haven for aristocrats and romantics on a splurge, the Clift is the luxury hotel that other hotels want to be when they grow up. The divine rooms have high ceilings, marble bathrooms, fine art, and meticulously restored woodwork and moldings, true to old San Francisco (circa 1915); the service is impeccable, not just for adult guests but for their children and pets as well. The art deco Redwood Room piano bar is an absolute must, especially if you're wooing your traveling companion.... *Tel 415/775–4700, 800/332–3442, fax 415/441–4621. 495 Geary St., San Francisco, CA 94102; Powell/Hyde and Powell/Mason cable car; 2, 3, 4, 30, 38, or 45 bus. 329 rooms, 25 suites. $$$$$*

Commodore Hotel. You have to go by this one just to check out the lobby. It's a goofball version of a cruise ship, complete with a giant Wheel of Fortune and lobby chairs that look like chaise longues covered in purple upholstery. Each room is furnished with post-modern pieces designed by Fun Displays (a company that specializes in Pee Wee Hermanstyle exhibits for trade shows), and has a local artist's painting of a favorite San Francisco "hidden spot"; every morning you get a tip sheet telling you what the hip happenings are in the city that day.... *Tel 415/932–6800, 800/338–6848. 825 Sutter St., San Francisco, CA 94109, California St. cable car. 113 rooms. $$–$$$*

Fairmont Hotel. This is probably the most famous hotel in San Francisco, at the very tip-top of Nob Hill, yet it's not incredibly expensive, provided you stay out of the suites. Rooms in the main building are more affordable than those in the tower, but don't miss the ride in the tower elevator; the view is incredible. The staff is friendly and helpful, but not annoyingly deferential. You will be pampered with all the typical luxury hotel amenities and wonderful bathrooms besides.... *Tel 415/772–5000, 800/524–4727, fax 415/772–5013. 950 Mason St., San Francisco, CA 94108, California St. cable car. 600 rooms, 62 suites, $$$$–$$$$$*

Grant Plaza. This bargain hotel in Chinatown is clean and comfortable, and convenient to North Beach, Union Square, downtown, and public transportation. The rooms tend to have dreary mauve carpeting and floral bedspreads, but the windows are large and let in plenty of light. The Super Saver package includes breakfast and free parking. It ain't fancy, but the price is right.... *Tel 415/434–3883, 800/472–6899, fax 415/434–3886. 465 Grant Ave., San Francisco, CA 94108. 15, 30, 45 MUNI bus. 72 rooms. $*

Green Tortoise Guest House. This non-smoking facility was originally made popular by super-cheap hippie bus trips from San Francisco to the Northwest and other destinations. The buses still exist, and the guesthouse, near the legendary Enrico's cafe as well as a few notorious strip joints, appears still to attract lots of young people looking for a cheap place to crash and some kindred souls. Dorm rates start at $10 and private rooms with shared bath start at $20, including breakfast. They also have a sauna, laundry, and organized tours.... *Tel 415/834–1000, 800/867–8647, fax 415/956–4900. 15, 30 MUNI bus. 100 beds, 10 rooms with shared bath. $*

Haus Kleebauer. First things first. There are only two available rooms in this private residence, so start dialing the phone right now if you want to get in. You'll be pampered with a

SAN FRANCISCO | ACCOMMODATIONS

basket of fruit, cheese, and wine in your room upon arrival, then fresh-baked chocolate chip cookies in the afternoon, chocolates on your pillow at night, and a full breakfast in the morning. (Did we mention queen-size brass beds with down comforters?) Pets are welcome.... *Tel 415/821–3866, fax 415/821–1417. 225 Clipper St., San Francisco, CA 94114, J Church MUNI Metro. 2 rooms. $$$*

Holland Motel. This budget motel is located along the Marina; the rooms are average, but freshly painted, and there's free parking.... *Tel 415/922–0810. 1 Richardson Ave. (off Lombard St.), San Francisco, CA 94123, 28 or 30 MUNI bus. 20 rooms. $–$$*

Hotel Astoria. This super-cheap Chinatown hotel has plain, but not shabby, rooms, some with shared bath, some with private bath (shared bathrooms start at $31). Many locals recommend this hotel to friends looking for a clean and comfortable sleep with no frills. Airport pickup and some business services are provided.... *Tel 415/434–8889, 800/666–6696, fax 415/434–8919. 510 Bush St., San Francisco, CA 94108; 30, 45 MUNI bus. 90 rooms, 40 with private bath. $*

Hotel Bohème. This Parisian-style beatnik villa is both comfortable and chic at the same time. It is right on Columbus Avenue, in the heart of North Beach, but the rooms are surprisingly quiet. The walls are lined with dozens of archival black-and-white photos of jazz and poetry legends doing their thing in local haunts in the Forties and Fifties. If you want to be in the thick of one of the most interesting neighborhoods in the city, this is the place to stay.... *Tel 415/433–9111, 800/566–4553, fax 415/362–6292. 444 Columbus Ave., San Francisco, CA 94133; 15, 30, 45 MUNI bus. 15 rooms. $$$*

Hotel Nikko. This Japanese hotel is perilously close to the Hilton and it has rubbed off. Most of the rooms are very Western, and the traditional Japanese suites are lovely but cost close to $1,000 a night. The hotel has its own swimming pool and fitness center.... *Tel 415/394–1111, 800/645–5687, fax 415/421–0455. 222 Mason St., San Francisco, CA 94102; Powell St. BART/MUNI Metro stop; Powell/Mason or Powell/Hyde cable car; 38 MUNI bus. 500 rooms, 22 suites. $$$$–$$$$$*

Hotel Richelieu. This turn-of-the-century hotel is just a few blocks from the Great American Music Hall, whose stars it usually puts up, and is often filled with hip, young music-lovers. The rooms are large but unremarkable—standard hotel-issue furnishings, complete with fitted bedspreads—but they do have coffee-makers, mini-bars, and private safes. The location is convenient to transportation and downtown, but watch which direction you wander—a few blocks down, Geary Boulevard starts looking pretty grim. The staff is hip and helpful.... *Tel 415/673–4711, 800/ 295–7424, fax 415/673–9362. 1050 Van Ness Ave., San Francisco, CA 94109, 38 MUNI bus. 150 rooms. $$$*

Hotel Triton. Plush, upholstered chairs that look like they came from Barbara Eden's bottle in "I Dream of Jeannie" sit next to the modern, angular front desk. Two huge columns that look like upside-down doric pillars make the royal blue carpet—splattered with gold stars—look like a right-side-up sky. The guests look as arty as the decor. Great location right across from the gate to Chinatown.... *Tel 415/394–0500, 800/ 433–6611, fax 415/394–0555. 342 Grant Ave., San Francisco, CA 94108; 30, 45 MUNI bus. 140 rooms. $$$–$$$$*

House O'Chicks. Admit it, the name alone makes you want to check it out. This Victorian house is a lesbian lodging in the Castro District; guests can feel free to use the kitchen, office, computer, and fax machine. Prices start at $50, but go up for holidays and Gay Pride.... *Tel 415/861–9849. 2162 15th St. (near Noe St.), San Francisco, CA 94114, Church St. MUNI Metro stop. $$*

Huntington Hotel. Guests in this Nob Hill landmark pay for the assurance of privacy, so don't expect to meet your future rich spouse or rub shoulders with anyone you may have seen on "Hard Copy". Rooms are exquisitely—and individually—appointed, with museum-quality works of art and a blend of antique and custom-designed furniture. The hotel is definitely ruling class, so mind your manners.... *Tel 415/ 474–5400, 800/227–4683 in California, fax 415/474– 6227. 1075 California St., San Francisco, CA 94108, California St. cable car, 1 MUNI bus. 140 rooms, 40 suites. $$$$–$$$$$*

Inn at the Opera. A favorite of Luciano Pavarotti, Placido Domingo, Mikhail Baryshnikov, and many other famous performers, this tiny European-style establishment is the most distinguished small luxury hotel in the city and one of the most romantic. A 25-foot wide Victorian jewel, nestled virtually in the backyard of the Opera house, it looks like a pen-and-ink illustration of a small rooming house in turn-of-the-century London or Paris. The staff is attentive but they don't fawn all over you, and the Act IV restaurant is one of the best in the area.... *Tel 415/863–8400, 800/325–2708, fax 415/861–0821. 333 Fulton St., San Francisco, CA 94102; Civic Center BART/MUNI Metro stop; 5, 21, 47, or 49 MUNI bus. 30 rooms, 18 suites. $$$–$$$$*

Inn San Francisco. This Italianate Victorian inn used to be a private mansion, and is now a very gracious bed-and-breakfast guesthouse with a garden hot tub, rooftop sun deck, fireplaces in the guest rooms, and complimentary buffet breakfast. Pets are "occasionally" welcome (check when you call for reservations).... *Tel 415/641–0188, 800/359–0913, fax 415/641–1701. 943 South Van Ness Ave., San Francisco, CA 94110, 5 MUNI bus. 22 rooms. $$–$$$$*

Inter-Club/Globe Hostel. If you want to stay South of Market and bask on a sundeck, try this hostel. It has a dorm and private rooms, plus a pool table, cafe, and bar. Rates start at $10; reservations are highly recommended.... *Tel 415/431–0540, fax 415/431–3286. 10 Hallam Place (off Folsom St., between 7th and 8th Sts.), San Francisco, CA 94103, Civic Center BART/MUNI Metro stop, 42 MUNI bus. 33 rooms. $*

Laurel Motor Inn. This Pacific Heights motel has a great location plus kitchens and a complimentary continental breakfast; rates start at $73. Parking is free and pets are welcome.... *Tel 415/567–8467, 800/552–8735, fax 415/928–1866. 444 Presidio Ave., San Francisco, CA 94115, 3 MUNI bus. 49 rooms. $$–$$$*

Leland Hotel. This Victorian Polk Street hotel is super cheap, considering that you get rooms with bay windows, private baths, televisions, and in-room phones. For $40–$58, that's almost luxurious.... *Tel 415/441–5141, 800/258–4458. 1315 Polk St., San Francisco, CA 94109, California St. cable car, 42 MUNI bus. 108 rooms. $*

Lombard Plaza Motel. This budget motel is located along the Marina and offers free parking. Among the 30 rooms are two suites with cathedral-beam ceilings and kitchens.... *Tel 415/ 921–2444, fax 415/921–5275. 2026 Lombard St., San Francisco, CA 94123, 28 or 30 MUNI bus. 32 rooms. $–$$*

Manka's Inverness Lodge & Restaurant. Locals rave about this small oceanside inn, with its remarkable restaurant, less than an hour from the city. The cheerful, rustic private cabins and garden suite are great favorites, but it's the game grilled in the fireplace, local line-caught fish, and garden-grown vegetables that bring people from all over the state to this wonderful retreat.... *Tel 415/669–1034. P.O. Box 1110, Inverness, CA 94937. On Point Reyes National Seashore. $$–$$$$*

Mansions Hotel. This peculiar little hideaway features rooms named after famous or infamous San Franciscans; it's a combination of whimsy and Victorian elegance. Some of the rooms feature priceless antiques, which kind of makes you wonder why they allow pets. There is a nightly magic show; breakfast is complimentary.... *Tel 415/929–9444, fax 415/567–9391. 2220 Sacramento St., San Francisco, CA 94115; 1,3, or 83 MUNI bus. 21 rooms. $$$*

Marina Motel. This California Colonial-style budget motel with a planted courtyard is located along the Marina and offers free parking.... *Tel 415/921–9406, 800/346–6118, fax 415/921–0364. 2576 Lombard St., San Francisco, CA 94123, 28 or 30 MUNI bus. 38 rooms. $–$$*

Mark Hopkins International. Sometimes overshadowed by its super-glam Nob Hill neighbor, the Fairmont, this classic 19-story luxury hotel should not be overlooked. Every room has a marvelous view, and the Jacuzzi suite has a private terrace with a view of the Golden Gate Bridge. The Mark Hopkins's low-key elegance makes it popular with locals, and the Top of the Mark cocktail lounge is an ultra-romantic tradition.... *Tel 415/392–3434, 800/327–0200, fax 415/421–3302. 1 Nob Hill, San Francisco, CA 94108, California St. cable car. 390 rooms, 27 suites. $$$$–$$$$$*

Mill Valley Inn. The perfect escape, only 12 miles from the city—it feels like a different world. The inn itself is a three-story European-style *pensione*—it looks like a cross between an Italian villa and a California Colonial lodge—at the foot of Mount Tamalpais, alongside a redwood grove. Breakfast is served at a popular local espresso cafe. Reserve a month in advance.... *Tel 415/389–6608, 800/595–2900, fax 415/389–5051. 165 Throckmorton Ave., Mill Valley, CA 94941. 16 rooms, 2 cottages. $$$*

"Minshuku" Suzume No Oyado. Situated in a quiet residential neighborhood three blocks from the ocean (between 45th and 46th Aves.), the small, white house looks like any other well-kept private home on the block, except for the Japanese-style trim above the bay window. For a panoramic view of the breakers, take a few steps to 46th Avenue and head downhill a block.... *Tel 415/752–3330. 8122 Geary Blvd., San Francisco, CA 94121, 38 MUNI bus. 6 rooms. $$–$$$*

Miyako Hotel. This is one of the most tranquil, gracious hotels in the city. Each room is definitely Japanese, but the Western rooms feature American-style beds and bathrooms. Forget those. The whole reason to go to the Miyako is to stay in the luxurious traditional Japanese rooms with their wonderful deep-soak tubs (shower first, then soak) and Zen gardens. American-style breakfast is included. (Don't confuse this hotel with the Best Western Miyako Inn nearby, a standard chain hotel that just happens to be in Japantown.).... *Tel 415/922–3200, 800/533–4567, fax 415/ 921–0417. 1625 Post St. (near Geary Blvd. and Laguna St.), San Francisco, CA 94115, 38 MUNI bus. 218 rooms, 11 suites. $$$–$$$$*

Nob Hill Lambourne. It looks like most any other small, sort-of-expensive hotel when you drive up to the entrance, but the minute you cross the threshold into the spare, modern lobby and catch a glimpse of the sleek little spa around the corner, it's an odds-on bet that you won't be dealing with flowered coverlets or pastel art prints in the rooms. A model hotel for the busy, health-conscious business traveler, this small property equips visitors with a personal computer, compact stereo unit, fax machine, 2-line phones, voice mail, and exercise equipment in each room. Yet prices are surprisingly reasonable when compared to similar accommodations elsewhere in the city.... *Tel 415/433–2287, fax*

415/433–0975. 725 Pine St., San Francisco, CA 94108, Powell BART stop. 20 rooms, 6 suites. $$$$–$$$$$

Pension San Francisco. A wide green awning welcomes you to this red brick Victorian perched at the crossroads of the Mission District, the Hayes Valley, and Upper Market Street. Though tropical palm trees down the center of the boulvard suggest the approaching Latino/Bohemian enclave, the feel of the pension itself is almost French Quarter, with wrought iron fire escapes on the front of the building and ornate white wood railings surrounding the rooftop.... *Tel 415/864–1271, 800/886–1271, fax 415/864–5786. 1668 Market St., San Francisco, CA 94102, Van Ness MUNI Metro stop or 7 bus. 36 rooms. $*

The Phoenix. One of the most wacked-out and popular lodgings in the city, this Tenderloin/Civic Center motel is best known for its famous guests. The decor is sort of Rancho Tropicale, with lots of rattan and art d'moderne. It's extremely popular, as is the adjoining Miss Pearl's Jam House, so make reservations far in advance. Otherwise, you could end up double-booked into a room with the Red Hot Chili Peppers. Stranger things have certainly happened here.... *Tel 415/776–1380, 800/248–9466, fax 415/885–3109. 601 Eddy St., San Francisco, CA 94109; 19, 31, or 38 MUNI bus. 44 rooms, 3 suites. $$–$$$*

Red Victorian Bed and Breakfast Inn. There should be a sign in front of this lovely and eccentric Haight-Ashbury inn that reads: Welcome Back to 1967. This is the Summer of Love all over again, so mellow out and dig the vibes. Each room has its own theme, documented in a photo book at the front desk, so you can take your pick.... *Tel 415/864–1978. 1665 Haight St., San Francisco, CA 94117; 7, 66, 71, or 73 MUNI bus. 18 rooms (4 with private bath), 1 suite. $$–$$$*

The Ritz-Carlton San Francisco. Handsome rooms, Italian marble bathrooms, plush terry bathrobes, and twice-daily maid service (once to turn down your bed) are just some of the comforts guests have come to expect from Ritz-Carltons, and this one is no exception. Business travelers can take full advantage of the fax machines in each room, and everyone can enjoy the fully equipped fitness center—with indoor

SAN FRANCISCO | ACCOMMODATIONS

pool, whirlpool, and sauna.... *Tel 415/296–7465. 600 Stockton St., San Francisco, CA 94108, Stockton St. BART stop. 336 rooms, 42 suites. $$$$$*

Rodeway Inn. You'll see it coming—a huge blue mural of a giant arrow points to the word "MOTEL" in letters big enough to be read clearly by low-flying planes. Next to the sign is a hint of what may be the motel's key attraction—a satellite dish. It's a bit more expensive than the other budget motels along Lombard Street, offering a restaurant, lounge, free parking, kitchens, and wheelchair accessibility. Pets are welcome.... *Tel 415/673–0691, 800/228–2000. 1450 Lombard St., San Francisco, CA 94123, 28 MUNI bus. 73 rooms. $$$*

San Francisco International Hostel (AYH). Fort Mason is a great location—a center of cultural activities (the Mexican Museum, theaters, galleries, and festivals) and hub of the beautifully scenic Golden Gate National Recreation Area. And right in the thick of it, this dormitory hostel is wheelchair accessible, provides free parking, and starts at $13 per person.... *Tel 415/771–7277, fax 415/771–1468. Building 240, Fort Mason, San Francisco, CA 94123; Powell/Hyde cable car; 30 or 42 MUNI bus. 150 beds. $*

San Francisco Marriott. One thing is certain—you can't miss this gigantic building, looming like a huge jukebox over the Financial District. Locals either love it or hate it, but you can't ignore it. Decor is typical Chain Hotel Moderne; there are 1,500 rooms, three restaurants, four lounges, a pool, health club, spa, gift shops, airline ticket desks, and some unbelievable views of both the bay and the Golden Gate. They also accept pets, but require a hefty deposit to do so.... *Tel 415/896–1600, 800/228–9290, fax 415/777–2799. 55 4th St., San Francisco, CA 94103, Powell St. BART/MUNI Metro stop, Powell St. cable car turnaround. 1,500 rooms. $$$–$$$$*

San Remo Hotel. This delightful, clean, European-style hotel starts at $35 and tops out at $85 for the rooftop penthouse cottage with its own sundeck and an unbeatable view of the city. The other rooms are furnished with antiques and have comfortable beds, windows that open to let in salty sea air, and ceiling fans to whoosh it around. The shared bathrooms on each floor are sparklingly clean and well kept, with redwood walls and shiny tiled floors (separate toilets are oak with brass pull-chains). It's also walking distance from Fisherman's Wharf.... *Tel 415/776–8688, 800/352–7366, fax 415/776–2811. 2237 Mason St., San Francisco, CA 94133, Powell/Mason cable car line, 15 or 30 MUNI bus. 62 rooms, all share bath. $–$$*

Sappho's Inn. This brown-and-beige Victorian set up as a safe haven for women could use a paint job and some new drapes, but the hand-painted sign over the door looks welcoming to those who don't mind staying in a neighborhood where most of the houses have bars on the ground-floor windows. Sappho's is on the edge of the Western Addition, which has improved considerably in recent years, but still requires some extra alertness around the housing projects. When you first check in, you might want to take a cab.... *Tel 415/775–3243. 859 Fulton St., San Francisco, CA 94117, 5 MUNI bus. 15 beds. $*

Sea Captain's Motel. This motel along the Marina offers room service, a Jacuzzi, and free parking.... *Tel 415/921–4980. 2322 Lombard St., San Francisco, CA 94123, 28 or 30 MUNI bus. 39 rooms. $–$$*

Sheraton Fisherman's Wharf. This hotel is not a pretty sight. With a little strategically placed graffiti, it could look like the city jail, which has, by the way, considerably more character. The rooms are bare-bones and expensive, presumably because the Fisherman's Wharf location appeals to unsuspecting tourists. However, there are a couple of redeeming factors, to wit: They have an outdoor heated pool and they accept pets.... *Tel 415/362–5500, 800/324–3535, fax 415/956–5275. 2500 Mason St., San Francisco, CA 94133; Powell/Mason cable car; 15, 42 MUNI bus. 525 rooms, 6 suites. $$$–$$$$$*

Sheraton Palace Hotel. Once the Palace Hotel, this San Francisco landmark has now been restored to its turn-of-the-century distinction, and you can bet your room rate is going to help pay for those $50,000 chandeliers. The antique-furnished rooms are beautiful and equipped with all the modern conveniences, and the health club boasts a lap pool along with all the standard fitness equipment.... *Tel 415/392–8600, 800/325–3535, fax 415/543–0671. 2 New Montgomery St., San Francisco, CA 94105; Montgomery St. BART/MUNI Metro stop; 7, 15, 30, 45 MUNI bus. 550 rooms, 32 suites. $$$$$*

Stouffer Renaissance Stanford Court Hotel. The Stanford Court is one of the most impressive hotels in the city, with a stained-glass dome in the lobby, antique furnishings in the rooms, and possibly the ghost of railroad baron Leland Stanford, founder of Stanford University, lurking in the hallways. The rooms are definitely deluxe, with bathrooms equipped with televisions and telephones. Services include on-call child care.... *Tel 415/989–3500, 800/227–4736, fax 415/391–0513. 905 California St., San Francisco, CA 94108, Powell/Hyde and Powell/Mason cable cars, 1 MUNI bus. 402 rooms, 18 suites. $$$$$*

Surf Motel. This horseshoe-shaped Fifties modern motel is located along the Marina (hence the name); it's wheelchair accessible and offers free parking.... *Tel 415/922–1950, 800/545–5333 California. 2265 Lombard St., San Francisco, CA 94123, 28 or 30 MUNI bus. 35 rooms. $–$$*

24 Henry Guesthouse. This very intimate little Victorian guesthouse (non-smoking) in the Castro District offers such amenities as libraries, sitting parlors, and a complimentary buffet breakfast.... *Tel 415/864–5686, 800/900–5686, fax 415/864–0286. 24 Henry St. (between Sanchez and Noe Sts.), San Francisco, CA 94114, J Church MUNI Metro. 5 rooms (4 with shared bath), 1 suite. $–$$$*

Victorian Inn on the Park. It's a bit misleading to call the narrow patch of grass between Fell and Oak Streets "the park," but since the Panhandle is technically attached to Golden Gate Park and the inn itself is so lovely, we'll let that go. The hotel is a beautifully restored historic landmark with 12 rooms, some of which have working fireplaces and terraces overlooking the Panhandle. If you like to flirt with the unwashed masses but go home to a reserved sanctuary, this is perfect. Breakfast and afternoon snacks are included.... *Tel 415/931–1830, 800/435–1967, fax 415/931–1830. 301 Lyon St., San Francisco, CA 94117, 7 MUNI bus. 12 rooms. $$$*

Westin Saint Francis. Perhaps the most venerable grande dame, the original old Saint Francis is architecturally exquisite. The new towers are not particularly remarkable, however, except for their super-fast elevators with magnificent views. It's extremely well located if you don't mind staying amid the thousands of Union Square shoppers and tourists. Rooms in the old building are preferable to those in the tower, and are slightly less expensive than their Nob Hill counterparts.... *Tel 415/397–7000, 800/228–3000, fax 415/774–0124. 335 Powell St., San Francisco, CA 94102; Powell/Hyde and Powell/Mason cable cars; 2, 3, 4, 30, 45, and 76 MUNI buses. 1,200 rooms, including 83 suites. $$$$–$$$$$*

York Hotel. The hotel's formal script logo, emblazoned on deep green awnings, belies the relaxed atmosphere that prevails at the York, a clean, peachy-colored Victorian that looks inviting from a block away.... *Tel 415/885–6800, 800/808–9675, fax 415/885–2115. 940 Sutter St., San Francisco, CA 94109, Powell/Mason or Powell/Hyde cable car, 38 MUNI bus. 96 rooms. $$$–$$$$*

San Francisco Accommodations

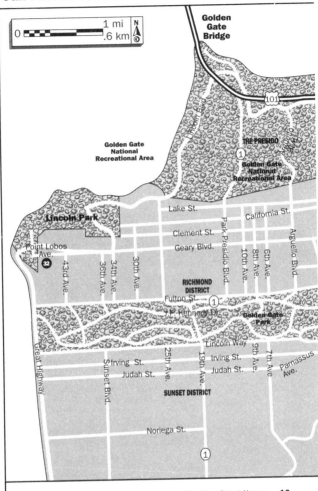

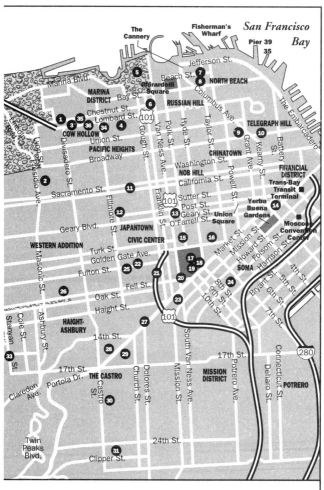

The Cannery

Fisherman's Wharf

San Francisco

Pier 39

35

7

Bay

Jefferson St.

Beach St. **NORTH BEACH**

5

MARINA DISTRICT Bay St.

Ghirardelli Square

8

Columbus Ave.

The Embarcadero

Chestnut St.

RUSSIAN HILL

6

1

35

Lombard St.

Hyde St.

Taylor St.

101

TELEGRAPH HILL

COW HOLLOW

34

4

Union St.

9

10

Grant Ave.

Kearny St.

Battery St.

PACIFIC HEIGHTS

Broadway

CHINATOWN

Washington St.

FINANCIAL DISTRICT

2

Sacramento St.

California St.

NOB HILL

Powell St.

Trans-Bay Transit Terminal

11

Franklin St.

Van Ness Ave.

Polk St.

Gough St.

101

Sutter St.

Post St.

Yerba Buena Gardens

14

12

13

Geary St.

Union Square

Moscone Convention Center

Geary Blvd.

Fillmore St.

JAPANTOWN

O'Farrell St.

Market St.

Mission St.

Howard St.

Folsom St.

Harrison St.

WESTERN ADDITION

CIVIC CENTER

15

16

Turk St.

Golden Gate Ave.

Masonic St.

25 **22**

17 **18**

SOMA

4th St.

5th St.

Fulton St.

19

Bryant St.

6th St.

26

21

20

24

9th St.

7th St.

Fell St.

23

10th St.

Oak St.

Haight St.

101

Stanyan St.

Cole St.

Ashbury St.

HAIGHT-ASHBURY

27

14th St.

South Van Ness Ave.

17th St.

Connecticut St.

280

33

28

29

POTRERO

17th St.

MISSION DISTRICT

Potrero Ave.

Deharo St.

Claredon Ave.

Portola Dr.

THE CASTRO

Church St.

Dolores St.

Mission St.

Twin Peaks Blvd.

30

Castro St.

24th St.

31

Clipper St.

Union Square/Nob Hill Accommodations

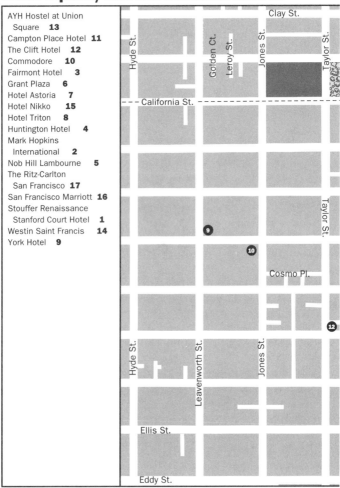

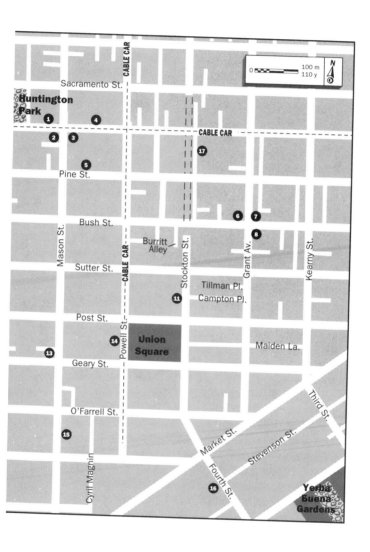

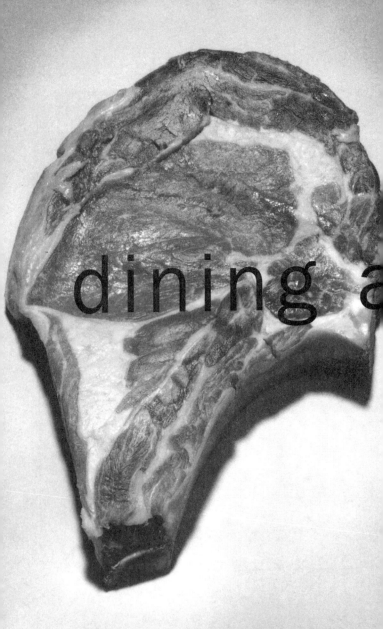

2

nd cafes

Welcome to one
of the best food
towns on the
planet. With some
3,500 restaurants
representing every
cuisine on earth

(and a few from outer space), the city that spawned California cuisine has become a magnet for ingenious chefs. They are drawn not only to the creative freedom that has always defined San Francisco, but also to the year-round abundance of fresh fruits, vegetables, herbs, fish, and seafood that are Northern California's unique bounty.

Oddly enough, it took local cooks until nearly the end of the twentieth century to figure out there was more to culinary life than steak and seafood, at which point they immediately went berserk with outlandish combinations of exotic ingredients and trickled raspberry vinegar on absolutely everything. Fortunately, most food fads—including that one—have the life span of a disposable razor, but there are some things you can always count on when you dine in San Francisco: a mélange of authentic ethnic eateries that is probably the most diverse in America; cafes, bistros, and formal dinner houses that serve extraordinary French food; a solid core of world-class restaurants inspired by California cuisine in all its transmutations; and, of course, the traditional grill fare that has been a staple since the Gold Rush. You could spend your entire vacation—and most of your money—eating at Masa's, and other high-profile spots that have gotten more press than the Internet, but the best way to enjoy San Francisco's lavish feast is to explore the nation's most exotic variety of ethnic food. Often the most interesting and delicious food is far less expensive than see-and-be-scene fare. There are far too many excellent restaurants than can be mentioned here, but the samples we offer will get you started on your own dining adventure.

Only in San Francisco

The sunny **Mission District** has long been famous for its Mexican restaurants and storefront taquerias, where locals take for granted lunchtime feasts of authentic barbecued pork *carnitas* and grilled steak (*carne asada*) for less than the price of a Big Mac. A steady stream of immigrants and refugees from Guatemala, El Salvador, Nicaragua, Chile, and Peru have brought dozens of new restaurants to the neighborhood, adding countless treats to the Latin American banquet table. Chinese food is also synonymous with San Francisco, but you can find that in almost every city. The true gems are the rarer **Asian/Pacific** cuisines such as Cambodia's complex mingling of coconut milk, lemongrass, lime, and fish sauce finished in the French tradition with butter and parsley; or Singapore's exotic seafood dishes that combine European, Indian, Chinese, and Malaysian influences.

Supper clubs are night creatures' latest raison d'être, so swanky drinks like martinis are very chic these days, but San Francisco's own naturally fermented **Anchor Steam beer** is high on the locals' list of favorite beverages—(get it on tap, not in the bottle). Beer has been big in the city since the raucous Barbary Coast days, when the **San Francisco Brewing Company** pub (corner of Columbus and Pacific avenues) first opened its doors. After Prohibition, the 1907 establishment started legally producing its own beer (we love the Shanghai Pale Ale), which is available only at the pub or in extremely limited bottled batches at two neighborhood liquor stores (the **Jug Shop**, 1576 Pacific Ave., and **Coit Liquors**, 585 Columbus Ave.). Don't try to take it home as a souvenir—the beer is not pasteurized, so it must be refrigerated to last even two weeks. Finally, though Irish coffee is far from a local invention, a visit to the **Buena Vista Cafe** for a cup of it—especially on a foggy late afternoon—is a time-honored tradition among locals and tourists alike.

Ethnic Eats

Sharon Silver and Frank Viviano's Exploring the Best Ethnic Restaurants of the Bay Area *(San Francisco Focus Books, tel 415/553–2800) is a lively and very helpful book put out by the city's public television station, KQED. It describes almost three dozen different varieties of ethnic cuisine available in the Bay Area, with glossaries that will help you find your way through a menu, and recommendations for the best restaurants in San Francisco and the rest of the Bay Area. There are also many helpful sidebars that explain in depth how particular dishes are made, so you'll know exactly what to order when you come to sample San Francisco's incredibly diverse cuisine.*

How to Dress

Jackets and ties are rarely mandatory at San Francisco restaurants, but common sense should dictate the obvious: If you're going to a fancy place, dress up a bit. You'll probably need some sort of jacket, anyway, simply because it is so cool at night, even in summer. At casual establishments, anything goes. As long as you don't look like you just climbed out of a dumpster, you'll probably be acceptable no matter what you're wearing.

When to Eat

Unlike their New York night-owl counterparts, San Franciscans tend to dine *before* they go to the opera or ballet, not afterward. That means you need to reserve weeks in advance if you want to have dinner before 8 in any popular restaurant near a major theater or concert hall. After 8:30, however, you

SAN FRANCISCO | DINING

can walk right into Backstage, the Hayes Street Grill or other popular "opera ghetto" restaurants (those clustered near the performing arts mecca centering on City Hall and the War Memorial Opera House) and get a table on the spot. That's a very important thing to remember when it's a Saturday night and you're dying for a great meal but forgot to make reservations anywhere. Very few restaurants serve dinner after 10, so get your grazing over with before you go out on the town, or you may be stuck with burgers or all-night coffee-shop food (see Eating with Insomniacs). Most breakfast places serve all day, with specials often ending at 11:30, and lunch tends to be whatever you feel like eating between then and mid-afternoon, when many restaurants begin to gear up for dinner. Mexican food seems to work for breakfast, lunch, and dinner, so you'll never have to go hungry if you can find your way to the Mission District.

Getting the Right Table

Unless your major objective in going to a restaurant is to gawk at celebrities—or perhaps be mistaken for one—the right table isn't much of an issue in San Francisco. Some few restaurants, such as Act IV at the Inn at the Opera (see Accommodations), have one exceptional table (theirs is by a fireplace) that is worth booking in advance for those who are planning a do-or-die romantic encounter, but the trendiest establishments tend to do the same thing as in every town—pack in the hoi polloi wherever they fit. (The Index notes where reservations are recommended.)

Where the Chefs Are

It's a small town, and it seems every star chef used to be somebody else's sous chef. **Richard Radcliffe** worked with Joyce Goldstein at Square One and Reed Harron at Lulu before honing his Mediterranean/California/International craft at Backstage (near the opera house); **Yahya Salih** was cultivated by superchef Jeremiah Tower (Stars, Balboa Cafe) before unleashing his distinctive Iraqi-inspired hybrid at his own Sunset District establishment, Yaya Cuisine. Then there are the switcheroos: **Rick Hackett** left Oliveto to resuscitate Enrico's Sidewalk Cafe in North Beach as an eclectic supper club; **Alain Rondelli** came all the way from a three-star restaurant in Paris to open his eponymous bistro in what was once Le St. Tropez, after **Gerald Hirigoyen** moved out of that Clement Street locale to open Fringale in the South of

Market district. After founder Masataha Kobayashi's death, chef **Julian Serrano** consoled the gourmet world with his culinary flawlessness, keeping Masa's (Union Square) on a par with the best French restaurants in the world.

Café Society

When you hear people raving about the café scene in San Francisco, they're not referring to posh bistros that call themselves cafés primarily to horn in on the French tradition of charging a small fortune for a dab of *je ne sais quoi*. They're talking about coffeehouses with names like **Jammin' Java**, **Red Dora's Bearded Lady**, and **Mad Magda's Russian Tea Room**—neighborhood caffeine dens that are often much more popular than bars as places to meet, hear music, listen to poetry, read, write, talk about art and politics, or just sit and watch the general buzz. The best cafés are basically ongoing block parties.

In recent years, Seattle has often been mislabeled by the media as America's gourmet coffee center—primarily due to the success of Starbucks coffee stores—but the problem with this whole Seattle blather is that coffee by itself is utterly insignificant. Seattle could sell enough coffee beans to fill up Mount St. Helens, and it would still never be San Francisco. San Francisco's coffeehouses and cafés are the hearts and souls of their communities. When **Radio Valencia**—a small corner café instrumental in the revitalization of the city's "New Bohemia," the Mission District's Valencia Street—was smashed by a fire truck in a head-on collision, countless charitable offers poured in from customers and merchants around the neighborhood.

Such small neighborhood cafés have been the center of the city's vital bohemian scene since the turn of the century,

The Ultimate Café Guide
There are hundreds of cafés in San Francisco, but just one book that tells about every single one, including 32 separate indexes that group the cafés according to what they serve, how they serve it, who goes there, whether or not there are bookstores or laundromats nearby, and scores of other categories. James M. Forbes' Café San Francisco— Or How to Stop Worrying and Live with Little Money offers an engaging history of coffeehouse culture and reviews each café in town, noting not only the ambiance, clientele, and decor, but specifying every detail down to the brand of coffee served. Check your local bookstore, or send $10.95 plus $4.50 shipping and handling to Café San Francisco, 715 Cole St. #168, San Francisco, CA 94117.

SAN FRANCISCO | DINING

and have enticed some of the most interesting artists and writers in the world to not only visit, but stay. Chain coffee stores owned by giant corporations miss the point—and the social experience—entirely.

Navigating the Coffee Trail

In many of San Francisco's neighborhoods, there are at least two cafés per block—parts of the Mission District and the Haight average twice that many. The key to your own adventures in café-land is to get a feel for a neighborhood, remember that most cafés are defined by who goes there, and discover your own favorite spots as you go.

North Beach has been a bohemian stronghold for more than a century, known best for the Beat movement that originated there in the Fifties, when Jack Kerouac and Allen Ginsberg were regulars at **Caffe Trieste** and **Enrico's**. Lawrence Ferlinghetti still hangs around—and displays his paintings—at Enrico's and **Caffe Puccini**. There are more than 20 cafés in one six-block area alone—bordered by Union Street and Broadway on the north and south, and Grant and Powell streets on the east and west. The coffee and pastries are very Italian, as is the opera music commonly heard on the jukeboxes, and the customers range from neighborhood residents having their afternoon coffee break to visitors from all over the world.

The **Mission District** café scene is funky, neighborhood-oriented, and the command post of Beatnik Central. Very few touristy types make it out to Valencia Street's hip coffeehouses, but locals come from all over the city to take in the live music and spoken word performances—and to congregate with young, anti-fashion fashion-setters. Most of the cafés (and bars) are concentrated in the area bordered by 16th and 24th streets on the north and south, and by Mission and Valencia streets on the east and west.

The **Haight** is still a hippie haven of sorts, but the post-punk species is far better suited than its flower-child predecessors to hours of angst-ridden malingering at local coffee joints. The neighborhood isn't all nose rings, purple hair, and Jerry Garcia murals, though. You'll find cafés for every taste, from tranquil little pastry shops to ultra-hip hangouts virtually vibrating from the blare of loud music and the jolt of caffeine. Walk along Haight Street from Central to Stanyan, and don't be afraid to venture a block or two up or down the side streets.

Other cafés we mention are located in three areas where you'd expect to find the city's café culture well-represented: **Hayes Valley**, a small, sunny neighborhood perfect for strolling because it basically involves just a few blocks along Hayes Street (between Franklin and Buchanan streets) with an occasional side-street detour; **South of Market**, an industrial neighborhood where artists, architects, multimedia gurus, filmmakers, and musicians live and work in warehouse lofts (below Market Street, between Second and Tenth streets); and the **Castro** district, San Francisco's infamous gay mecca (mostly south of Market to about 20th Street., between Castro and Sanchez streets).

Finally, there are the refuges—cafés that provide escapes from neighborhoods that are often overrun by tourists or other consumption-crazed breeds. The ones we mention are located in the **Financial District** (Grant Ave. at Sutter St.) and the gentrified section of **Fillmore Street** (near Steiner St.).

The Real Poop on Starbucks

When every Denny's in America serves cappuccino with the breakfast special, blame it on Seattle. Not so long ago, a decent shot of espresso was a rare pleasure in that neck of the woods (and we do mean woods). Then suddenly, Seattle was hailed nationwide as the undisputed coffee heaven of the New World. They had discovered espresso sort of like Columbus discovered America—with little or no acknowledgement of those who had already cultivated it for generations. The most obvious player, Starbucks, is a publicly held company with a huge chain of coffee bars that are about as avant-garde as Mrs. Field's. The company was started by a former San Franciscan who first imitated Berkeley's beloved family-owned Peet's coffee store, then bought Peet's, then sold Starbucks to venture capitalists (but kept Peet's), and now has to compete with Starbucks to try to stay alive. David created Goliath.

SAN FRANCISCO | DINING

The Lowdown

Grills in the mist... Long before there was California cuisine or nouvelle anything, mesquite-grilled seafood was the most popular item at **Tadich Grill**, where mesquite has been the charcoal of choice since the 1920s. The juicy steaks and fresh seafood at this turn-of-the-century Financial District landmark are still so enticing that most savvy locals prefer to eat at the counter than endure the long wait at the mahogany bar for a table (no reservations are accepted). Still, the wait is worth it for the coveted private booths that have hosted scandalous trysts and backroom power deals almost since time began. As you'll learn if you go on any of the Dashiell Hammett walking tours, **John's Grill** is the place where Sam Spade ate his chops (actually rack of lamb) while in pursuit of the Maltese falcon—a replica of the black bird, donated by Warner Brothers, sits in a display case outside John's small Hammett museum. Founded in 1908, this downtown dinner house has wood-paneled walls, period furnishings, and perfectly grilled, tender steaks. South of Market's **Fly Trap Restaurant** has moved a few blocks away from its original 1898 address, where fly paper was tacked to the tables to keep the horses' pesky companions off the steaks, but it still bases its menu on traditional San Francisco grill fare. The decor is conventional but not stuffy—small cloth-covered tables with cafe chairs and a variety of maps and architectural drawings on the walls—and its comfort-food specialties follow suit.

For committed carnivores... The best pure-and-simple steak house in town is definitely **Harris'**, midway between Russian Hill and Pacific Heights on Van Ness Avenue, where luscious cuts of Midwestern corn-fed beef are dry-aged on the premises, martinis flow by the barrel, and the gigantic booths can swallow you whole. **Izzy's Steaks and Chops** is also a meat-eater's dream, but its true glory is its status as a lively Marina watering hole. The steaks, though tender and delicious, may not be quite as luxurious as those at Harris', but they cost a lot less.

If you're George Jetson on an expense account... The least traditional food in San Francisco is served at the Mission District's ultra-hip, ultra-crowded **Flying Saucer**, where chefs from other restaurants line up with other customers to sample food that tastes out of this world and looks like what George Jetson might order on an expense account. Squid, papaya, and vermicelli become basic elements of one of Chef Albert Tordjman's sculptured entrees, with cilantro, lime, and mint as added texture and color, and Thai vinaigrette as auxiliary rocket fuel. The menu is based in his French background, but from there it sprouts wildly with California, Latin, and Asian flavors.

See-and-be-scenes... Where you go to be seen depends largely on whom you hope to see—and how long it takes the trendies to get bored with the place. For years, Jeremiah Tower's **Stars** (near Civic Center) has been the easiest place for commoners to rub shoulders with celebrities. If you're feeling Absolutely Fabulous, snag a seat at the long bar and have either a martini or a glass of champagne while you watch people watch each other. **Moose's** (North Beach) is a good place to go if you want to stare at fashion models and young Republicans—and you don't mind eating in a room that feels big enough to host a national convention. The best people-watching is on crowded weekend nights, when the long wait for a table leaves people milling around in the foyer near the bar. **Enrico's Sidewalk Cafe** (see "North Beach classics" below) has always been a great place to people-watch, and nightly jazz makes it even more fun. You can have a full dinner or just stop in for a drink, but you'll always find someone to look at.

Hold the hype... No matter how endlessly food critics lavish praise on the super-restaurants, there are some sacred cows, like Berkeley's **Chez Panisse**, that aren't always worth the money and effort. To give credit where it's due, Chez Panisse has been the most important restaurant in the Bay Area's culinary development in the past two decades. But sometimes the students catch up with the teachers, and there are plenty of other restaurants with more innovative chefs and less expensive tabs. The fact that you have to reserve a month in advance for a weekend dinner may be a testament to the restaurant's reputation, but it's also a pain in the neck, especially when you don't know if you'll be in the mood for the prix-fixe meal when the day finally arrives. The above-mentioned **Stars** is also untouchably popular with critics—and publicity agents—despite the fact that it is so loud you can not carry on a conversation without shouting and the commoners-hoping-to-hobnob-with-celebrities factor can make you feel like you're having a nightmare about Los Angeles.

Some like it hot... For authentic four-alarm Thai food that is unbelievably delicious but not watered down for uninitiated Western tongues, the Upper Haight's **Thep Phanom** can't be beat. The Thai wait staff, whose traditional garb suits the gracious, antique-laden dining room, usually try to warn you when a dish is hot. Believe them. They mean it. The super-hot delicacies include *larb ped* (duck salad with mint, hot chili peppers, red onion, and lemon); even the milder dishes, such as charbroiled catfish or deep-fried quail, are served with a variety of hot dipping sauces. For cooler options, try any of the mild curries, especially those made with coconut milk. **Cha Cha Cha** is a Haight hot spot in more ways than one— it's an exhaustingly popular place, especially if you indulge in the house special Sangria in the funky bar area during your inevitable hour-or-so-long wait for a table. And the Cajun/Caribbean food (mostly tapas) is absolutely fiery. That's saying something in San Francisco, where Mexican food has numbed most locals to anything cooler than a jalapeño. If the huge plates of flawless spicy ribs, beef and chicken didn't already qualify **Flint's** of North Oakland as the undisputed barbecue-joint champion of the world, the fact that it serves until 4 in the morning would definitely clinch the title. If you even *think* you like barbecue, hop on BART and ride over to North Oakland (Flint's is two blocks south of the Ashby stop)—there's nothing even close to this in San Francisco. It's all take-out, though, so if your craving comes at 3am, you may have to smuggle your greasy treasures back to your hotel room.

Tastiest tapas... Cities everywhere have gone a bit mad for those little Spanish tidbits that are more than an appetizer but less than a main dish. **Cha Cha Cha** serves a blazing Caribbean/Cajun version, while the Mission District's boisterous **Esperpento**, decorated like somebody's surrealistic dream about a childhood piñata party, remains steadfastly and authentically Spanish. All of the tapas are worth tasting, so share them family-style; the most popular main dish here is probably the paella, a steaming mountain of shellfish, pork, chicken, and saffron-flavored rice served in the pan. But the ultimate tapas in town may be those at **Timo's**, an eccentric, semi-Bohemian place that shares its Mission District home with a neighborhood bar called the Zanzibar, and appreciates a good cigar (a tobacco menu is available for discriminating smoke-eaters) as much as a perfect salsa. The tapas are just like the ones you get in Spain—treats such as roasted new potatoes in aioli, and potato cakes and fish with cilantro-mint salsa—and the crowd is interesting, artistic, and decidedly local.

Pass the dumplings, darling... The other little morsels that make tastebuds quiver in ecstasy are served from dim sum carts—tender shrimp wrapped in paper-thin dumplings, tiny crab cakes, octopus with hot peppers, and dozens of other Chinese delicacies. For exceptionally delicate dumplings, **Yank Sing** has long been the favorite of locals on the weekends—Financial District types tend to crowd into its modern, somewhat upscale dining room during the week—but nearby **Harbor Village** is a more serene and majestic alternative at lunch time (11–2:30). You won't find any unidentified steamed objects on their carts; instead you'll find dozens of authentic delicacies served by a meticulous wait staff. Every porcelain dish and carved chopstick reflects the Imperial aesthetic Harbor Village claims to have brought from Hong Kong, and the dim sum tradition allows you to enjoy all its refinement without the high tab of its exquisite dinners.

Best Chinese in Chinatown... **R & G Lounge** serves probably the best food in Chinatown. The dining room used to be in the basement of a commercial building, but a brighter, upstairs room has been opened to accommodate the burgeoning clientele drawn primarily by super-fresh seafood. If you think Maine has a corner on the lobster market, do yourself a favor and try a live one from R & G's tank. One huge plus at the R & G Lounge is that the waiters will gladly translate the Chinese menu for Westerners, which expands the choices considerably.

South of the border in the Mission... The Mission District is crammed with Central and South American food that is sometimes even tastier than its native version because of the wonderful fresh ingredients that abound in San Francisco. Even the most ordinary taqueria beats a fast-food lunch by a mile. Start with our suggestions, then graze your own way through the neighborhood. **Los Jarritos** makes wonderful fresh tortillas and other home-cooked Mexican delights for a loyal following of local customers, many of whom travel across the city—and sometimes the bridges—for its food and friendly ambiance. Call in advance to find out when they'll be serving posole, a spicy chicken and pork stew that takes all day to prepare and is rarely available outside of home kitchens. If you want to get in a good mood fast, go to **La Rondalla**. It serves standard Mexican fare such as enchiladas, chiles rellenos (stuffed chili peppers baked in egg batter), and other recognizable dishes, but there's nothing standard about the atmosphere, from the year-round Christmas ornaments to the strolling mariachis who serenade on weekends. **La Taqueria** is an immaculate neighborhood favorite famous for its shredded pork *carnitas*, which fill soft, fluffy tortillas to make the perfect taco.

Chef/owner Gus Shinzato of **Fina Estampa**, another comfortable storefront establishment, is Japanese-Peruvian, and his menu relies heavily on Peru's spicy cross-cultural coastal cuisine, made with fresh local catch. Specialties include *parihuela*, a tomato and chili soup laced with the freshest seafood he can find, including mussels, clams, shrimp, squid, and other Pacific delicacies. Modest **El Nuevo Frutilandia** is one of the few places in the city to get home-cooked Puerto Rican and Cuban food (the fresh fruit shakes are wonderful, as are the Puerto Rican dumplings made of crushed plantain and yuca, filled with shredded pork). And right next door you can get one of the best dinner deals in town at **El Trebol**, a Formica-table kind of place that serves Salvadoran/Nicaraguan treats like *pupusas* (handmade corn patties stuffed with cheese or meat or both) for less than a dollar and full meals (including rice and beans) for less than $4.

Seoul food... Do-it-yourself Korean barbecue joints have become extremely popular, partially because many of them are inexpensive all-you-can-eat propositions, but mostly because the food is delicious and it's as much fun to cook as it is to eat. You barbecue marinated beef and pork on grills built into the tables, wrap the meat in a lettuce leaf and add whatever condiments you like—kind of a Korean burrito. **Kyung Bok Palace** has made a name for itself among the many Korean eateries along Geary Boulevard (Richmond District) by offering at least 10 different varieties of kimchee (spicy, pickled cabbage) to go with dinner. It packs the house with a mix of local Koreans and non-Korean students and families. **Brothers Restaurant** is a bit smaller and less hectic, catering to a primarily Korean clientele—it's probably the most popular Geary Boulevard place with local Koreans, and the staff sometimes proves its own authenticity when you're making reservations in English. You can grill meats at its tables' wood-fired hibachis or sample from the rest of its small menu. Brothers' kimchee is truly outstanding.

A passage to India... Many of the best Indian eateries in the Bay Area are outside San Francisco in the Indian and Pakistani communities of the East and South Bay, but the best in the city, **Gaylord of India**, is in an unlikely spot—the middle of touristy Ghirardelli Square. Unfortunately, you'll pay rather dearly for the gourmet quality (about $40 per person, à la carte) and its wonderful view of the bay. One way to economize is to order the *thali* plates (about $25 a person), which allow you to sample a wide variety of either vegetarian or tandoori dishes; then you can splurge on a luscious dessert, such as *kulfi* (homemade pistachio ice cream). A much less costly alternative is a multicourse meatless feast at **Ganges Vegetarian Restaurant**, a cozy refuge in a Victorian house near the Haight. There are low tables with floor cushions in back and Western-style tables and chairs in front. Owner Malvi Doshi's vegetarian dinners include classic yogurt/cucumber salad, vegetables with assorted chutneys, stew or soup, curries, a variety of main dishes (vegetarian, of course), and finally dessert.

Asian delights... One of the first places you should go on your San Francisco ethnic-food adventure tour is **Angkor Borei**, the perfect place to sample Cambodia's intricate cuisine at the modest price tag locals have come to expect in the Mission District. The combination of spices in most any dish on the menu is intriguing—typically, sweet basil and tangy lemongrass are first to hit the tongue, then a short blast of hot chili pepper bursts through, and finally soothing coconut milk brings the whole blend together. If the combination of tropical flavors and French culinary techniques make you want to try even more sophisticated Cambodian cuisine (at a considerably higher price), try **Angkor Wat**, an elegant Richmond District dinner house. To economize, take advantage of the weekday lunch special (call for current specifics). Geary Boulevard's tropical, romantic **Straits Cafe** features extraordinary food from Singapore, an exotic hybrid of European, Indian, Chinese, and Malaysian tastes that mixes spicy-hot peanut sauces with cool cucumbers and coconut milk curries. Chef Chris Yeo uses all those flavors and textures to create extraordinary dishes like *laksa* (tamarind-scented broth with fish, chili peppers, onions, and rice noodles), and *satays* (chunks of meat). For great Vietnamese food, check out the **Golden Turtle**, a modestly elegant restaurant near Russian Hill that looks and tastes much more expensive than it is. You will be offered a choice of several French wines to complement the delicately spiced entrees, ranging from steamed sea bass with fresh ginger to grilled beef with lemongrass. The **Saigon Sandwich Cafe** is a Civic Center take-out deli with incredible Vietnamese sandwiches—baguettes full of pork or chicken with spicy sauces, cilantro, and peppers, or the popular Vietnamese-style meatball sandwiches—for around $2.

Japanese jewels... For a variety of Japanese country-style food—fluffy tempura, savory noodles, and dumplings—go to **Sanppo** in the heart of Japantown, a favorite of local Japanese, where you may be asked to share a table when the regular crowd elbows in. Sanppo's rustic, home-like decor is instantly cozy. The tempura is consistently excellent and the *gyoza nabe* (pot stickers in a savory broth with noodles and bean curd) is a wonderful meal in itself. **Cho-Cho**'s tempura bar makes it popular with the Financial District crowd for after-work martinis and snacks, but it's the shabu-shabu—an audience-participation delicacy that involves sitting at a large, low table and cooking pieces of seafood, fish, meat, and vegetables by dipping them into a steaming caldron of tasty broth—that makes it such a fun place to stay for dinner. For the freshest sushi in town, call in advance to **Hama-Ko**, a gracious little Cole Valley restaurant, and ask chef Ted Kashiyama to prepare his special deluxe meal of hot and cold dishes; the exact contents depend on what local fishermen have available that morning.

The French connection... Three-star **Masa's** is the name you'll hear bandied about most often when people are bragging about the best restaurants in town—chef Julian Serrano is virtually worshipped by food critics and fledgling chefs for his unflagging dedication to authentic, perfectly executed French cuisine. His foie gras (with cognac and black truffles) and his roast squab have been described in near-religious terms. But you can easily find more innovative and far less expensive French food in more modest bistros such as **Alain Rondelli** (Clement Street) and **Fringale** (South of Market). Rondelli, who once cooked for the president of France and ran a three-star kitchen of his own in Paris, is so in love with food that he often serves complimentary samples of unusual items to patrons, and he regularly offers a $45 six-course tasting menu to acquaint people with his approach. The fresh scallops in plum-lime marmalade (seared to a crispy gold on top and served with arugula), and the braised pork shank in vinegar–juniper berry broth evoke audible moans of pleasure. Fringale's menu reflects its chef's Basque origins as well as his classic training; the place is reasonably priced, and so friendly and comfortable that you never feel self-conscious, despite the studied indifference of much of the too-hip-for-words clientele. The frisée salad with warm bacon dressing and croutons is exquisite—soft but not soggy—and the pork tenderloin with onion and apple marmalade is rich and velvety without being overly sweet. If you want to feel as though you *are* in Paris, stop in at a Financial District treasure, **Cafe Claude**, where every fixture, chair, dish, and spoon was imported from France. It's jammed with a lively, youngish crowd who come to enjoy both the atmosphere and the inexpensive but oh-so-French sandwiches along with a glass or two of Rhine, Beaujolais, or Mâcon Blanc wine.

Aria hungry?... The Civic Center opera ghetto, which surrounds the symphony hall and opera house, is dotted with splendid restaurants that are jammed to the rafters until 8 on performance nights, and often up for grabs between 8:30 and 10. Take advantage of that quirky schedule to enjoy superb meals at Backstage and the Hayes Street Grill. Stylish **Backstage**'s chef Richard Radcliffe, author of perhaps the best crème brûlée in the city, is the Sam Shepard of cooking—his meticulous attention to detail produces sumptuous, uncontrived dishes such as a delicious Tuscany-inspired Muscovy duck ragout with wild herb pappardelle, featuring local Sonoma County duck (chosen for its subtle flavor and

SAN FRANCISCO | DINING

lack of gaminess). His eclectic Mediterranean/California/International menu changes monthly, so ask for his suggestions before you order; Radcliffe is rapidly becoming a superchef, but he still loves to share his food and advice with patrons. Fish and seafood are the mainstays of the **Hayes Street Grill** menu—which changes daily—and they may be sautéed or mesquite-grilled with a Mexican, American, French, Italian, or Asian accent, depending on which accompanying vegetables are freshest that day. Grilled Alaskan king salmon and pan-fried Hama-Hama oysters are typical favorites. Some purists bemoan the loss of the older, funkier decor—creaky floors and cafe chairs—to the carpeting and chic little banquettes of the new and improved Hayes Street Grill, but the food is just as good as ever.

Vegging out... The Mother of All Vegetarian Restaurants must be **Greens**, where there is a 2-week waiting list to sample the fare that has spawned several cookbooks, international acclaim, and a devoted following that brings people hundreds of miles just for dinner. This is no hippie-veggie-health-food cafe; it is meatless *haute cuisine*, combining the best of French, Mediterranean, and California cookery. The menu changes regularly, but past favorites have included a puffy vegetable cake laced with ricotta and gruyère cheeses, topped with a tangy-sweet tomato and sherry sauce, and finished with a spoonful of crème fraîche. Add the gracious dining room with its enchanting view of the Marina, and you'll see why this brainchild of San Francisco's Zen Center is considered one of the best vegetarian restaurants in the world.

Still, we'd rather go to **Millennium** in the Civic Center's hip Abigail Hotel, where the menu is smaller but more whimsical—with items like Dr. Dunphy's Chinese Herbal Aphrodisiac Love Potion, which you're not likely to find at dignified Greens. Though the white linen is sufficiently upscale, the staff is mercifully less serene. Every ingredient is organic and purely vegan, so don't expect any butter with your fresh-baked herb bread. **Ganges Vegetarian Restaurant** is a great spot for people who love traditional Indian food but would prefer not to lay their eyes on any cooked flesh.

North Beach classics... Cafes are the heart and soul of North Beach, but only **Enrico's Sidewalk Cafe** is a first-class restaurant and supper club as well, with live jazz every night (no cover charge). The dinner menu stretches from roasted turnip salad to Spanish seafood paella and duck breast gumbo, but hungry locals gobble Enrico's trade-mark hamburgers (served on Italian focaccia) until closing time. When Broadway turned so seedy in the 1980s that owner Enrico Banducci pulled his chairs in off the side-walk and boarded up his windows, most people figured his classic coffeehouse was dead, but the new owners have surely turned things around. Everybody loves Enrico's, all day and all night, every day and every night.

Columbus Avenue's main strip (between Broadway and Washington Square) is loaded with calzone joints and trattorias, but if you pass them all by on your way to Greenwich Street, you'll find rich, authentic Tuscan food that locals rave about at **Buca Giovanni**. Chef Giovanni Leoni works with produce he grows himself, and garlic lovers should be in heaven here—the smell of the stinking rose greets you well before you descend into the down-stairs dining room (*buca* means "hole" in Italian) that gave the place its name. Plan on two to three hours for din-ner—Leoni's hearty, mega-caloric cuisine (like veal ravio-li slathered in *panzerotti salsa di noci*, a rich white sauce with walnuts) requires plenty of time to savor and digest.

Athens al fresco... What could be better than feather-light filo dough, made from scratch and layered into sweet, delicate baklava that melts in your mouth? Try all that plus a sunny afternoon in the outdoor garden upstairs at **Stoyanof**, a cheery Sunset District cafe. Georgi Stoyanof and his son Angel also wrap their delicate filo around Greek cheeses, spinach, and lamb; dinner is a bit more formal, featuring classic Macedonian seafood dish-es and exotic appetizers.

The rest of the world... You've enjoyed many specialties of the city's global kitchen, from Geary Boulevard's hibachis to the Mission District's tapas, but you'd be miss-ing out on three of San Francisco's most fun—and unusu-al—dining experiences if you bypassed Suppenküche, Yaya Cuisine, or Helmand. Fans of German food may find **Suppenküche** one of the only places in town to satisfy their appetite. A small, spirited Hayes Valley beer hall and cafe, it serves delicious German food and drink to a good-humored, youngish crowd. The staples, served at plain wood tables, are variations of sauerkraut and sausage—flanked by baskets full of fresh-baked breads or mounds of buttery Bavarian-style mashed potatoes—supplemented by the more refined choices on the daily special chalkboard. At **Yaya Cuisine**, Chef Yahya Salih, who learned his culinary wizardry from superchef Jeremiah Tower, has transformed the cuisine of his native Iraq into a mouth-watering Mediterranean/California hybrid. Salih's enthusiasm is evident in every aspect of this Sunset District restaurant—his giant mural of Babylon that covers an entire wall, his habit of leaving the kitchen to chat with customers, and an ambitious menu. Tables are set with Iraqi-style flatbread to be dipped in thyme-sesame olive oil and savored while you mull over your order; try the steamed oysters or vegetarian dolmas (his are whole vegetables stuffed with bulgur and chili peppers), both dressed in yogurt-mint sauce, or such main dishes as a hearty lamb stew or the California-style roasted baby chicken. The Helmand River flows out of Iran through Afghanistan; the formal dinner house **Helmand** rests on the shores of Broadway, which flows from North Beach to Pacific Heights. The Afghani food here is exquisite, with flavors from Central Asia, India, and the Middle East, and owner Mahmood Karzai has done Westerners the favor of removing much of the fat from the traditional recipes. We recommend *aushak,* a delicate, triangular-shaped wheat dumpling filled with leek and served in a yogurt-mint or beef sauce reminiscent of the Far East, and *chowpan seekh,* a grilled rack of lamb on Iranian-style flatbread; don't be afraid to try lots of new things, like *kaddo borawni,* an appetizer of baked pumpkin with garlic yogurt sauce.

Goofy decor, fabulous food... **Miss Pearl's Jam House** looks like a movie set for the cartoon version of Abbott and Costello Go to Gilligan's Island, and the rainbow-colored drinks are often tricked up with paper umbrellas, but the food at this wacky Civic Center hangout is definitely the genuine article. Delectable Caribbean dishes like jerked chicken, cold squid with ginger, chili, lime, and peppers, or a salad of jicama (a delicate root that tastes like a cross between an apple and a parsnip) will get you in the mood for the carousing that follows dinner. Many artists, musicians, and otherwise irresistible riff-raff join the youngish crowd here, so the dancing and socializing are definitely an important part of the experience (but watch out for that limbo).

The **Cypress Club**, though reminiscent of a grand, baroque opium den, is the opposite of funky. The ultrachic backdrop once made this North Beach dining room a temple of trendiness, with more patrons jockeying for a strategic spot at the see-and-be-seen bar than ordering food at the tables. The Trend Factor has waned a bit, but the menu remains impressive; it's as rich as the decor. Don't miss the venison.

Kid pleasers... Dining with the family can be tricky business, especially if your children vary in age, but you're always safe in any of the neighborhood eateries in the Mission District, where there is usually at least one six-year-old running between tables while apologetic parents try to pull in the reins. **El Nuevo Frutilandia** (24th St.) is an especially good choice, because the fruit shakes will appeal to all ages, even if the Puerto Rican food is a bit too spicy for the younger palate. **La Rondalla** (Valencia St.) is fun for lunch or early dinner because of the goofy decorations, and the traditional Mexican food familiar to most kids—and not too fiery. (Later in the evening, the bar livens up and the atmosphere is less suitable for younger children.) If the kids do like hot-and-spicy treats, take them to **Kyung Bok Palace** (Richmond District), where they can have a ball playing chef and cooking their own meat on the grills. You'll have to sign up on a waiting list at the door, but if you go early enough, the wait won't be long.

It is actually possible to please teenagers if you take them to the right places and pretend to be Hollywood agents instead of their parents. Try **Hamburger Mary's**, a funky South of Market spot that attracts a lot of hip X-Generation types and serves great burgers and other American standards with humor and aplomb. Another cool spot is **Miss Pearl's Jam House** (near Civic Center). It's more like a Caribbean party boat than a restaurant, and it's attached to the Phoenix, *the* motel where all the rock stars stay. There's no telling who might be at the table next to you—at Miss Pearl's, the Red Hot Chili Peppers are not just a spice, they're a band (your teenagers

SAN FRANCISCO | DINING

already know that). Again, it's probably better earlier in the evening, before the bar becomes the focal point.

Where to seal a deal... This, of course, depends upon the client. The old-boy network tends to be wary of fancy food and effusive waiters, which you'll never find at **Harris'** (Van Ness Ave.). It's not cheap, but it's the best steak house in the city, and a few of Harris' martinis can soften up even the toughest old buzzard. If your client is of the artistic persuasion, go to the **Cypress Club** (North Beach), where the ingenious, surrealistic decor is matched by the superb menu. Attorneys love the **Fly Trap**, the traditional San Francisco grill (with a few culinary updates) across the street from the courthouse. If your clients are food lovers who don't want to be bothered with trendy trappings, take them to our favorite small French bistros—**Alain Rondelli** (Clement St.) and **Fringale** (South of Market)—or for the créme brûlée at **Backstage** (near the opera house).

Cheap eats... The Mission District is jammed with great food at very inexpensive prices, but the best buy of all is **El Trebol** (24th St.), where a full Salvadoran dinner including rice and beans comes in at around $4. Other Mission haunts famous for good food for next to nothing are **La Taqueria** (Mission St. near 24th), a family-oriented Mexican cafe, and **El Nuevo Frutilandia** (next door to El Trebol), where the fruit shakes are as popular as the Puerto Rican food. The best Vietnamese deli in the city is the **Saigon Sandwich Cafe** (near Civic Center), where $2 will buy a delectable pork or chicken sandwich with spicy sauce.

Eating with insomniacs... San Francisco is not known as a late-night town, but there are a couple of spots that stay open until the wee hours, if not all night, and are a cut above the 24-hour Market Street joints where the coffee is as greasy as the bacon and eggs. **Hamburger Mary's** is our first choice, though you may have to wait a bit on weekends, when the South of Market club crowd drops in to chow down and sober up. Floral wallpaper that looks like your Great Aunt Ida's drapes, family portraits of nobody in particular, and unmatched salt and pepper shakers have made Mary's a funky favorite for years. The classic burgers here are topped with whatever you like, from grilled mushrooms to chili and cheese. It's hip, full of thrift-store knickknacks, and it serves a wicked margarita—but it closes at 2. If you're still hungry after the bars shut down, head for **Sparky's**, a 24-hour Church Street diner that serves a decent burger and a hearty breakfast to Castro and Upper Market locals. The lights are sometimes a bit too bright and the wait staff a bit too dim, but at least the breakfasts here avoid the white-bread toast and frozen hashbrown-type food substance that seem to be standard issue at all-night coffee shops.

The morning after... Two breakfast stops are mandatory when you visit San Francisco—Sear's, in Union Square, and Kate's, in the Upper Haight. **Sear's Fine Foods** is best visited after 9 on weekday mornings, when the Financial District crowd has had time to get to work. Their coin-size Swedish pancakes are marvelous—thin and sweet like the best French crêpes—and you get almost a million of them (well, 18) stacked high on your plate. **Kate's Kitchen** is famous for buttermilk cornmeal pancakes, with lots of butter and real maple syrup. The place is funky and honest, with furniture that has seen better days, floors that could use refinishing, and simple, delicious food.

The café superhighway... Don't let the ubiquitous thrift-shop furnishings and hand-scribbled signs on tattered old bulletin boards fool you—the future has arrived in San Francisco cafés, and its name is **SF Net**. SF Net connects computer terminals at more than a dozen coffeehouses in town—including **Jammin' Java**, **Ground Zero**, **Horseshoe Coffee House**, **Mad Magda's Russian Tea Room**, **Muddy Waters**, and **Brain Wash**—so you can chat with other coffee-chugging café rats all over town. First you have to give the computer money (usually a quarter), then you log on with an exotic alias, and presto!, you can blab away with whoever is online at the moment. Periodically, the computer will demand more coins—like some greedy "Twilight Zone" carnival game—so be sure you have plenty of change, or you might lose contact with your new cyberpals. The cybercafé that's gotten the most notice from the international media is the **Icon Byte**, a South of Market haunt popular with multimedia types who work in

SAN FRANCISCO | DINING

the neighborhood. You can visit the Icon before you leave home—their Internet address is *icon@bytebar.com*.

Wake-up call: cafés that open before 8am... When you're up and at 'em at the crack of dawn—and you need a serious caffeine jolt—only a select number of cafés are open and ready to pamper you with a perfectly frothy cappuccino or café au lait, airy croissants, and the morning paper to boot. If you're staying in a downtown hotel, try the Financial District's **Café de la Presse**, a subdued French-owned refuge that is also an international newsstand. In North Beach, **Caffe Greco**, **Caffe Trieste**, and **Stella Café & Pastry** are early-morning favorites. There are even a few bohemian types who open their eyes before noon—**Café La Bohème** and **Muddy Waters Coffee House** serve daybreak espresso in the Mission District, while Haight Street early-birds go to **Jammin' Java Coffee House** or **Tassajara Café & Bakery**.

How about a little fresh air?... San Francisco's narrow sidewalks don't leave much room for outdoor seating, and some neighborhoods strictly enforce ordinances against al fresco impediments to pedestrian traffic. A typical sidewalk seat is a bench—without tables—in front of the building. There are some notable exceptions, however, beginning with the granddaddy of the city's sidewalk cafés, **Enrico's** (North Beach). Huge awnings overhang the table-seating area that provides Broadway's best people-watching—you feel as though you have box seats at the opera. Then there's the elevated wooden deck outside **Café Flore** in the Castro. On a foggy day, it's like being in one of those pensive, French B-movies. On a sunny day, it's like being on the French Riviera. But no matter what the weather, it's almost impossible to get a deck seat unless you are there at opening time (8am) or have the patience to wait for someone to leave—and can sprint to the open table faster than anyone else. Our favorite backyard "gardens" are at **Mad Magda's Russian Tea Room** in the sunny Hayes Valley, where customers have been known to sunbathe topless, and **Red Dora's Bearded Lady** in the city's other sun belt, the Mission District.

Sturm und drang... Every once in a while, every self-respecting café-dweller must disregard the sheer bliss of everyday life and slump over a coffee-stained table to ago-nize over some irresolvable existential dilemma. The best place to do that in San Francisco is **Ground Zero**, a stark, modern Haight Street café. If that's a little too sturmy for you, **Brain Wash** is an acceptable alternative, surrounded as it is by not only the endless spinning of clothes in dry-ers, but by the barren industrial architecture of South of Market warehouses. Still haven't met your angst quota? Go back to the Haight and listen to the lyrics blasting from the sound system at the **Horseshoe Coffee House**. If the Horseshoe's whining, dysfunctional, alternative soundtrack doesn't send you running for the Prozac, nothing will.

Quick escapes from retail madness... When the shopping frenzy at Union Square gets unbearable, dash over to **Café de la Presse**, an international newsstand—and oasis—in the midst of the consumer dementia. You'll meet up with lots of other travelers, but they will not be of the Hawaiian-shirt-and-Instamatic-camera variety. It's also entirely possible to go temporarily insane on the super-gentrified section of Fillmore Street (between Sutter and Jackson), where boutique overdose can be a major problem. Relief is available just a block away at the **Blue Monkey**, an unpretentious, yup-free café with mag-azines to read and a few outdoor tables.

All-day hangouts... One of the unwritten rules of café life is that customers get to linger as long as they wish, even if all they buy is one cup of coffee. But certain places are more conducive than others to the all-day, write-in-your-journal, plan-out-your-future type of pause. **Café La Bohème** (Mission District) is the ultimate spot to waste a day—dozens of unemployed poets, artists, and general layabouts have made a career of it. If you sit there long enough, you'll see—and probably meet—people of all different ages, ethnic backgrounds, professions, and tal-ents. (You'll probably also be asked for spare change a dozen times.) The location of **South Park Café** makes it possible to hang out all day within arm's length of an espresso without having to stay inside the whole time. The Mission District's **Radio Valencia** is at its all-day best on Sunday, when you can start the day with brunch and top off the evening with a wheat beer and live jazz.

Some people like to watch the waitstaff change shifts to see if listless service is an aberration or is simply genetic to twenty-something hipsters.

The spoken word... If you've ever been to a big wedding, you probably know that a microphone can transform even the most bashful ingenue into a dead ringer for Ethel Merman. And if you've ever been to an open-mike poetry reading, you know there are worse transmutations to witness than that. Nevertheless, the spoken word is big in San Francisco, whether it's poetry, prose, story-telling, or free-form ranting. Most cafés that have caught the wave book featured poets or storytellers, occasionally opening the mike afterward. Among the scattered cafés that feature the spoken word: the **Blue Monkey**, **Café Beano**, **Brain Wash**, and **Red Dora's Bearded Lady**. Call ahead for details.

Live music... The Most Eclectic Assortment of Quirky Music award goes to **Radio Valencia**, where, before the aforementioned fire-truck mishap interrupted the performance calendar, the regular house bands played swing, bluegrass, and "outside" jazz, with special performances by many top jazz musicians whose material was a bit too eccentric for other venues. We fully expect the resurrected café (which was due to reopen in November 1995) will continue the tradition. Meanwhile, **Enrico's**, a North Beach institution (see Nightlife), presents live jazz seven nights a week (no cover charge), ranging from Brazilian, bebop, and swing to Dixieland and jump & jive; North Beach's **Caffe Trieste** presents live opera music on Sunday afternoons; and the Mission District's **Café Istanbul** regularly offers live Middle Eastern music and belly dancing (call for details). Other cafés that occasionally present live music include **Brain Wash**, **Red Dora's Bearded Lady**, the **Blue Monkey**, and **Mad Magda's Russian Tea Room**.

Jack Kerouac woke up here... Legendary writers have scribbled in notebooks and on napkins all over North Beach. Jack Kerouac and Allen Ginsberg were regulars at **Caffe Trieste**; Richard Brautigan hawked homemade copies of his poems and stories there. Francis Ford Coppola drafted a screenplay at one of the small tables at

Mario's Bohemian Cigar Store, though a debate still rages over whether or not it was *The Godfather*. Lawrence Ferlinghetti is a regular at **Caffe Puccini**, where every seat is a window seat, and he still displays his art work at both Puccini and **Enrico's**.

Hippie holdouts... One of the few true hippie cafés left over from the Sixties—it was a crash-pad then—is **Sacred Grounds**, a Haight Ashbury classic that will make you want to tie-dye your entire wardrobe. The atmosphere is gentle, but not nostalgic. **Tassajara Café & Bakery** is hardly a hippie tradition—it's not old enough to remember the Summer of Love and it's usually well-stocked with medical students and other polo-shirted Cole Valley denizens—but because it serves organic food, its clientele includes a sizable contingent of diehard hippies among its clean-living vegetarians. The Mission District's **Café La Bohème** welcomes virtually everybody, and always has its share of customers who look like extras from *Woodstock*.

SAN FRANCISCO | DINING

The Index

$$$$	over $25
$$$	$15–$25
$$	$7–$14
$	under $7

Alain Rondelli. Named after its extraordinary expatriate Parisian chef, this unpretentious Clement Street bistro is arguably the city's best French restaurant. The warm, sensual decor—tawny-colored walls, cushy banquettes, and an intimate bar—enhances Rondelli's seductive, ever-changing menu and unforgettable six-course tasting menu ($45 per person).... *Tel 415/387–0408. 126 Clement St., 2 or 38 MUNI bus. Reservations essential. AE, DC not accepted. $$$*

Angkor Borei. This small, unpretentious, neighborhood restaurant serves fine Cambodian cuisine at Mission District prices. Try the delicate vegetable-filled spring rolls to warm up, then go for a spicy noodle dish or anything with green curry.... *Tel 415/550–8417. 3471 Mission St., 14 or 49 MUNI bus. DC not accepted. $*

Angkor Wat. Possibly the best Cambodian restaurant in the western hemisphere. If you can afford to go on a Friday or Saturday night, you'll be treated not only to exquisite dishes that burst with tropical and French flavors, but also to performances by the Cambodian Royal Ballet.... *Tel 415/ 221–7887. 4217 Geary Blvd., 38 MUNI bus. Reservations recommended. $$–$$$*

Backstage. The eclectic Mediterranean/Californian/International menu changes monthly at chef Richard Radcliffe's stylish opera ghetto bistro; don't be shy about asking him for suggestions.... *Tel 415/673–9353. 687 McAllister St., Civic Center BART/MUNI Metro station, 50 MUNI bus. Reservations highly recommended for tables before 8:30pm. $$*

Blue Monkey. If you overlooked our tip in "Shopping" and went browsing in the self-proclaimed "five-star neighborhood" along Fillmore Street, here's a chance to redeem your day: Go west one block. On Steiner Street (between Sutter and Post streets) you'll find the Blue Monkey, at the edge of the *un*gentrified Fillmore District. Enjoy the wall mural and the funky, non-yuppie atmosphere.... *Tel 415/929–7117. 1777 Steiner St.; 2, 3, or 4 MUNI bus.*

Brain Wash Café. This is becoming the "in" place South of Market, mostly because you can hang with the post-punkers or log onto SF Net while your whites, colors, and mixed loads are tumbling dry just footsteps away. You can sip a latte or guzzle a beer while the café's washers and dryers do the work—and they'll do it until 11pm. Now there's a concept.... *Tel 415/861–3663. 1122 Folsom St. (near 7th St.), Civic Center BART stop, 12 or 19 MUNI bus.*

Brothers Restaurant. This Korean barbecue spot has wood-fired hibachis at each table, dozens of choices to grill, and a host of other dishes for those who choose not to barbecue, including a variety of hot and cold noodles. Brothers' kimchee is some of the best outside of Seoul.... *Tel 415/ 387–7991. 4128 Geary Blvd., 38 MUNI bus. Reservations recommended. AE, DC not accepted. $$*

Buca Giovanni. If you're looking for a light supper, sup else-where. Chef Giovanni Leoni's authentic Tuscan cuisine—cre-ated from produce he grows himself—is sinfully rich and hearty. The dining room is downstairs in a simple little North Beach cottage-style building.... *Tel 415/776–7766. 800 Greenwich St., Powell-Mason cable car, 30 MUNI bus. Reservations recommended. $$*

Café Beano. The spoken word is big at the Mission District's Beano, which attracts a sort of poetic/bohemian/literary crowd in addition to the usual neighborhood artists and les-bians. Like most Valencia Street cafés, Beano covers its walls with local art and is a comfortable place to linger as long as you like. It's clean, and mercifully uninfatuated with itself.... *Tel 415/878 Valencia St. (near 19th St.), 16th or 24th St. BART stop, or 26 MUNI bus.*

Cafe Claude. This great lunch spot tucked away in the Financial District is the most authentic Parisian-style cafe in the city; wonderful sandwiches and wines by the glass.... *Tel 415/ 392–3505. 7 Claude Lane (near Bush and Kearny sts.), Montgomery St. BART/MUNI Metro stop, 38 MUNI bus. $*

Café de la Presse. Escape from the shopping frenzy of Union Square into this oh-so-French café. It's one of few places in the city where a "latte" is a "café au lait," and because it doubles as a terrific international newsstand, it's about the only place where you can enjoy full daily coverage of the Tour de France. Many European visitors find refuge in this Financial District haven, which is open 7am–11pm every day.... *Tel 415/398–2680. 342 Grant Ave. (near Sutter St.); 2, 3, 4, or 76 MUNI bus.*

Café Flore. This is the most nicknamed café in town, mostly because the many gay men who frequent it love to make fun of it, of themselves, and of everyone else who goes there. So don't be discouraged if you hear someone refer to it as Café Whore or Café Bore—it usually indicates that the barb-throw-er has logged way too much time there. The food is good (a bit pricey) and the outside sundeck is one of the prime peo-ple-watching spots in the Castro District—but you may never know that first-hand unless you are truly aggressive; it is next to impossible to get a seat there on any halfway sunny day.... *Tel 415/621–8579. 2298 Market St. (at Noe St.); Castro St. MUNI Metro stop; 8, 24, or 37 MUNI bus.*

Café Istanbul. Free belly-dancing is the main attraction on Wednesday and Saturday nights, but the Middle Eastern atmosphere—in the middle of the Mission District—is reason enough to come on any night. Sit cross-legged on the pillow platform, swig a pot of thick Turkish coffee or tea, and feel free to pretend you are in Istanbul. Reservations are essential to see the belly dancing.... *Tel 415/863–8854. 525 Valencia St. (near 16th St.), 16th St. BART stop, 26 MUNI bus.*

Café La Bohème. If you're in the mood to share big, wooden tables with artistic and often terminally unemployed café-dwellers, La Bohème is the quintessential all-day hangout. The crowd is multi-everything—multicultural, multiracial, and multigenerational—and though the café is decidedly Mission District, its location directly across from the 24th Street BART stop attracts visitors from all over the city.... *Tel 415/285–4122. 3318 24th St., 24th St. BART stop.*

Caffe Greco. It's not the oldest coffeehouse in North Beach by a long shot (opened in 1988), but it has become one of the most popular among neighborhood residents, partially because of its peerless espresso (imported Illy Caffe, touted as the world's finest). Regulars tend to gather in the afternoon, but early-risers start filing in at 7am (8 on weekends) for a morning jolt and first dibs on the house copies of the newspaper.... *Tel 415/397–6261. 413 Columbus Ave.; 15, 30, 41, or 45 MUNI bus.*

Caffe Puccini. Beat legend Lawrence Ferlinghetti has exhibited his paintings at Puccini, as have many local artists. Named after the great opera composer, Giacomo Puccini, this café is deep Italian—as any good North Beach spot should be—and manages to avoid becoming a trend trap despite its fair share of noted patrons and artistic types. The pastries are terrific, and every table on its triangular floor sits near a picture window.... *Tel 415/989–7033. 411 Columbus Ave.; 15, 30, 41, or 45 MUNI bus.*

Caffe Trieste. One of the last remaining haunts of the young beatniks—Jack Kerouac and Allen Ginsberg were regulars—this legendary little café is a must for visiting coffeehounds. Past, present, and future literary geniuses still scribble at the tables. On Saturday afternoons, the owners sing arias from their favorite Italian operas. They also roast their own coffee—among the best in North Beach—but if you smell a faint scorch when you walk by, you may be disappointed. Let your nostrils be your guide.... *Tel 415/982–6223. 601 Vallejo St. (at Grant St.), 15 or 41 MUNI bus.*

Cha Cha Cha. Every dish in this super-popular, semi-trendy, funky Caribbean tapas joint is a tongue-burner to some degree, which is as it should be in a Cuban/Cajun restaurant that looks like it was decorated by a voodoo queen on a Sangria binge. Check out the daily specials board for serious entrees (such as pan-fried Cajun trout) but be sure to try some of the tapas, too. The fried plantains are a nice way to finish.... *Tel 415/386–5758. 1801 Haight St.; 6, 7, 33, 66, or 71 MUNI bus. No reservations or credit cards.* $

Chez Panisse. Among restaurant reviewers, Berkeley's Chez Panisse is a sacred cow. But locals who have eaten there for years will tell you that it isn't consistent. You also have to reserve at least a month in advance for a weekend dinner.... *Tel 510/548–5525. 1517 Shattuck Ave., Berkeley, North Berkeley BART station and a cab. Reservations essential.* $$$

Cho-Cho. True to its classic Japanese theme and decor, Cho-Cho offers shabu-shabu and other traditional Japanese foods, including marvelous tempura, cooked to order at the tempura bar. Lots of Financial District types stop in after work for a martini and a snack.... *Tel 415/397–3066. 1020 Kearny St.; 15, 30, or 41 MUNI bus. DC not accepted.* $$

Cypress Club. You've got to see this place to believe it. When you step through the thick velvet curtain doorway, you've entered what looks like Salvador Dali's impression of the Mad Hatter's tea party. But after one glance at the menu, you can rest assured this is a serious place to eat, with some of the best game dishes in the city (the venison is to die for) and a superb wine list.... *Tel 415/296–8555. 1500 Jackson St., 15 or 30 MUNI bus. Reservations recommended.* $$$

El Nuevo Frutilandia. A casual, friendly neighborhood bistro, this brightly painted Mission District storefront is one of the few places in San Francisco that serve authentic Puerto Rican and Cuban home cooking, including a generous assortment of tropical fruit shakes. The odds of running into a horde of tourists here are extremely slim.... *Tel 415/648–2958. 3077 24th St., 24th St. BART/MUNI Metro stop. No credit cards. $*

El Trebol. This delightful little Salvadoran/Nicaraguan eatery on 24th Street in the Castro District is one of the best deals in the city—friendly service, Formica tables, and a full dinner including rice and beans for as little as $4. The decor is very plain, just the way locals like it, and the food is excellent.... *Tel 415/285–6298. 3324 24th St., 24th St. BART/MUNI Metro stop. No credit cards. $*

Enrico's Sidewalk Cafe. New owners resurrected what may be the city's favorite cafe and transformed it into a casual supper club that's both an excellent restaurant and an extremely popular spot for coffee, cocktails, and live jazz. If you're having drinks, be sure to try the lip-puckering Mojito, a rum, mint and lime juice concoction.... *Tel 415/982–6223. 504 Broadway; 15, 30, 41, 45, or 83 MUNI bus. Reservations recommended for dinner (essential on week-ends), available same-day only (call after 11am). DC not accepted. $$*

Esperpento. A perfect fit for its artistic Latin/beatnik/urban-chic neighborhood, Esperpento serves authentic, inexpensive Spanish paella and tapas in a jam-packed Mission District storefront. Bonus: The Spanish wines are relatively inexpensive. Sometimes lunch (11–3 daily) is less crowded than dinner.... *Tel 415/282–8867. 3205 22nd St., 24th St. BART/MUNI Metro stop, 26 MUNI bus. Reservations recommended. No credit cards. $*

Fina Estampa. Some of the most delectable Peruvian food you'll ever taste is prepared at Fina Estampa by chef Gus Shinzato, a Japanese-Peruvian. It's a typical Mission District store-front—casual, comfortable, and completely unpretentious—but the food is extraordinary and inexpensive besides.... *Tel 415/824–4437. 2374 Mission St., 16th St. BART/MUNI Metro stop, 14 or 49 MUNI bus. AE, DC not accepted. $*

Flint's. It's worth a trip to Oakland to this famed barbecue hit where the sauce comes in a few choices—hot, hotter, and hottest—and the ribs are piled so high you can barely carry them on the paper plates. It's strictly takeout, but you can sit outside during the day. Open weekdays until 2am, weekends until 4am.... *Tel 510/653–0593. 6609 Shattuck Ave. (at 66th St.), Ashby BART stop. $*

Fly Trap Restaurant. A long history of good humor and a menu based on traditional San Francisco grill food make this institution a refreshing choice amid the glut of tony, food-fad eateries South of Market. If you like comfort food, you'll love the warm apple crisp.... *Tel 415/243–0589. 606 Folsom St., Montgomery St. BART/MUNI Metro stop, 15 MUNI bus. Reservations recommended. $$*

Flying Saucer. If Captain Kirk beamed the *Star Trek* crew to earth for dinner, the Flying Saucer would be a perfect site—as long as he remembered to make reservations three weeks in advance. This tiny Mission District bistro may be the most "in" restaurant in town. Chef Albert Tordjman is a space-age Picasso, whose eccentric, exotically flavored creations double as culinary sculptures.... *Tel 415/641–9955. 1000 Guerrero St., 24th St. BART/MUNI Metro stop, 26 MUNI bus. Reservations essential (2–3 weeks in advance, possibly same-day for weeknight off-hours). $$*

Fringale. A cozy, curved blond-wood bar greets you the moment you open the door and makes you feel comfortable in this chic South of Market bistro. The food—French/Basque—is delightful, the wait staff is smart and friendly, and the price is downright reasonable.... *Tel 415/543–0573. 570 Fourth St.; 30, 45, or 76 MUNI bus. DC not accepted. $$*

Ganges Vegetarian Restaurant. Malvi Doshi runs her small Indian restaurant near the Haight as though it were her own kitchen and each patron a long-lost friend. Don't miss her *kulfi*—homemade cardamom ice cream.... *Tel 415/661–7290. 775 Frederick St., 33 MUNI bus. AE, DC not accepted. $*

Gaylord of India. Surprisingly enough, the most cultivated Indian food in the city can be found right in Ghirardelli Square (third floor). The furnishings are elegant and the view

SAN FRANCISCO | DINING

of the bay exquisite, but the prices are somewhat high.... *Tel 415/771–8822. Ghirardelli Square, 900 North Point; Powell/Hyde cable car; 19, 30, or 42 MUNI bus. Reservations recommended. $$$*

Golden Turtle. Even the toughest food critics hail this modest but formal restaurant near Russian Hill for its elegant Vietnamese food and inexpensive prices.... *Tel 415/441–4419. 2211 Van Ness Ave.; 42, 47, 49, or 76 MUNI bus. DC not accepted. $*

Greens. Ten years ago—when California cuisine was still a baby—there was a six-month waiting list for reservations at this legendary vegetarian restaurant overlooking the Marina, but three cookbooks and a couple of chefs later, Greens can usually accommodate guests with just two weeks' notice.... *Tel 415/771–6222. Fort Mason, Bldg. A, Buchanan St. at Marina Blvd., 28 MUNI bus. Reservations essential. AE not accepted. $$*

Ground Zero. Before most of San Francisco was designated a no-smoking zone, Ground Zero used to be a great place to hunker down with one of those extra-stinky French cigarettes and bemoan the futility of life. Now you can't dangle the smokes off the corner of your mouth anymore, but it's still a great place to log on to SF Net and ponder whether or not George Orwell was too optimistic in forecasting life in the late 20th century.... *Tel 415/861–1985. 783 Haight St. (near Scott St.); 6, 7, 33, 66, or 71 MUNI bus.*

Hama-Ko. Chef Ted Kashiyama's little Cole Valley restaurant offers a limited sushi bar menu; for a full meal, you must order in advance. It's all the freshest in town.... *Tel 415/753–6808. 1088 Carl St., 37 or 43 MUNI bus. Reservations essential except for sushi bar. AE, DC not accepted. $$*

Hamburger Mary's. When you've got to have a burger and it's got to be thick and juicy, but it's past midnight (and you want a beer as well), this funky South of Market institution is the place to go. The trendies come and go, but Mary's thrift-store decor and classic burgers never grow old. The breakfasts are also delish.... *Tel 415/626–5767. 1582 Folsom St., Van Ness MUNI Metro station, 12 MUNI bus. Reservations accepted but not always practical. DC not accepted. $*

Harbor Village. If the major appeal of Chinese food to you is its customary inexpensive price tag, don't bother with Harbor Village—they don't pay the rent on their fancy Embarcadero Center digs by offering budget meals. The dinners are exquisite, but the real reason to go to Harbor Village is for the dim sum, served only at lunch (11–2:30, 10:30–2:30 Sun.).... *Tel 415/781–8833. 4 Embarcadero Center; Embarcadero BART/MUNI Metro stop; 15, 45, or 76 MUNI bus. Reservations recommended.* $$–$$$

Harris'. Anne Harris cooks and serves damn fine steaks. That's about the long and short of Harris', except for the luxurious, gigantic booths and killer martinis. The best steak house in the city.... *Tel 415/673–1888. 2100 Van Ness Ave.; 42, 47, 49, or 76 MUNI bus. Reservations recommended.* $$$

Hayes Street Grill. Superb fish and seafood are the mainstays of the menu, sautéed or mesquite-grilled with a Mexican, American, French, Italian, or Asian accent. A loyal clientele dines here before opera, ballet, or symphony performances across the street.... *Tel 415/863–5545. 320 Hayes St., Civic Center BART/MUNI Metro stop, 21 MUNI bus. Reservations essential for tables before 8:30pm.* $$

Helmand. A formal dinner house on a stretch of Broadway between North Beach and Pacific Heights. Owner Mahmood Karzai's Afghani menu—easily the best in the city—incorporates tastes of Central Asia, India, and the Middle East.... *Tel 415/362–0641. 430 Broadway; 15, 30 or 45 MUNI bus. Reservations recommended.* $

Horseshoe Coffee House. This is the nose-ring and tattoo capital of the city, hands down. We're talking all pierced up and nowhere to go—except one of the most happening coffee houses in town, if you like loud music (mostly alternative rock), huge lattes, cheap food, and bulletin boards that read like a stream-of-consciousness urban novel. If you're looking for mondo-hip, check this place out.... *Tel 415/626–8852. 566 Haight St. (near Fillmore St.); 6, 7, 66, or 71 MUNI bus.*

Icon Byte. Even though the Icon is also a restaurant and night spot, we're including it here because it meets the major requirements of a café—it serves good, strong coffee; it is a primary neighborhood gathering spot; and you can hang out as long as you want. This "Multimedia Gulch" (South of Market) joint was the original state-of-the-art cybercafé, with in-house computer hardware that can project digital images onto the walls and dozens of patrons regularly clacking away on their personal laptops. The customers are not your typical computer nerds with pen protectors in their pockets and Band-Aids holding their eyeglasses together: They are local multimedia gurus, neighborhood cyber-punks—the Digerati.... *Tel 415/861–2983. 297 Ninth St. (at Folsom St.), Civic Center BART/MUNI Metro stop, 12 or 19 MUNI bus.*

Izzy's Steaks and Chops. If you like a good, stiff drink with your T-bone, you'll like Izzy's. The steaks are thick, the drinks plentiful, the wait staff very friendly. A very popular Marina watering hole.... *Tel 415/563–0487. 3345 Steiner St.; 10, 20, 30, 43, 60, 70, or 80 MUNI bus. Reservations recommended. $$*

Jammin' Java Coffee House. What a difference a block makes—just a few steps up from Haight Street, the deci-bel and frenzy level drop remarkably. A sidewalk seat at Jammin' Java can soothe your spirit and rejuvenate your trend-weary soul—especially on a sunny afternoon. The clientele is a harmonious blend of young hipsters and older bohemians, as well as your average taxpayer who happens to live in the neighborhood.... *Tel 415/668–5282. 701 Cole St. (at Waller St.); 6, 7, 33, 37, 43, 66, and 71 MUNI bus.*

John's Grill. Now nearly 90 years old, this is a terrifically fun place to get a juicy steak (the homemade vanilla ice cream is heavenly, too) or have a late-afternoon cocktail. The dark wooden walls, period furnishings, and old photographs of dozens of celebrities who have eaten there reflect its authentic role in San Francisco's notorious past.... *Tel 415/ 986–0069. 63 Ellis St., Powell St. BART/MUNI Metro stop. Reservations recommended. $$*

Kate's Kitchen. The decor is a bit worn-in, but that works well with the home-style cooking and seems to suit the Haight neighborhood regulars just fine. The light buttermilk pan-cakes come with real maple syrup and lots of gooey butter, and the corned beef hash is glorious.... *Tel 415/626–*

3984. 471 Haight St.; 6, 7, 22, 66, or 71 MUNI bus. No credit cards. $

Kyung Bok Palace. A smorgasbord of pickles, salads, and sauces accompanies the marinated beef and pork you cook to your own liking on live-coal grills built into the tables. You can go back as many times as you like, and eat as much as you want. Dinner starts at 5, and don't be fashionably late or your name may be at the end of a very long waiting list.... *Tel 415/221–0685. 6314 Geary Blvd., 38 MUNI bus. No reservations. AE, DC not accepted. $$*

La Rondalla. It's always fiesta time here; the Christmas lights and gaudy ornaments shine through the front window all year long. The traditional Mexican fare is tasty and substantial, a perfect prelude to a few gigantic margaritas at the crowded, lively bar. On weekend nights, mariachi bands stroll between the tables and play songs on request.... *Tel 415/647–7474. 901 Valencia St., 16th or 24th St. BART stop, 26 MUNI bus. No credit cards. $–$$*

La Taqueria. The Mission District is full of little taquerias, almost any of which will serve you a decent taco or burrito for a couple of dollars or less. La Taqueria, with its clean, comfortable cantina-style atmosphere—adobe walls, colorful murals, chunky wooden tables—is a local favorite. Try the delicious shredded pork *carnitas.... Tel 415/285–7117. 2889 Mission St., 24th St. BART/MUNI Metro stop, 14 or 49 MUNI bus. No credit cards. $*

Los Jarritos. Anything you order at this friendly Mexican eatery will be authentic and tasty, but make sure you don't miss the homemade tortillas.... *Tel 415/648–8383. 901 South Van Ness, 16th or 24th St. BART/MUNI Metro stop, 33 MUNI bus. AE, DC not accepted. $*

Mad Magda's Russian Tea Room. Not only can you drink your tea any way you like it at Mad Magda's, you can have your leaves read and find out what the future holds. If you're a devout coffee drinker, they'll read your tarot cards instead. The whole place is sort of *Fantasia* meets the Kremlin. The bathrooms are a bit too out-house for us, and the service is just a tiny bit too mellow, but the backyard is such a welcome respite from busy city streets that we forgive every-

SAN FRANCISCO | DINING

thing.... *Tel 415/864–7654. 579 Hayes St. (near Octavia St.), Civic Center Bart stop or 21 MUNI bus.*

Mario's Bohemian Cigar Store Café. This is our favorite North Beach café, not just because Francis Ford Coppola allegedly drafted an ingenious screenplay there, or because it has the best focaccia sandwiches in the city, but because, despite the fact that it currently sells no cigars, it is still much what it was when it opened in the early part of the century—a closet-size corner café, with one six-stool bar and a half-dozen tables. The windows open out to Washington Square, and a set of narrow, glass-paned double doors lets you peek in to see who is there or how crowded it is before you go in. (P.S. There are hardly any tourists.)... *Tel 415/362–0536. 566 Columbus Ave. (at Union St.); 15, 30, 41, or 45 MUNI bus.*

Masa's. If you want a three-star meal so classically French it will rival the best of Paris—and you don't mind spending $300 or so for two people—by all means, sign up three weeks in advance for dinner at Masa's.... *Tel 415/989–7154. Hotel Vintage Court, 648 Bush St., any Powell St. cable car. Jacket required, tie optional but preferred; reservations essential. $$$$*

Millennium. The hip, international Abigail Hotel is a perfect setting for the city's latest vegetarian attraction: a stylish vegan restaurant with an inventive menu that's the culinary equivalent of a world-beat concert. The feel of the dining room is a bit upscale—white linen tablecloths and a voguish wait staff—but the service is very friendly and the prices are reasonable.... *Tel 415/487–9800. 246 McAllister St.; Civic Center BART/MUNI Metro stop; 5, 10, 20, 60, 70, or 80 MUNI bus. Reservations accepted. $–$$*

Miss Pearl's Jam House. Some of the best dinners at Miss Pearl's have been forgotten in the haze that follows one too many of those tantalizing tropical drinks. The dancing and socializing are definitely worthwhile at this wacky Caribbean hangout adjacent to the Phoenix Motel, but the food shouldn't be overlooked. Jerked chicken is very popular, as are the tapas.... *Tel 415/775–5267. 601 Eddy St.; Civic Center BART/MUNI Metro stop; 19, 31, or 38 MUNI bus. Dinner reservations recommended on weekends. AE not accepted. $$*

Moose's. Ed Moose used to own the venerable Washington Square Bar & Grill—just across the Square—so it's no surprise his new restaurant became an instant hit. The innovative menu—combining Southwestern, Italian, and Californian delicacies—is exceptional, but the mammoth dining room would feel like a refugee center if it weren't for all the Armani suits and fashion models.... *Tel 415/989–7800. 1652 Stockton St., 15, or 30 MUNI bus. Reservations essential. $$–$$$*

Muddy Waters Coffee House. You won't have any trouble finding this Mission District café—its name is emblazoned in giant letters across the front window. Inside, the atmosphere is funky, bohemian, punked-out cybernerd—with an eclectic clientele to match. You can log on to SF Net (a computer chat network that connects many Bay Area cafés) or settle into a thrift-shop sofa in the back room.... *Tel 415/863–8006. 521 Valencia St. (near 16th St.), 16th St. BART stop or 26 MUNI bus.*

R & G Lounge. The name sounds like a booze joint where a guy named Sam might be playing the piano, but it's actually a Chinatown restaurant offering some of the best seafood in the area. A rather upscale clientele has found its way to R & G's bright new dining room, drawn by super-fresh seafood (live lobster, prawns, and fish from a tank) and lesser-known delicacies such as steamed winter melon with greens and shredded dried scallops.... *Tel 415/433–1817. 760 Clay St.; 15, 30, or 45 MUNI bus. $–$$*

Radio Valencia. The small café that helped launch the hip revitalization of Valencia Street was redecorated rather abruptly in the summer of 1995 by a fire truck that smashed through the corner window and ran right into the middle of the café. The temporary loss of the café was mourned throughout the city, by regular customers and by music aficionados who recognized it as a rare venue for live, non-mainstream jazz. The resurrection was scheduled for November 1995.... *Tel 415/826–1199. 1199 Valencia St. (at 23rd St.), 24th St. BART stop or 26 MUNI bus.*

Red Dora's Bearded Lady. This is a popular lesbian hangout, but the crowd is definitely mixed at this delightful, eccentric, Mission District café near the projects. There's a great sense of humor about the Bearded Lady, from the name itself, to the goofy, mishmash decor—plus there's good home-cooking and a rare backyard garden. Weekend nights often feature live music or spoken word performances, but call to confirm.... *Tel 415/626–2805. 485 14th St. (at Guerrero St.), 16th St. BART stop.*

Sacred Grounds Café. Across the Panhandle from Haight Street, this Sixties throwback—eclectic furnishings and works by local artists share the room with fine, Victorian-style wood paneling—is still a vital part of the Haight Ashbury scene. Live music and poetry readings continue to attract a dynamic crowd, especially students.... *Tel 415/387–3859. 2095 Hayes St. (at Cole St.), 21 MUNI bus.*

Saigon Sandwich Cafe. This isn't a restaurant, but it makes the best Vietnamese sandwiches in town—for around $2. Lunch only (7–4:30, 8–4 weekends).... *Tel 415/474–5698. 560 Larkin St.; Civic Center BART/MUNI Metro stop; 19, 31, or 38 MUNI bus. No credit cards. $*

Sanppo. For a wide variety of country-style Japanese food, do what the local Japanese do—go to Sanppo. Comfortable, inexpensive, and very good, it's right in the heart of Japantown. You may have to share a table if it gets crowded—that's just part of the fun.... *Tel 415/346–3486. Japan Center, 1702 Post St., 38 MUNI bus. AE, DC not accepted. $*

Sear's Fine Foods. If you're anywhere near Union Square at breakfast time, it is mandatory to eat at Sear's diner, beloved for its teeny-tiny, rich, sweet Swedish pancakes. Warning: Go after 9 to avoid the pre-workday rush.... *Tel 415/986–1160. 439 Powell St., Powell St. BART/MUNI Metro stop, any Powell St. cable car, 76 MUNI bus. No credit cards. $*

South Park Café. This little South of Market spot has a delightful multiple-personality disorder. It starts as a casual café in the morning, then turns into a super-hip lunch bistro, then goes back to its casual café persona (at least in the front section) for the rest of the day. If you become intrigued and stay all day long, you won't be sorry: The restaurant serves exquisite food (French) at decent prices, and the setting—a Victorian necklace of stylish eateries that circle the oval lawn of South Park—is downright quaint.... *Tel 415/495–7275. 108 South Park (near 2nd and Bryant Sts.); Montgomery St. BART stop; 15, 30, or 45 MUNI bus.*

Sparky's Diner. One of the few places you can go 24 hours a day for a decent burger or breakfast. The wee-hours crowd at Sparky's can be a bit eccentric—and sometimes a tad inebriated, especially on weekends—but they're harmless, so just mind your own business and pass the ketchup.... *Tel 415/621–6001. 242 Church St., Church St. MUNI Metro stop. DC not accepted. $*

Stars. Chef/owner Jeremiah Tower, the self-proclaimed inventor of California Cuisine, created Stars, commonly considered one of the top restaurants in the city. It's a little loud, though, and suffers from the customers' celebrity mania.... *Tel 415/861–7827. 150 Redwood Alley (near Van Ness Ave.), Civic Center BART stop. Reservations highly recommended. $$$*

Stella Pastry & Caffe. Owner Franco Santucci will be happy to expound on the virtues of his patented *Sacripantina*, Luciano Pavorotti's favorite San Francisco dessert and one of many delectable pastries baked on Stella's premises. You won't find a bohemian crowd at Stella, but if you settle at one of the six tables, you'll see dozens of savvy locals come in to pick up pastries and coffee to go. There are also a couple of outside tables for afternoon java breaks.... *Tel 415/986–2914. 446 Columbus Ave.; 15, 30, 41, or 45 MUNI bus.*

Stoyanof. Georgi Stoyanof, now in his seventies, was making his own delicate filo dough before *Zorba the Greek* was a concept, much less a movie. Now he and his son Angel run a bright, cheery, neighborhood cafe in the Sunset District that serves the best Greek pastries in San Francisco.... *Tel 415/664–3664. 1240 Ninth Ave., N. Judah MUNI Metro streetcar, 71 MUNI bus. Credit cards for dinner only; DC not accepted. $*

Straits Cafe. Singapore is a melting pot of European, Indian, Chinese, and Malaysian culture—and food. The coconut-milk chicken curry is as exotically delicious as the decor, which is almost like a film set of a Singapore street.... *Tel 415/668–1783. 3300 Geary Blvd., 38 MUNI bus. Reservations recommended. $$*

SAN FRANCISCO | DINING

Suppenküche. Good German food is not a contradiction in terms, though the scarcity of decent German restaurants in San Francisco could make you wonder. This small, inviting (often crowded and noisy) Hayes Valley beer hall/dining room steadily attracts a young crowd looking for good food, good beer, and good company all in the same place.... *Tel 415/252–9289. 601 Hayes St., Civic Center BART/MUNI Metro stop, 21 MUNI bus. DC not accepted. $$*

Tadich Grill. This enormously popular steak-and-seafood house is a landmark—it's been run by the same family since the turn of the century, and probably never redecorated. You can't go wrong with the day's fresh catch, grilled on mesquite charcoal. The french fries are a must, and the fresh seafood salads make an excellent light meal.... *Tel 415/391–2373. 240 California St., Embarcadero St. BART/MUNI Metro stop. Jacket suggested. No reservations accepted. AE, DC not accepted. $$–$$$*

Tassajara Café & Bakery. A bit up the hill from the Haight, in the quieter, less bohemian Cole Valley, a banquet in the simple dining area of Tassajara Café is ideal for a relaxing break when you want good coffee without the trend factor. The cookies and pastries are about the best you can get— they're also served in most of the best restaurants in town—and are blessedly inexpensive. Neighborhood residents often spend hours at a time here.... *Tel 415/664–8947. 1000 Cole St. (at Parnassus St.); 6, 37, 43, or 66 MUNI bus; or N. Judah MUNI/Metro streetcar.*

Thep Phanom. It's a good thing Thep Phanom is located in California, land of a zillion chili farmers, because they use tons of the red-hot peppers in their fiery Thai food. Keep plenty of water at your table—you'll need it. The decor and wait staff are also totally Thai, with heirloom antiques and authentic Thai clothing.... *Tel 415/431–2526. 900 Waller St.; 3, 6, 7, 22, 66, or 71 MUNI bus. DC not accepted. $–$$*

Timo's in the Zanzibar. There are two major draws to quirky, artistic Timo's: The tapas, which locals insist are the best in town, and the adjoining bar, the Zanzibar, which thumbs its nose at San Francisco's anti-smoking forces by not only selling a potpourri of legal smokables, but also offering patrons a tobacco menu.... *Tel 415/647–0558. 842 Valencia St., 16th St. BART/MUNI Metro stop, 26 MUNI bus. AE, DC not accepted. $$*

Yank Sing. A guidebook staple that's worth the trip. The dim sum is always satisfying, especially the dumplings, which include many vegetarian options. The modern atmosphere is a bit upscale and the weekday crowd is dominated by business suits, but on weekends Yank Sing is jammed with far more casual customers. The wait staff is friendly and helpful, so don't be shy.... *Tel 415/362–1640. 427 Battery St., Embarcadero BART/MUNI Metro stop. $–$$*

Yaya Cuisine. At this Sunset District restaurant, Chef Yahya Salih's native Iraq flavors the exuberant Mediterranean/California hybrid he honed as a protégé of superchef Jeremiah Tower.... *Tel 415/566–6966. 1220 Ninth Ave., 66 or 71 MUNI bus. Reservations recommended. DC not accepted. $$*

San Francisco Dining

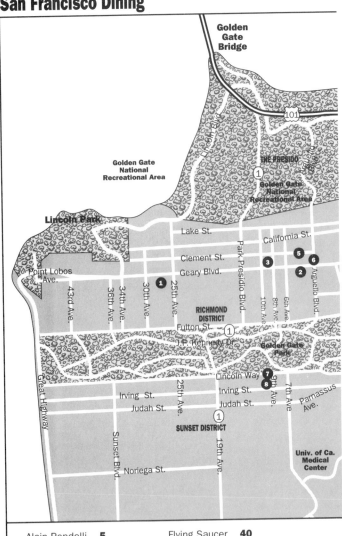

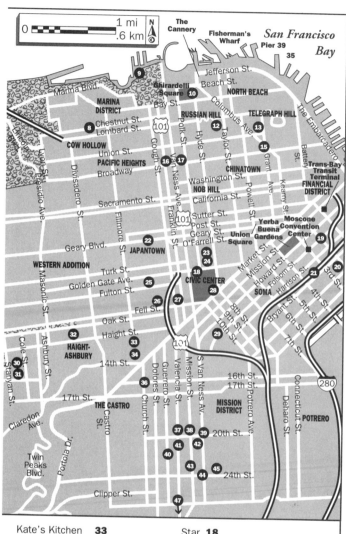

Kate's Kitchen **33**
Kyung Bok Palace **1**
La Rondalla **41**
La Taqueria **43**
Los Jarritos **39**
Millennium **28**
Miss Pearl's Jam House **23**
Moose's **13**
Saigon Sandwich Cafe **24**
Sanppo **22**
South Park Café **20**
Sparky's Diner **36**

Star **18**
Stoyanof **8**
Straits Cafe **6**
Suppenküche **26**
Thep Phanom **34**
Timo's in the Zanzibar **37**
Yaya Cuisine **7**

Union Square & Financial District Dining

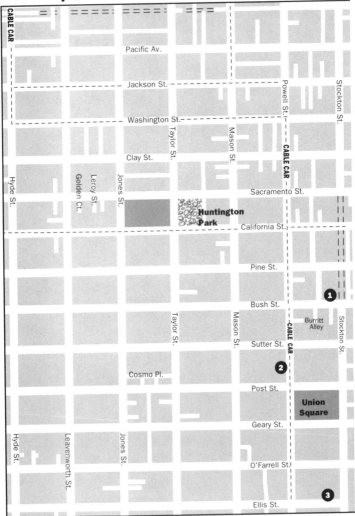

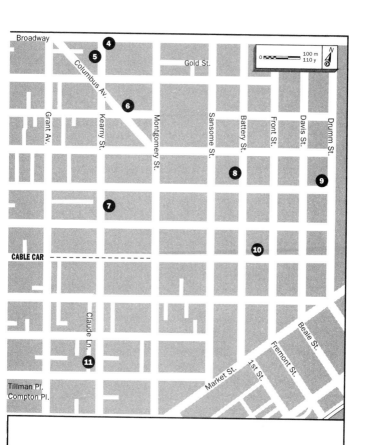

Cafe Claude **11**
Cho-Cho **5**
Cypress Club **6**
Enrico's Sidewalk
  Cafe **4**

Harbor Village **9**
John's Grill **3**
Masa's **1**
R & G Lounge **7**

Sear's Fine Foods **2**
Tadich Grill **10**
Yank Sing **8**

3

sions

Unless your purpose in traveling all the way to San Francisco is to rub elbows with throngs of tourists—

shivering in their shorts and souvenir tank tops despite repeated warnings about how cold it is in July—stay away from Fisherman's Wharf, Pier 39, and the cable car turn-arounds. If you brought the kids, that may be tough to do; our best advice is to get your wharf duty out of the way as quickly as possible (we give you a few survival tips later on in the chapter) so you can move on to the city's true delights.

There are a few things that are so utterly San Francisco that they absolutely must be experienced at some point during your visit—a cable car ride to the Buena Vista Café for a cup of Irish coffee, a trip to Coit tower, a walk across the Golden Gate Bridge, the view from the elevator at the top of the Fairmont Hotel—but the best way to really get to know the city is to explore the neighborhoods where people actually live. Skip the taxi cabs (unless it's after dark or you are in a questionable neighborhood): Take a bus or a streetcar instead, then poke around on foot. Wander around the Haight and count the shrines to Jerry Garcia. Take in the Spoken Word or a punk cha-cha band at a hip, side-street bar in the Mission District. Practice your tai chi with the Chinese senior citizens in Washington Square (North Beach). Gawk at the mansions in Pacific Heights. Visit the Castro for an undiluted dose of the predominant—and wonderfully irreverent—influence gay culture has on every aspect of life in San Francisco.

Lombard Street

The zigzags of "the crookedest street in the world" have been negotiated by so many tourists that the bricks finally started cracking and popping out of the pavement. That means the famous block between Hyde and Leavenworth streets will be closed to automobile traffic for at least another year while repairs are made—bad news for rental car drivers, but great news for pedestrians. The best way to enjoy Lombard Street has always been to walk down the staircases on either side and enjoy the view, and now there aren't any noxious car exhaust fumes to choke you along the way.

No matter what neighborhood you visit, the best seat in the house is any table at a cozy café (see Dining and Cafés). Pull up a chair. Have a nice, frothy cappuccino. There is plenty of time for that trip to the museum—mañana.

Getting Your Bearings

Get a map. There's no other way to visualize San Francisco's irregular layout. The city is not one big grid like Manhattan; it is totally akimbo with sub-grids that skirt its many hills and valleys in a roundabout way. You can rarely see what's over the next hill, so you may not realize that North Beach is the uphill next-door neighbor of Fisherman's Wharf (north) and China-town (south). That may not seem important to you yet, but when you think you're trapped at Pier 39, you'll be relieved to realize that the inviting cafes of North Beach are just a few blocks away.

When it comes to maps, you need two kinds—an over-all view of the neighborhoods in relation to each other, and a comprehensive street map. A neighborhood map will show clearly, for example, that Haight Ashbury is right next to Golden Gate Park, which stretches from the middle of the city all the way to the Pacific Ocean (at Ocean Beach, near the Cliff House). You'll see that the Castro and the Mission District—right next to each other, and not too far east of Haight Ashbury—are both south of Market Street, but the neighborhood officially known as South of Market is quite a distance farther east, in the downtown area.

You'll also see that San Francisco—a city and county unto itself—is at the northern tip of a peninsula flanked by the San Francisco Bay on the east and the Pacific Ocean on the west. The Financial District sits on the eastern

Pick a Card, Any Card
If you've already seen the in-flight movie nine times—before the airline censored it—and you're looking for a good way to amuse yourself on the plane ride to San Francisco, why not play cards? Forget Solitaire and Old Maid—you'll have much more fun with Lynn Gordon's special deck, 52 Adventures in San Francisco. There are no hearts, diamonds, clubs, or spades, but each card does bear a lively illustration on the front and directions for an enticing adventure on the back. Pick cards at random and find the best places to get ice cream—or to go bird-watching—or go through the whole deck and relish the thought of how much fun you're going to have when you finally land in the city. The decks are inexpensive ($5.95) and also double as souvenirs or substitutes for all those postcards you didn't send because you were having way too much fun to stop at the post office. Find them at your local bookstore or contact Chronicle Books, tel 800/722-6657.

SAN FRANCISCO | DIVERSIONS

shore of the city, which curves northward as the Embarcadero passes North Beach and Fisherman's Wharf, eventually turning almost due west to the Golden Gate, where the Pacific Ocean meets the bay. If you stand just about anywhere in the city, you can see a tower that looks like a miniature space needle sitting atop Twin Peaks, the geographical center of the city.

The front section of the San Francisco Yellow Pages has several excellent maps, including transit maps, but if you want to get your bearings in advance, send $2 for a complete packet including useful booklets and a comprehensive visitor map to: San Francisco Convention and Visitors Bureau, P.O. Box 429097, San Francisco, CA 94102-9097 (allow three weeks for U.S. delivery; international mail sent via surface). You can also pick up a copy of the visitor map for free at the Visitor Center at Hallidie Plaza when you arrive. To get the official transit map by mail, send $2.50 to: MUNI MAP, 949 Presidio Ave., San Francisco, CA 94115 (allow two weeks for delivery). It includes all MUNI routes (cable cars, buses, and Metro street-cars), regional transit connections, frequency guide, travel hints, and points of interest. Ask them to include a copy of their excellent booklet, "Tours of Discovery," which features eight different routes you can ride on MUNI that will intro-duce you to San Francisco's most interesting views and neigh-borhoods—all for the price of a single fare (and a transfer).

The Lowdown

Must-sees for first-time visitors from Peoria...

There is one sure-fire perfect way to spend your first after-noon in San Francisco—take $2 out of your pocket, walk five or ten blocks up Powell from Market Street (away from the turnaround), and hop on the **Powell-Hyde cable car**. Don't even think about not doing it because it seems too "touristy"—locals have been known to invite out-of-town guests purely for an excuse to take this ride. The Powell-Hyde line is our favorite because it ends up just footsteps away from the Buena Vista Café (2765 Hyde St., tel 415/474-5044), a National Historic Landmark where a post-cable-car Irish coffee is an esteemed tradi-tion, especially on a foggy afternoon. (The first Irish cof-fees ever served in America were mixed at the Buena Vista in 1952.) The ride itself twists through the city, climbing "halfway to the stars" atop Nob Hill, then plummeting back down on a breathtaking roller-coaster ride that levels out around the famous crooked section of Lombard Street ("The Crookedest Street in the World") before coasting down to the bay. No postcard can possibly capture what it feels like the first moment you glimpse that million-dollar view. (By the way, watch your teeth—many first-timers smile so broadly they collect stray bugs like radiator-grills.)

Another mandatory awe-inspiring adventure is a bracing 15-minute walk across the **Golden Gate Bridge**. There is simply no other way to truly appreciate its immense scale and beauty. The best part is that the weather is absolutely predictable—it always feels cold and windy on the bridge (wear layers). To get an unbelievable view before you actually set foot on the bridge, take the 28 MUNI bus to Fort Point—a brick and granite stronghold built in 1861—where you can climb up to the roof and behold the bridge above you before you set out on the pedestrian walkway. Once you are on the bridge, you'll feel it sway and vibrate as gusty ocean winds whip through its cables. Don't be alarmed. The bridge is not about to collapse. It held up under the ballast of more than a hundred thousand revelers who congregated there to celebrate its 50th anniversary (1987), and it didn't flinch during the 1989 earthquake.

Unless you take the lazy—and boring—way out (the 30, 39, or 45 MUNI bus), you'll probably need to fuel up for the steep hike to **Coit Tower**. We suggest starting out with a cup of super-strength coffee at Caffe Trieste (601 Vallejo St., tel 415/392–6739) because it's right on the corner of Grant Street, the most interesting route to the famous fire-hose-nozzle spire atop Telegraph Hill. Between the cafe and Greenwich Street (where you turn right and head up the hill to the tower) you'll pass some notorious Grant Street goofatoriums—don't miss the Schlock Shop or Quantity Postcards. Once you've actually begun the ascent, you may want to distract yourself from the daunting incline by imagining the tower's namesake—Lillie Hitchcock Coit (1843–1929)—dressed as a fireman and racing around town with the volunteer brigade. Rumor has it that Ms. Coit found men's clothes appealing in other circumstances as well, particularly when she wanted to get into places where "ladies" weren't allowed. Though Ms. Coit's greatest achievement was to be made mascot of Engine Company 5—a reward for her help in fighting a fire—we love to think of Ms. Coit as San Francisco's most famous cross-dresser. No one really knows if Coit Tower was deliberately designed in the shape of a fire-hose nozzle. Up close, it doesn't matter. The Depression-era murals inside the lobby at the base of the tower are haunting images of Americans at labor, and the 360-degree view from the top of the tower (elevator ride $3) is unbeatable.

SAN FRANCISCO | DIVERSIONS

Only in San Francisco... San Francisco is full of sights and sounds that simply don't exist in other cities. Where else would a major league baseball team blast a foghorn to celebrate home runs, or a county fair include a "fog calling" contest? The fog and the hills are San Francisco's natural treasures.

One of the best ways to enjoy the trademark topography is to hike down some of the stairways that have been built into the city's steep sidewalks and pathways. Allow at least an hour or two to walk the **Filbert Street Steps** (between Sansome Street and Telegraph Hill), a romantic favorite with locals because the path feels hidden from urban clamor as it winds past enchanting hundred-year-old cottages and lush gardens. The breathtaking view of the bay from the top of the hill has attracted artists, writers, and singers for years (Joan Baez and Armistead Maupin are among past residents). Start there, at Telegraph Hill Boulevard near Coit Tower, and work your way down. When you cross Montgomery Street to the lower steps, take a look at the art deco apartment complex at 1930 Montgomery—you might recognize it from the movie *Dark Passage* (Humphrey Bogart and Lauren Bacall). You may want to take a sidetrack along Napier Lane, a lovely wooden walkway that leads to the public Grace Marchant Gardens, a particularly enchanting sight on Halloween, when more than 200 jack-o-lanterns light up the night for local trick-or-treaters.

Chinatown is one of the most celebrated neighborhoods in San Francisco, but it has never become merely a tourist trap—above all else it is a place people *live*, the largest Chinese community outside of Asia. As soon as you cross under the ornate, dragon-crested gateway on Grant Avenue (at Bush Street), you're no longer in the Western world. Street signs are marked in Chinese characters, lamp posts are encircled by dragons, and store windows display strange medicinal herbs and animal parts you'd never find at a suburban drug store. The best way to see this teeming neighborhood is early in the morning, when merchants deliver their wares in pushcarts and mothers rush down the street toting live chickens for that night's dinner. Wander up Grant Avenue or Stockton Street to Sacramento and find Waverly Place, where you'll find **Tien Hon Temple** (125 Waverly Place, top floor) among the many brightly painted balconies. Back on

Grant Avenue, a tiny bar with the single word "**Buddha**" on a sign over the door sits on the corner of Washington Street. Look inside. Old men with long braids and "thinking caps" sit at the bar. You're not only on a different continent, you're in a different century.

Every city has churches, but only San Francisco has the **Church of John Coltrane** (351 Divisadero St., tel 415/621–2054), an African Orthodox church that has been using Coltrane's music for the divine liturgy—and serving free food three days a week—for more than 22 years. Jazz lovers from all over the world flock to the small storefront church, where the house band, Ohnedaruth (the Sanskrit word for compassion and the spiritual name Alice Coltrane gave her husband when he died), plays their patron saint's music every Sunday. You never know who will be in attendance—or sitting in with the band. Bobby Hutcherson has stopped by more than once, as has Rashid Ali, Coltrane's last drummer. Once you get inside, you'll be in Coltrane heaven—the walls are adorned with more than a dozen contemporary versions of traditional Russian-style icons, including, of course, ones of Coltrane. The music seems to come from everywhere—the band sits near the altar, the choir takes up the entire first row of seats, and there are saxophones and other instruments spread throughout the congregation. It really is a divine spectacle. Come early to get a good seat; services usually start around noon and last for at least an hour-and-a-half.

Special moments... If a ride on the Powell-Hyde cable car or the view from Coit Tower hasn't already made you fall hopelessly in love with San Francisco, perhaps what you need is a view of the sun virtually melting into an orange-red-fuchsia pool as it sets on the blue Pacific. The ultimate spot is a window table at the pub in the **Cliff House** restaurant (1090 Point Lobos Ave., tel 415/386–3330), facing directly out to sea. The funky-nautical motif pub is a bit tacky, but it fades into the distant background the moment the sun begins its dazzling nightly show. Even the most jaded urbanites ooh and ahh at the display, so be sure to go at least an hour before sundown if you expect to get a good seat—or go outside and find a spot along the cliff.

If you have access to a car, don't leave the Bay Area without watching a sunset from the top of **Grizzly Peak** in the Berkeley Hills. Cars start lining up about a half-hour before sundown to watch the transformation from daylight to shimmering night lights—a magnificent sight in any weather, clear or foggy. The vista covers the entire bay, from San Mateo to the south, the city and the Golden Gate Bridge straight ahead, and Marin County to the north.

On Sundays, soak up the true "spirit" of the city with hundreds of other foot-tapping, hand-clapping, shoulder-swaying sinners at **Glide Memorial Church**'s morning celebrations. An hour or so with Reverend Cecil Williams and his exuberant gospel choir will surely shake your soul and let the glory out, no matter what your religious beliefs may be—everybody leaves this Tenderloin church wearing a major smile. Glide brings out the best in everyone—Bobby McFerrin drops by often, Maya Angelou visits when she's in town; even President Clinton has joined the crowd (fortunately he left his saxophone at home).

Morbid landmarks... For those who enjoy excursions to the dark side, here are a few points of interest that will never make it into San Francisco's public relations hall of fame.

The People's Temple, where crusader Jim Jones gathered disciples before leading them to their eventual death at a tragic mass suicide in Guyana, still stands at 1859 Geary Street. (It is now a Korean Presbyterian Church.)

It's hard to believe that **Charles Manson** recruited some of his deadliest "family" members—including Susan Atkins and Squeaky Fromme—during the peak of Haight Ashbury's peace-and-love scene, but he lived at 636 Cole Street for a few months in 1967 before heading to Southern California to organize his horrifying killing spree. (Manson now lives about 80 miles north of San Francisco at Folsom Prison, isolated from other inmates for his own protection.)

San Quentin State Prison, fondly known to its residents simply as "Q," has hosted some of California's most notorious criminals, including the aforementioned Mr. Manson, Sirhan Sirhan, and William Harris (one of Patty Hearst's kidnappers). They don't give tours of death row or anything like that, but you can take a ferry to Larkspur and hoof it to the prison, where there is a small museum (gas chamber mementos and such) and a gift shop that sells items made by prisoners (no license plates).

Every hotel has gruesome moments it would rather not recall, but the **Westin Saint Francis** has a couple of whoppers—**President Ford's assassination attempt** (September 23, 1975) and **Fatty Arbuckle's lost weekend** (Labor Day weekend, 1921). President Ford was leaving the hotel through the Post Street entrance when Sara Jane Moore whipped out a gun and fired at him from across the street, but an ex-Marine standing next to her grabbed her arm, redirecting the bullet. (It was the second assassination attempt in one two-week trip to California.) Fatty Arbuckle was celebrating a multimillion-dollar movie contract inside the hotel at what has often been described as a drunken orgy when a young female guest was found unconscious in Room 1219. She died a few days later and Arbuckle was tried three times for her murder before finally being acquitted.

The roar of the fish stalls, the smell of the crowd... It has been decades since **Fisherman's Wharf** was actually a bustling fresh fish market, and equally as long since **Pier 39** and the Port of San Francisco were a thriving part of the city's mercantile economy. Yet these two tourist traps are the first stop for most sightseers. (Pier 39, converted just over 15 years ago to an outdoor mall of shops and restaurants, is third on the list of the world's top 10 attractions, with about 10.5 million guests each year.) There are precious few reasons to go near either place, but if you must (your kids will probably insist), here are some ways to make the best of it. Buy a fresh, whole crab at **Nick's** seafood stall (make sure it's still alive and wiggling), get them to cook and crack it for you on the spot, then pick up a sourdough baguette from **Boudin Sourdough Bakery**, and savor one of the best crab sandwiches around. Visit the sea lions—hundreds of them hang around Pier 39's K Dock, where docents from the Marine Mammal Center (remember it from *Star Trek IV*?) give out free books and teach visitors all about the barking pinnipeds (11–5). Then escape to **Pier 23 Cafe**, an almost-unnoticeable shack that attracts a local crowd with jazz, reggae, and calypso, as well as a beautiful view.

Looking for a few good whales: Marine World... One of the best ways to take the family to Pier 39 without actually lingering there is a ferry excursion on the Blue & Gold Fleet to **Marine World/Africa USA**, a

SAN FRANCISCO | DIVERSIONS

unique, hands-on wildlife park across the bay in Vallejo. The hour-long passenger-ferry ride provides incredible views of the city, Alcatraz, Angel Island, four bridges, and many tiny islets, some with lighthouses. One of the most popular park features is its spectacular whale and dolphin show—where kids love getting splashed by giant killer whales—but there are plenty of other fine entertainers among its sea lions, walruses, lions and tigers, primates, and exotic and predatory birds. You can ride elephants, feed giraffes, walk though a glass atrium filled with butterflies from all over the world, or roam through a "walkabout" with kangaroos, wallaroos, wallabies, and an occasional emu.

Urban ferry tales... There are plenty of bay cruises that pick up tourists at Fisherman's Wharf and Pier 39, but it's more fun to go to the Ferry Building at the foot of Market Street and ride with the locals on an afternoon **Golden Gate Ferry** to the seaside village of Sausalito. You can do a one-hour round-tripper, or stop to explore Sausalito. There is really just one main street—Bridgeway—so it's easy to walk around the yuppie/nautical/ex-Bohemian enclave and find a perfect spot to watch the sun set behind the San Francisco skyline. **Cafe Sausalito**, on the top floor of the Village Fair building, is a good vantage point, and relatively inexpensive. If sunsets aren't your thing, and you'd sooner toss back a pint at a rowdy tavern full of live music and boisterous baby boomers, try the **No Name Bar**, but don't drink too many happy-hour specials unless you intend to spend the night—the last ferry departs for San Francisco just after 7.

Cruising Golden Gate Park... San Francisco is so abundant in natural beauty and outdoor treasures that no one park bears the entire burden of maintaining urban residents' need to see grass and trees every now and then, but Golden Gate Park is the city's reigning playground. It has been home to the 49ers football team and all the city's major hippie happenings (including Jerry Garcia's memorial service in 1995); it still is home to Sunday strollers, skaters, and joggers, to museums, to free operas, even to a herd of buffalo.

Most of the park's recreational facilities are covered in the "Getting Outside" chapter, but Golden Gate also probably has more museums than any other urban oasis in the world. The **Asian Art Museum** (John F. Kennedy Dr., opposite 11th Ave.) is the largest museum outside of Asia devoted exclusively to Asian art (more than 12,000 pieces in the permanent collection). There are more than 500 Korean and Chinese masterpieces on display—including the world's oldest dated Chinese Buddha—plus hundreds of exquisite works from India, Tibet, Nepal, Pakistan, and Southeast Asia. The massive **California Academy of Sciences** complex (off Martin Luther King Jr. Dr., opposite 9th Ave.) is a great place to take your kids, but be sure to allow plenty of time—it includes the Natural History Museum, the Steinhart Aquarium, and the Morrison Planetarium. The most fun shows at the Natural History Museum are in the Earth and Space Hall, which features a simulated earthquake and has lots of good "Star Trek" souvenirs in the gift shop. The planetarium's 50-minute sky shows—projected on a huge domed ceiling—are a hit with adults, but young children tend to get bored and restless. Teenagers love the nighttime laser shows at the planetarium, which feature the recorded works of bands like Metallica and Pink Floyd. The **M.H. de Young Memorial Museum** (next to the Asian Art Museum) is San Francisco's scaled-down, unobtrusive answer to New York's Metropolitan Museum of Art. The major international exhibits bring art-lovers from miles around, but it is the museum's exhaustive collection of American art—from Paul Revere to Georgia O'Keeffe—that puts it on the museum map. There is also a magnificent textile collection, including rugs to die for. While you're there, be sure to stop by the garden cafe for the yummy daily specials.

Then there are the gardens. The five-acre **Japanese Tea Garden** (adjacent to the Asian Art Museum) is the oldest in America. When you enter through the hand-carved gate, you really feel as though you are in Japan. The bamboo-lined footpaths and bridges pass ponds full of koi fish, tiny Bonsai trees, stone lanterns, Shinto shrines, and a serene 18th-century Buddha. In early spring, the garden is ablaze with cherry blossoms. (Go early in the morning to avoid crowds.) Cap your visit with a rest stop at the tea pavilion for a fortune cookie (they were first introduced there) and a relaxing cup of green tea served by women in traditional Japanese costume. The **Conservatory of Flowers** (on Conservatory Way, near Arguello Blvd.) is a massive glass Victorian greenhouse that was built in

Ireland and shipped to San Francisco piece by piece. It is stunning from the outside, and utterly magnificent on the inside, where beautiful exotic flowers and tropical trees are always in season. We suspect the orchids possess magic restorative powers—especially on drab, foggy days.

Museum meccas outside Golden Gate Park...
From a half-block away, the huge circular skylight atop Swiss architect Mario Botta's **Museum of Modern Art** (South of Market) looks like some sort of signaling device for extra-terrestrial art collectors. Inside, earthlings have been known to be utterly dazzled by the West Coast's most extensive collection of 20th-century art, which fills 50,000 square feet of gallery space. Botta's magnificent structure is a work of art in itself, and one of the primary reasons to visit.

The city's ethnic diversity and social compassion fuel most of the art displayed in the celebrated **Center for the Arts at Yerba Buena Gardens,** a multi-gallery center adjacent to the new Museum of Modern Art. Exhibits have included panels from the NAMES Project Memorial Quilt and works by prison inmates and residents of local halfway houses. There is also a theater, which hosts a variety of local performances from multicultural groups, and is one of the sites used by the San Francisco Ballet while the city's opera house is undergoing repairs.

The **Palace of Fine Arts** is a must-see, not just because it houses the Exploratorium, but because it looks just like an ancient Roman temple—where's Nero when we really need him?—and it is the only building that remains from the 1915 Panama Pacific Exposition (held to celebrate the opening of the Panama Canal). A trip to the **Exploratorium** is also mandatory. (If you brought your kids, it is a ticket to heaven.) Seasoned locals will assure you it's the most fun you can have without hallucinogenic drugs, especially if you crawl through the dark, sensual Tactile Dome or try any of the other hands-on games designed to totally twist your mind. You never know what the mad scientists will have in store for you at this wonderfully fun, interactive science museum—and the gift shop is the best of any museum in the galaxy.

San Francisco's cable car system is still run out of a three-story red brick barn, and you can watch it in action from several special spectator galleries. The **Cable Car**

Barn and Museum includes the original prototype cable car (1873) along with other cars and models. Yes, there is a gift shop full of cable-car souvenirs.

The literally ship-shape **Maritime Museum** looks like a set for an old Hollywood romantic-cruise movie. Nautical types will go nuts when they see all the ship models, relics, figureheads, photographs, scrimshaw—you know, your basic sailor stuff.

Freebies at the major museums... Most major museums set aside special free-admission days; some are free year-round. The free days tend to occur during the first week of the month, so keep that in mind when planning your trip, and always call for the most current schedule. The **Asian Art Museum** in Golden Gate Park is free the first Wednesday of every month and first Saturday from 10 to noon; the **Cable Car Barn and Museum** is free every day from 10 to 6; the **California Academy of Sciences** in Golden Gate Park is free the first Wednesday of every month; the **Center for the Arts at Yerba Buena Gardens** offers free gallery admission the first Thursday of every month from 6 to 8pm, and to seniors every Thursday from 11 to 3; the **M.H. de Young Memorial Museum** in Golden Gate Park is free the first Wednesday of every month and the first Saturday from 10 to noon; the **Exploratorium** at the Palace of Fine Arts is free the first Wednesday of every month from 10 to 9:30; the **Museum of Modern Art** is free the first Tuesday of every month from 11 to 6; and the **Maritime Museum** at Aquatic Park is free every day from 10 to 5. (See the Index for descriptions of each museum.)

Local exhibitionists... When Pogo would make a more entertaining afternoon companion than Picasso, it's time to quit the cathedrals of culture and head for smaller houses of object worship, like the **Cartoon Art Museum** (814 Mission St.). Once tucked away in a largely ignored warehouse space, the museum is now an esteemed neighbor of the Museum of Modern Art, with thousands of pieces in its permanent collection, from original Krazy Kat watercolors and Pogo comic strips to storyboards from the Disney classic, *Fantasia*. Some of the donors include "Peanuts" artist Charles Schulz and rock star Graham Nash.

SAN FRANCISCO | DIVERSIONS

Ghia Gallery/Discount Caskets and Urns (2648 Third St.) is a favorite among necro-kitsch fans, but you don't have to be morbid to like designer coffins. Just ask Cher—she bought two of Ghia's "King Tut" sarcophaguses and turned them into wine bars. Other creative coffins include the all-glass "Here's Lookin' At You" models and a variety of custom designs that have been used as phone booths, vanity tables, and night stands. Some people have been so inspired by Ghia's furniture for the hereafter, they've staged their own funerals while they were still alive.

If you can't resist penny arcades, you'll love the quirky little **Musée Mecanique** at the Cliff House (1090 Point Lobos Ave.). It's packed with antique mechanical gadgets, from old carnival fortune-tellers to marionette shows and player pianos. Admission is free, which is a good thing, because you easily drop a small fortune in coins playing with all the doohickeys and thingamabobs. One really strange exhibit is a miniature amusement park made out of toothpicks. The fact that the piece was glued together by prisoners at San Quentin kind of makes you wonder.

For flesh freaks, we have two recommendations: **Lyle Tuttle's Tattoo Museum** (841 Columbus Ave.) and **Good Vibrations** (1210 Valencia St.). Lyle Tuttle, undisputed king of the San Francisco tattoo empire, moved his mini-museum from a seedy location at Seventh and Market Streets long after he had already engraved Janis Joplin's flesh, but you can still see his collection of tattoo art—including candid shots of himself, covered head-to-toe with indelible designs—at his tiny little shop in North Beach. More pleasurable pleasures of the flesh are explored at Good Vibrations, where the contraptions in the window display look like old-time hair dryers or permanent-wave doodads, but are actually part of an eclectic collection of sex toys and vibratorana, including the "Queen Victoria," a wooden hand-crank model from turn-of-the-century London. The museum/store—which tends to favor women's interests—is almost cheery; if it weren't for the dozens of plastic penises on the shelves, you'd expect a young Henry Fonda to appear from behind the counter and offer you an ice cream soda.

Galeria de la Raza (2857 24th St.) and the **Mexican Museum** (Fort Mason, Bldg. D) showcase

Mexican and Chicano art. The Mexican Museum's permanent collection—more than 9,000 pieces—makes it a "serious" museum, but the atmosphere is as informal and friendly as Mexico itself. It showcases the best in Mexican and Chicano culture, from folk art to Frida Kahlo, and has one of the best gift shops in the city. Be sure to check out the many whimsical Dia de los Muertos (Day of the Dead) objects, including the perfect wedding gift—a skeleton bride-and-groom to top the cake. The Galeria de la Raza was the first Mexican museum in the United States. It is more locally oriented than the Mexican Museum, and often more innovative, presenting fine examples of work by community artists, as well as major national exhibits.

The **Jewish Community Museum** (121 Stuart St.) has two primary focal points—history and art. Exhibits have featured a variety of works by Jewish artists, from emerging current artists to masters like Marc Chagall. The gallery is known for presenting shows that challenge visitors to critically examine what they see.

The West Coast's largest photography collection is housed at the **Ansel Adams Center** (250 Fourth St.). From Annie Liebovitz's irreverent portraits to Ansel Adams' awesome images of the American West, this remarkable museum houses five exhibition halls, an extensive bookstore, and the largest collection of photography on the West Coast. Exhibits change, but one of the galleries is devoted solely to Adams' own work.

If low art is more to your taste, you must make a stop at the **Keane Eyes Gallery** (651 Market St.), where those tacky bug-eyed waif paintings from the 1960s—portrait after portrait of small children with oversized heads and eyes so huge and round they make Liza Minelli look like a squinter—are celebrated as high kitsch.

It makes sense that a museum devoted strictly to "automotive art" would find a home in California, land of the freeway. Most of the paintings, photos, and sculptures at the tiny **Steering Wheel West** museum (1701 Van Ness Ave.) focus on the opulent "Class Era" (1927–1937).

To get a virtually private glimpse of the history of one of San Francisco's most intriguing neighborhoods, go to the **North Beach Museum**, tucked away on the mezzanine of the Eureka Federal Savings Bank (1435 Stockton St.). This delightful little museum traces North

Beach's past with photographs and artifacts dating back to the turn of the century. Hardly anybody knows the museum is there, so you may have it all to yourself, but you must go during regular banking hours.

Finally, it ain't Fort Knox, but the **Old Mint** (88 Fifth St.) did survive the 1906 earthquake and it does have an 1869 coin press you can use to strike your own souvenir coin (sorry, it's not legal tender) and minting machines that once churned out more nickels and dimes than we could ever count. The building itself—a national historic landmark—is a superb example of Federal classical revival architecture.

The Bongo-Rama Beatnik tour... Bohemian-history buffs won't want to leave San Francisco without paying homage to some of the hallowed grounds that have made the city a capital of late 20th-century counterculture. One might say the beat movement, for instance, was born in 1953, when Allen Ginsberg moved to San Francisco and Lawrence Ferlinghetti opened **City Lights Booksellers** at 261 Columbus Avenue, even though Neal Cassady and Jack Kerouac already lived in the city at **29 Russell Street** (a small alley off Hyde Street between Union and Grand). One weekend in 1955, stoned to the gills, Ginsberg wrote his magnum opus, "Howl," in his apartment at **1214 Polk Street** (between Bush and Sutter streets), and read it for the first time two weeks later to a spellbound audience at the tiny **Six Gallery** at 3119 Fillmore Street (between Filbert and Greenwich streets). City Lights published the poem in 1956, and the police immediately declared it obscene, focusing national attention on North Beach. *Chronicle* columnist Herb Caen coined the term "beatnik" to describe the disheveled literati, who dug poetry and jazz at places like **Vesuvio's** (255 Columbus Ave.), on the corner of what is now Jack Kerouac Alley; **The Place** (1546 Grant Ave.), which Jack Kerouac described in *The Dharma Bums* as "the favorite bar of the hepcats around the Beach"; the **Cellar** (576 Green St.); and **Specs** (12 Adler Place). In 1958, after Kerouac's *On the Road* became a best-seller and Hollywood producers came up with the watered-down TV series "Route 66" to exploit the theme, tour-bus gawkers descended on North Beach to stare at the beatniks, making popular hangouts like **Caffe Trieste** (601 Vallejo St.), the now defunct **Co-**

Existence Bagel Shop (1398 Grant Ave.), and **Enrico's** (504 Broadway) feel like zoos for the caged poets. In 1960, The Place and the Co-Existence Bagel Shop closed, and the fuss over beatniks died for a while.

Tune in, turn on, trip out... Just a few years later, the city was the center of a cultural convulsion of a more Day-Glo shade. By the time the infamous Summer of Love rolled around in 1967, San Francisco's psychedelic scene had actually been in full swing for more than two years, since *One Flew Over the Cuckoo's Nest* author Ken Kesey introduced Owsley acid (known as the Cadillac of LSD) to the Grateful Dead, and acid rock was born. Another acid-powered band, the Jefferson Airplane, first played at a little club called the **Matrix** (3138 Fillmore St., near Union St.) in August 1965, but the club got too loud for the neighbors, so the acid-heads moved on and it evolved into a rowdy singles bar still doing business as **Pierce Street Annex**.

Examiner writer Michael Fallon coined the term "hippie" to distinguish the new hipsters from their beatnik predecessors shortly before the first big psychedelic concert was staged in October 1965 at **Longshoreman's Hall** in Fisherman's Wharf (400 North Point) by Chet Helms and his production company, the Family Dog. Later, the Family Dog moved its gigs to the **Avalon Ballroom** at 1268 Sutter Street (near Van Ness Avenue), now a multiplex movie theater. Meanwhile, Bill Graham entered the scene with a benefit for the San Francisco Mime Troupe (December 1965) at the **Fillmore Auditorium** (1805 Geary Blvd., at the corner of Fillmore), which would become his virtual kingdom and the undisputed center of the psychedelic rock universe.

In January 1967, 20,000 people showed up for the first "Human Be-In" at the **Polo Field** (just off Middle Dr. between 30th and 36th aves.) in Golden Gate Park, covered in luminous detail by the *Oracle*, a popular underground newspaper headquartered at **1371 Haight Street**. The Haight had become the center of hippie culture— Janis Joplin lived at **112 Lyon Street** (corner of Oak Street), the Grateful Dead around the corner at **710 Ashbury Street** (near Haight Street), and the Jefferson Airplane at **2400 Fulton Street** (closer to the park). By the summer of 1967, the whole world was watching the

Haight, especially when Rudolf Nureyev and Margot Fonteyn were arrested at a pot party at **42 Belvedere Street** (near Haight Street). Drug busts became a priority—if not a sport—for San Francisco's finest, and the October 1967 raid of the Dead house was the top feature of the premiere issue of *Rolling Stone*, which was produced in a small loft at 746 Brannan Street, South of Market. Drug busts and a massive influx of unenlightened strangers were ruining the scene; that same month, the Psychedelic Shop (1535 Haight St.) closed its doors and a march through the neighborhood declared the death of the true hippie movement. The party was over.

The last-call saloon crawl... The party is never over at some good old watering holes—these historic saloons are still full of characters and stories. There are at least a half-dozen classic booze joints in North Beach, from beatnik haunts that orbit City Lights—**Specs**, **Tosca**, and **Vesuvio's**—to beloved neighborhood dives like **Gino and Carlo** and literary hangouts like **Washington Square Bar & Grill**. Many of the best old downtown retreats, like the Templebar (1 Tillman Place, now a popular restaurant called Rumpus), have given way to more stylish ventures, but a few remnants of Old San Francisco remain, the best of which is **Harrington's**, a landmark Irish bar that has never been tamed by the genteel Financial District that surrounds it. If you get a chance, finish your tour at the **Mission Rock Resort** in China Basin and settle in for an afternoon beer on the deck, where you'll be hard-pressed to figure out how the word "resort" ever made its way into the name of this funky waterfront joint.

Painted ladies... Some 14,000 Victorian buildings—mostly private homes—are scattered throughout San Francisco, but the ones you usually see on the postcards (the 700 block of Steiner Street) are lined up around Alamo Square, the center of a small, wealthy neighborhood bordered by Golden Gate Avenue on the north, Fell Street on the south, Webster Street on the east, and Divisadero Street on the west. These ornate wooden homes range from gracious to almost garish, depending upon how much gingerbread is involved and who has been choosing the color scheme, but most of them have been meticulously restored. For a famous view, with the painted ladies in the foreground with the city and the bay in the background, find a high spot anywhere in Alamo Square and face due east (toward Steiner Street), or stand on the corner of Hayes and Steiner streets. The Archbishop's Mansion (1000 Fell St., see Accommodations), now an exclusive bed-and-breakfast inn, is a huge blue Victorian mansion right at the northern edge of the Painted Ladies postcard block. (A word of caution: This affluent area is the southwestern neighbor of the Western Addition, which can be dangerous near the public housing projects, especially at night. If you're not familiar with the area, you may prefer to take a bus or a cab instead of walking.)

If picture-pretty private residences are less intriguing to you than time-worn structures in a working-class neighborhood, head over to the inner Mission District, where several types of the city's oldest Victorians—stick, Italianate, and Queen Anne—can be found on or near Liberty Street, a small side street between 20th and 21st streets. These structures survived the 1906 earthquake because the fires stopped at 20th Street. An 1878 stick-style building, characterized by square bay windows with flat wooden "sticks" that have carved scrolls, leaves, and flowers, stands at 956 Valencia Street, on the corner of Liberty. Head north on Liberty, and you'll see rows of Victorians built between 1870 and 1894. At least five of them (19, 23, 35, 43, and 77) are Italianate style, distinguished by ornate porticos, façades above the rooflines, and slanted bay windows designed to bring in more light on foggy San Francisco days. The house at 27 Liberty is a local adaptation of a Queen Anne, identifiable primarily because of the shingled walls (most Queen Annes have rounded corner towers, but there are many variations on that theme). Some of the most interesting houses in the Mission District combined several architectural styles to get just the right amount of gewgaw and curlicues—the house at 827 Guerrero Street (corner of Liberty) has a Queen Anne tower, a Gothic front window, and a Moorish doorway. The Mission is full of wonderful houses. Walk around and explore for yourself, or get a little scholarly advice from Judith Waldhorn's *Take a Walk Through Mission History*, available for $1 from the Stanford Research Institute along with a free 11-page reading list about San Francisco Victorians (Victorian Booklets, M2308, Stanford Research Institute, Menlo Park, CA 94025, tel 415/326–6200).

Mural, mural on the wall... The 200 or so brilliant murals painted on the walls, fences, and sides of buildings in the Mission District are famous around the world, but often overlooked by visitors and locals alike. There are at least 250 more murals in other neighborhoods around the city—including the stunning Depression-era murals that cover the interior walls of the base of Coit tower. Keep your eyes open wherever you venture, but here's a tip for quick total immersion in the art of the streets: Take BART to the 24th Street stop and head up 24th toward Potrero Hill—you'll see it looming in front of you—until you come to Balmy Alley, nestled between Treat Avenue and Harrison Street. This one-block lane has one of the most dense collections of murals anywhere in the world—practically every inch of every fence, wall, and garage door is covered with color. Many of the alley's most cherished murals were defaced or destroyed by vandals in the past, but local muralists have painted new images and restored old ones. After you've marveled at Balmy Alley, go back out to 24th Street and head farther toward the hill, until you reach York Street, about four blocks away. Again you will be treated to a marvelous assortment of brilliantly colored murals. **Precita Eyes Mural Center**, a community resource center, hosts a tour of this area that will show you at least 60 Mission District murals in one eight-block stretch.

Are we there yet? (Fun with the kids)... The top family attractions besides Fisherman's Wharf and Pier 39 (sorry) are the **Exploratorium**, Alcatraz, the Zoo (**San Francisco Zoological Gardens and Children's Zoo**), and the **Steinhart Aquarium**. You simply cannot escape those places if your kids are even slightly persuasive. But there are other places they're likely to enjoy as well, depending on their ages. Youngsters love the Children's Playground in Golden Gate Park, just off Waller Street, opposite Arguello Boulevard, with all the requisite paraphernalia, plus wheelchair-accessible equipment. If they get bored with the slides/swings/sandbox routine, there is a restored 1912 carousel right next door (tel 415/666–7201). Other options for the under-14 set include CyberMind, a hyper-modern video arcade, and The Jungle, 15,000 square feet of crawling, jumping, and climbing. The last thing most teenagers want to do is go *anywhere* with their parents, but if you promise to hide completely across the room and pretend not to know them, they might just love you for taking them to the Hard Rock Cafe, where you'll need earplugs and they'll need enough money to buy expensive souvenir T-shirts, or Rock 'n' Bowl, a super-hip Haight Ashbury hangout where punkers and real-life bowlers go on weekend nights to watch rock videos on huge screens while they try to get those spares and strikes.

Fabulous footsteps... Hills, schmills. Don't let a few slopes here and there deter you from one of San Francisco's greatest pleasures—walking around the neighborhoods and exploring the city for yourself. Before you set out on your own, however, pick up some free walking-tour guides from the Visitor Information Center (Hallidie Plaza, Powell St. BART/MUNI Metro stop, tel 415/391–2000). The public library also offers about 20 free walking tours led by **City Guides**, volunteers who have completed an exhaustive training program in San Franciscan history, art, and architecture. Tours range from hidden rooftop gardens to brothels and boardinghouses. Some of the city's most unusual tours are organized by local individuals who love to show off their favorite parts of San Francisco. Rachel Heller leads the **Flower Power** Haight Ashbury tour, with stops at erstwhile crash pads of famous hippies (Janis Joplin and the Grateful Dead) and other lost psychedelic ports of call, such as the Straight Theater, where Bill Graham first staged his dance concerts. Host Trevor Hailey, a beloved—and very friendly—local historian, will take you **Cruisin' the Castro**, where you'll visit only-in-San-Francisco businesses, chat with the shopkeepers, enjoy brunch in a local hot spot, and discover why gay men have been migrating to San Francisco since the Gold Rush. Television chef and cookbook author Shirley Fong-Torres is the mastermind of the **I Can't Believe I Ate My Way Through Chinatown** tour, which treats walkers to a private tea ceremony, snacks, a visit to a rice-noodle factory, more snacks, visits with local food merchants, just one last snack, and a full Chinese luncheon. There are no hills to climb in Elaine Sosa's **Javawalk**, a two-hour jaunt through Union Square, Chinatown, Jackson Square, and North Beach, with pit stops along the way for—what else?—cups of joe. A multi-course lunch at Enrico's Sidewalk Cafe is the highlight of *Chronicle* food writer GraceAnn Walden's tour that goes behind the scenes at brick-oven bakeries, delis, and sausage makers to show what life is like for **The Italians of North Beach**. For lust and crime, get up early and join author John McCarroll on his **A.M. Walks** through the Barbary Coast, Chinatown, and Union Square, where gold rushers found "the best bad things obtainable in America." Then hook up with another local author, Mark Gordon, on his **Frisco Productions Crime Tour**, where you'll visit infamous crime scenes like the Hibernia Bank, robbed by Patty Hearst and the Symbionese Liberation Army in the mid-1970s.

The Index

A.M. Walks. You've got to get up at about 8am to find a little peace and quiet while you roam Chinatown, Union Square, and the Barbary Coast as your guide recounts tales of unbridled lust, scandal, and crime. Oh, how we love the city's naughty past. Host: author John McCarroll.... *Tel 415/928–5965.*

Ansel Adams Center for Photography. This is the largest collection of photography on the West Coast including one gallery devoted solely to Adams' work.... *Tel 415/495–7000. 250 Fourth St., Powell St. BART/MUNI Metro stop, 30, 45, or 76 MUNI bus. Open Tue–Sun 11–5, until 8 first Thur of every month. Admission charged.*

Asian Art Museum. Asiaphiles take note: Do not miss this under any circumstances. It is the largest museum outside of Asia devoted exclusively to Asian art.... *Tel 415/668–8921 or 415/668–7855; TDD 415/752–2635. Golden Gate Park, next to the de Young Museum and the Japanese Tea Garden,* *near Tenth Ave. and Fulton St. 44 MUNI bus. Open Wed–Sun 10–5, first Thur of each month until 8. Admission free first Wed of every month and first Sat 10–noon.*

Boudin Sourdough Bakery. When you're at Fisherman's Wharf or Pier 39, nothing tastes better than a San Francisco–style round sourdough bread from Boudin's. The crust is crisp and delicious, and the bread tears easily by hand for impromptu cracked crab sandwiches…. *Tel 415/928–1849. 156 Jefferson St., 32 MUNI bus. Open weekdays until 8, weekends until 9.*

Cable Car Barn and Museum. San Francisco's cable car system is still run out of this museum, which also houses the original prototype cable car…. *Tel 415/474–1887. 1201 Mason St., Powell/Hyde or Powell/Mason cable car. Open daily 10–6, Nov–Mar 10–5. Admission free.*

Cafe Sausalito. For a beautiful sunset view of San Francisco, take a ferry (see Golden Gate Ferry) to the seaside village of Sausalito, go to the top of the Village Fair (a beautiful, four-story gourmet shopping mall), and settle in at this inexpensive cafe…. *Tel 415/332–6579. 777 Bridgeway, Sausalito.*

California Academy of Sciences. This huge science museum complex is a major kid-pleaser, even if it isn't as goofy as the Exploratorium. The fish roundabout at Steinhart Aquarium puts you inside a huge tank that is almost an ocean; the Earth and Space hall at the Natural History Museum lets you experience a fake earthquake; and the Morrison Planetarium turns almost psychedelic at night when the Laserium projects vivid laser displays to the tunes of bands like Metallica. Don't miss cartoonist Gary Larson's "Far Side of Science" gallery…. *Tel 415/221–5610 or 415/750–7145 (recorded message); 415/750–7138 for Laserium. Golden Gate Park, near Eighth Ave. and Lincoln Way, 44 MUNI bus. Open 10–5. Admission free first Wed of every month, except Laserium.*

Cartoon Art Museum. Now that they've moved into fancy new digs near the spectacular new Museum of Modern Art, cartoon artists are being taken more seriously, even if their work is purposely whimsical. This one if the few art museums where your kids will have as much fun as you do…. *Tel 415/CARTOON (227–8666) or 415/456–3922. 814*

Mission St.; Montgomery St. BART/MUNI Metro stop; 15, 30, or 45 MUNI bus. Open Wed–Fri 11–5, Sat 10–5, Sun 1–5. Admission charged.

Center for the Arts at Yerba Buena Gardens. This dynamic multi-gallery center focuses on emerging local and regional artists, from Tenderloin painters and prison inmates to high-tech theater and dance. While the opera house is being repaired (probably until 1997), the San Francisco Ballet will perform here often.... *Tel 415/978–2700. 701 Mission St.; Montgomery St. BART/MUNI Metro stop; 14, 15, 30, or 45 MUNI bus. Open Tue–Sun 11–6. Gallery admission free first Thur of every month.*

City Guides. These free walking tours offered by the public library are very popular with locals as well as visitors, because the volunteer hosts are experts in the art, architecture, and lore of the city. Tours range from Mission murals, hidden rooftop gardens, and Pacific Heights mansions, to brothels, boardinghouses, and bawds.... *Tel 415/557–4266.*

Coit Tower. Supposedly shaped like a fire-hose nozzle to please Lillie Coit, an inveterate pyrophile and city benefactor, Coit Tower is a curious sight from a distance, and a marvel up close. Depression-era murals cover the interior walls at the base of the tower, while the top offers a 360-degree view. You can take the bus, but it's much more fun to hike up Grant and Greenwich streets.... *Tel 415/362–0808. 39 MUNI bus. Open daily 10–6:30. Base admission free, elevator $3.*

Cruisin' the Castro. Walk through the city's gay mecca with a local historian who knows every nook and cranny and will introduce you to the local shopkeepers along the way. Brunch at a popular cafe included. Host: Trevor Bailey.... *Tel 415/550–8110.*

CyberMind. This is a dads-and-sons kind of place, where some strange sort of high-tech male bonding occurs through the act of maneuvering joy sticks and killing imaginary enemies. Kids are crazy about this stuff. It's Nintendo to the nth power.... *Tel 415/693–0348. 1 Embarcadero Center, second floor, Embarcadero BART/MUNI Metro stop. Open* *weekdays 10am–10pm, Fri and Sat until 1am, Sun until 9 pm. Admission free.*

M. H. de Young Memorial Museum. This beautiful Golden Gate Park art museum hosts most of the major international- al shows that come to town, but is best known for an impressive collection of American art that dates back to the 1600s…. *Tel 415/750–3600 or 415/863–3330 (recorded message). Golden Gate Park, near Tenth Ave. and Fulton St., 44 MUNI bus. Open Thur–Sun 10–5, Wed until 8:45. Admission free first Wed of every month.*

Exploratorium. Kids love this wacky, blow-your-mind science circus—especially the dark and often creepy crawl-through Tactile Dome. Adults usually make things fairly equal by turning into kids themselves. The gift shop, by the way, is probably the best you'll ever encounter at a museum. (Don't miss the Einstein relativity theory wristwatches.)…. *Tel 415/561–0360. Palace of Fine Arts, 3601 Lyon St., 30 MUNI bus. Open Tue–Sun 10–5. Admission free first Wed of every month.*

Fisherman's Wharf. It's a tacky tourist trap, but if you have to go there, try to save your sanity by feasting on some fresh crab from a sidewalk stall and remembering that it used to be a real fishing port. Meanwhile, your kids are going to want to hit the Wax Museum and the Ripley's Believe It or Not Museum, but you can find at least mild amusement watching the hordes of tourists who pass by. To get to the wharf, take any Powell Street cable car, or the 15, 30, or 42 MUNI bus.

Flower Power. Take a walking tour through Haight Ashbury, checking out the sites where crash pads, concert halls, and psychedelic shops gave birth to the Hippie era. Host: Rachel Heller…. *Tel 415/221–8442. Admission charged.*

Frisco Productions Crime Tour. Get a vicarious thrill as you visit infamous crime scenes—real and fictional—with a local author who also offers a Bar Crawl tour, a Sentimental Journey Nostalgia tour, and a Hollywood in San Francisco tour. (He gets three demerits for calling it "Frisco," though.) Host: Mark Gordon…. *Tel 415/681–5555.*

SAN FRANCISCO | DIVERSIONS

Galeria de la Raza. This was the first Mexican museum in the United States, and it is still a major art and cultural center in the Latino community. Most of the work presented in the major exhibits is created by local artists, and is usually top quality.... *Tel 415/826–8009. 2857 24th St., 24th St. BART station, 48 or 67 MUNI bus. Open Tue–Sat noon–6. Admission free.*

Ghia Gallery/Discount Caskets and Urns. If the Addams Family had an art gallery, there is no question this would be it. Not only is the gallows humor entirely good-natured, the coffins are actually really fun to look at, and the show openings are major social events that often attract local politicians as well as other more artistic celebrities. (Cher is a customer—is that a surprise?) Exhibits change every six weeks; call for details and hours.... *Tel 415/282–2832. 2648 Third St.; 15, 30, or 45 MUNI bus. Admission free.*

Gino and Carlo. No bar in North Beach has more loyal regulars than Gino and Carlo, a classic neighborhood dive that is almost invariably free of tourists. If you venture through the double doors for a few drinks—just one would be viewed as trifling—be prepared for spirited arguments (mostly about sports) and patrons who will undoubtedly retell at least one episode from the bar's long history.... *Tel 415/421–0896. 548 Green St.*

Glide Memorial Church. Charismatic civic leader Reverend Cecil Williams and his gospel choir host services every Sunday morning that seem to lift the spirits of the whole city.... *Tel 415/771–6300. 330 Ellis St. Services Sun at 9 and 11.*

Golden Gate Ferry. Join the locals who ride from San Francisco's Ferry Building at the foot of Market Street to downtown Sausalito, a scenic seaside village with lots of expensive stores, expensive restaurants, expensive real estate, expensive boats—and gorgeous sunsets. The ride takes about a half-hour. Fare is $4.25 each way for adults, $3.20 for children, and $2.10 for seniors. Call for schedule.... *Tel 415/332–6600, TDD 415/257–4554. Embarcadero BART/MUNI Metro stop.*

Good Vibrations. The contraptions on display in the window may look like old-time hair dryers or permanent-wave doodads, but they actually belong to an eclectic collection of sex toys and vibrators. More than half the visitors are women, and the museum/store's extensive library tends to favor female interests. Workshops offered after hours range from safer sex education (led by the Safer Sex Sluts) to erotic reading circles.... *Tel 415/974–8980. 1210 Valencia St., 25th St. BART stop, 26 MUNI bus. Open daily 11–7. Admission free.*

Grizzly Peak. A popular Berkeley Hills perch for a great sunset vista of the entire bay. To get there from San Francisco, drive across the Oakland–San Francisco Bay Bridge, follow the signs to Highway 24 toward Walnut Creek (via Interstate 580), go through the Caldecott Tunnel (stay to the far right), and exit immediately after the tunnel at Fish Ranch Road. (The exit turns sharply right, then right again over the freeway.) Drive up to the top of the hill on Fish Ranch Road (to the stop sign), turn right on Grizzly Peak Boulevard, and drive about a half-mile or so until you find a turnout that appeals to you (the view parking spots will be on your left).

Hard Rock Cafe. In truth, the crowd at the Hard Rock is mostly tourists, but teenagers don't seem to care about that at all. They love the super-loud rock music, juicy hamburgers, and T-shirts that prove they've been there. In fact, there is usually a line out in front just for the shirts.... *Tel 415/885–1699. 1699 Van Ness Ave. (at Sacramento St.), California St. cable car, 1 MUNI bus. Reservations not accepted.*

Harrington's. When original owner Leo Harrington died in 1959, a procession of motorcycle police led a mile-long cortege in his honor, if that gives you any idea of how beloved this Irish bar is. The old building is wonderfully creaky and the floors have been known to get ankle-deep in green beer on St. Patrick's Day, but regulars consider that a testament to their resolute rowdiness in the face of their gentrified surroundings.... *Tel 415/392–7595. 245 Front St., California St. cable car.*

I Can't Believe I Ate My Way Through Chinatown. A well-known television chef and cookbook author lets you in on a private tea ceremony, among other gustatory delights, before you reach your final destination: a huge Chinese luncheon. Host: Shirley Fong-Torres.... *Tel 415/355–9657. Admission charged.*

SAN FRANCISCO | DIVERSIONS

The Italians of North Beach. Even if you don't give a hoot about seeing the inside of a brick-oven bakery, a sausage-making company, or a local italian deli, this four-hour tour is worth taking for one simple reason: It ends up with a full, multi-course lunch at Enrico's Sidewalk Cafe (see Dining). Host: GraceAnn Walden.... *Tel 415/397–8530. Saturdays only; during the week by prior arrangement. Admission charged.*

Javawalk. Walk the coffee trail in Chinatown, Jackson Square, and North Beach with a woman who swears there are no hills involved, and she'll tell you local secrets besides. Host: Elaine Sosa.... *Tel 415/673–9255. Admission charged.*

Jewish Community Museum. The idea of this fine museum is to highlight important events in Jewish history, including the works of Jewish artists. They don't shy away from controversy—one past exhibit focused on the relationship between Jews and African Americans. Call for exhibit schedule.... *Tel 415/543–2090 or 415/543–8880 (recorded message). 121 Stuart St., Embarcadero BART/MUNI Metro stop. Open Sun–Wed 11–5, Thur until 7 (closed on all Jewish holidays). Admission charged.*

The Jungle. This spot is just for kids 14 and under. It is a huge indoor playground (15,000 square feet) where kids can crawl, jump, climb, and basically be kids.... *Tel 415/552–4386. 555 Ninth St. (above Toys R Us), Civic Center BART/MUNI Metro stop. Open 10am–9pm, Sat 9–9, Sun 10–8. Admission $4.95 until 5pm weekdays, then $2.95; $5.95 weekends (two hours).*

Keane Eyes Gallery. In the 1960s, while counterculture icon Richard Brautigan was roaming North Beach, reading and giving away mimeographed sheaves of his poems, Mr. and Mrs. Keane were busily pumping out portrait after portrait of small children with oversized heads and eyes so huge and round they made Liza Minnelli look like a squinter. Then it was merely tacky—now it's high kitsch.... *Tel 415/495–3263. 651 Market St.; 6, 7, 8, 9, 21, or 66 MUNI bus. Open Mon–Fri 10–6, Sat until 4. Admission free.*

Lyle Tuttle's Tattoo Museum. Lyle Tuttle, undisputed king of the San Francisco tattoo empire, engraved Janis Joplin's flesh in a seedier, now-defunct location at Seventh and Market streets, but you can still see his collection of tattoo art at his tiny little shop in North Beach. Tuttle's list of satisfied clients includes Gregg Allman, Cher, Joan Baez, and Peter Fonda.... *Tel 415/775–4991. 841 Columbus Ave., 15 or 30 MUNI bus. Open Mon–Thur noon–9, Fri and Sat until 10, Sun until 8. Admission free.*

Marine World/Africa USA. Kiss a whale, let an exotic butterfly land on your nose, ride an elephant, feed a giraffe, or get soaked by a mighty splash from the tail of a gigantic killer whale in a million-gallon pool. The wildlife park is an hour from the city via high-speed Blue & Gold ferry from Pier 39; the fleet's package deal—round-trip ferry transportation, shuttle to the park, and all-day park admission—costs $36 adults, $30 seniors and ages 13–18, $20.50 ages 5–12, under 5 free. Reservations recommended.... *Tel 415/707– 5555 (ferry information), 707/643–6722 (park information, including driving directions).*

Maritime Museum. Kids like it because it looks like a life-size plaster model of a ship. Inside, the nautical exhibits—models, relics, and other inanimate sailor stuff—might bore the youngsters, but the macramé knots are kind of fun for parents with a twinge of 1970s arts-and-crafts nostalgia..... *Tel 415/929–0202. Fisherman's Wharf, 901 Beach St., Powell-Hyde cable car; 15, 30, 42, or 69 MUNI bus. Open daily 10–5. Admission free.*

Mexican Museum. Some people go for the huge permanent collection, others go for the changing exhibits that range from Diego Rivera to graffiti art, but we go for the gift shop. The folk art is absolutely wonderful, and many of the less expensive pieces make fabulous souvenirs—especially the Day of the Dead toys and statues.... *Tel 415/441–0404. Fort Mason Center, Bldg. D, 28 MUNI bus. Open Wed–Sun noon–5. Admission charged.*

Mission Rock Resort. The China Basin waterfront is hardly the Riviera, and the Mission Rock is far from a resort—refurbished bait shop is more like it. Yet that funkiness is precisely what draws locals here on sunny afternoons for no-frills burgers and beers on the huge deck.... *Tel 415/621– 5538. 817 China Basin, 15 MUNI bus.*

Musée Mecanique. If you're headed out to Ocean Beach for dinner, a drink, or an unforgettable sunset at the Cliff House, don't miss this ingenious little museum inside the restaurant. It's full of mechanical gadgets you can actually play with, from player pianos and old carnival fortune-tellers to an entire miniature amusement park. Bring your own quarters.... *Tel 415/386–1170. 1090 Point Lobos Ave., 18 or 38 MUNI bus. Open Mon–Fri 11–7, weekends 10–8. Admission free.*

Museum of Modern Art. No one has stopped talking about this art hall since it opened in 1995. The most obvious attraction is the building itself, an ultramodern skylighted structure designed by a famous Swiss architect (Mario Botta) and set in the middle of the city's art center, South of Market. The permanent collection features all the major modern and postmodern artists, but the best part is its huge collection of art photography.... *Tel 415/357–4000. 151 Third St.; Montgomery St. BART/MUNI Metro stop; 15, 30, or 45 MUNI bus. Open Tue–Sun 11–6, Thur until 9. Admission free first Tue of every month.*

Nick's. Located right on Fisherman's Wharf, Nick's sidewalk seafood stall is just outside the main restaurant, Nick's Lighthouse. It looks funky and the cooks can seem a bit gruff at times, but it's all part of the way things used to be when the area was still a bustling wharf. Make sure you get a whole, live crab—if it doesn't wiggle, demand another one—and have them cook it for you on the spot.... *Tel 415/929–1300. Fisherman's Wharf (Jefferson St.), 32 MUNI bus.*

No Name Bar. If you're over thirty but you still love to boogie, the No Name Bar in Sausalito may be just the spot for you. The music is live (blues and jazz) and the rowdy baby boomers are always in the mood to dance, seven nights a week. This is not a good place to go on a romantic date, but it may be a great place to find one.... *Tel 415/332–1392. 757 Bridgeway, Sausalito.*

North Beach Museum. Tucked away on the mezzanine of a small bank, this delightful little museum traces North Beach's history with photographs and artifacts dating back to the turn of the century. Call for schedule.... *Tel 415/ 391–6210. Eureka Federal Savings, 1435 Stockton St. (at Columbus Ave.); 15, 30, or 45 MUNI bus. Closed weekends. Admission free.*

Old Mint Museum. This was the city's second mint and is now a national historic landmark. The minting equipment is especially interesting.... *Tel 415/744–6830. 88 Fifth St., Powell St. BART/MUNI Metro stop. Open Mon–Fri 10–4. Admission free.*

Palace of Fine Arts. This wonderful old building that looks like a Roman ruin is home of the Exploratorium and the sole surviving structure from the 1915 Panama Pacific Exposition. It was also the site of the presidential debate between Jimmy Carter and Gerald Ford.... *Tel 415/567–6642. 3601 Lyon St., 30 MUNI bus. Open Tue–Sun 10–5.*

Pier 23 Cafe. Perhaps the most satisfying part of going to Pier 23 is that it looks a bit like an old shanty, so most Pier 39–bound tourists pass it by. Once you get inside, you'll be treated to great views of the bay and live jazz with no cover charge (5–8pm, every night except Friday). Locals love to enjoy the twilight at this simple, friendly little cafe.... *Tel 415/362–5125. Pier 23 (the Embarcadero), 32 MUNI bus.*

Pier 39. Believe it or not, this is the biggest tourist attraction in the city, and the third biggest in the world (after Disney World and Disneyland). That means you have to take your kids there, whether you like it or not. It's basically a glorified shopping mall/carnival, but it's not so bad if you direct them toward the sea lions (K-dock). A new attraction called Underwater World, a "multi-sensory aquarium," is set to open in 1996.... *Tel 415/705–5500. 15, 30, or 42 MUNI bus. Open Mon–Fri 9–5, longer on weekends.*

Precita Eyes Mural Center. This community resource center for murals and muralists offers information, tours, and workshops. It is a wonderful way to learn about the history of the Mission District murals in particular.... *Tel 415/285–2287. 348 Precita Ave. (near Folsom St.), 27 MUNI bus. Tours Sat 1:30pm. Admission charged.*

Rock 'n' Bowl. Big-screen rock videos and hard-rockin' bowlers are the key elements at this wild Haight Ashbury institution. (For one of their anniversary parties they hired a live band called Buck Naked and His Bare-Bottomed Boys.) The main event, though, is still simply bowling. It's busy on weekends;

SAN FRANCISCO | DIVERSIONS

reservations are recommended.... *Tel 415/826–2695. 1855 Haight St., 7 MUNI bus.*

San Francisco Zoological Gardens and Children's Zoo.

One of the most innovative features of this 65-acre zoo is the Primate Discovery Center that cares for many rare and endangered species, but nothing can top Gorilla World, one of the world's largest assortments of the big guys. There are plenty of other delights, including the Children's Zoo, adjacent to the main park, where kids can pet many animals and get up close to babies in the zoo nursery, or visit the Insect Zoo (more than 6,000 specimens).... *Tel 415/753–7080, 415/753–7083 for recorded information. Sloat Blvd. and 45th Ave., L Taraval MUNI Metro streetcar to the end of the line. Open daily 10–5, children's zoo 11–4. Admission charged, under 5 free; children's zoo, admission charged, under 3 free. Free first Wed of every month.*

Specs. This tiny brick-walled bar, a beatnik landmark, is still cluttered with mementos, yellowed newspaper clippings, and occasionally blessed with brilliant poetic bathroom graffiti. Its irreverent past (and present) is perhaps best expressed by the whale's penis bone that hangs over the bar.... *Tel 415/421–4112. 12 Adler Place.*

Steering Wheel West. This museum is devoted strictly to "automotive art." Most of the paintings, photos, and sculptures focus on the "Class Era" (1927–1937).... *Tel 415/474–8000. 1701 Van Ness Ave.; 42, 47, or 49 MUNI bus. Open Sat–Sun 10:30–5:30, weekdays by appointment only. Admission free.*

Steinhart Aquarium. This is part of the California Academy of Sciences, but it's such a favorite with kids that it deserves its own listing. The aquarium is one of the largest in the United States—more than 14,000 species. It's tough to say which is most popular with kids—the 10,000-gallon fish roundabout (a miniature ocean that surrounds you) or the feeding of the dolphins, seals, and penguins. There are also tidepools and a living coral reef, plus a hands-on area where kids can touch creatures living in the water.... *Tel 415/221–5100, 415/750–7145 for recorded information. California Academy of Sciences, Golden Gate Park, near Eighth Ave. and Lincoln Way., 44 MUNI bus. Open 10–5. Admission free first Wed of every month.*

Tosca. Everyone who stays in San Francisco long enough even-tually ends up at Tosca, where the jukebox plays Pavarotti and the cappuccino automatically comes with a shot of booze. The mirror behind the bar is like a history-class chalk-board—stickers from the 1939 World's Fair remain exactly where they were originally stuck.... *Tel 415/986–9651 (pay phone). 252 Columbus Ave.; 15,30 MUNI bus.*

Vesuvio's. The list of poets who have spent hours at Vesuvio's getting anywhere from pleasantly buzzed to totally soused stretches from Dylan Thomas (soused) and his namesake Bob Dylan (buzzed) to Jack Kerouac (soused) and Allen Ginsberg (soused and buzzed). No matter where you sit—especially in the balcony—any of the aforementioned are likely to have sat before you.... *Tel 415/362–3370. 255 Columbus Ave.; 15,30 MUNI bus.*

Washington Square Bar & Grill. Whatever it is, it has already been done at the WSB&G—weddings, wakes, funerals, huge business deals, political and marital scandals—during the past quarter-century. It's a bit heavy on the celebrity side, but you might not notice unless you recognize writers and local socialites by sight.... *Tel 415/982–8123. 1707 Powell St.; 15,30 MUNI bus.*

SAN FRANCISCO | DIVERSIONS

San Francisco Diversions

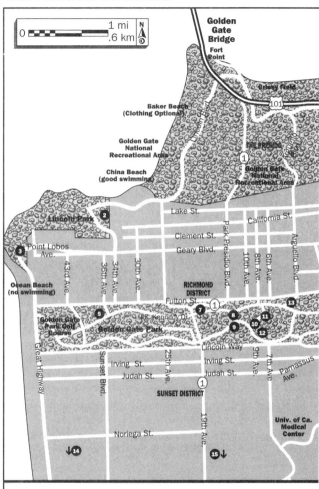

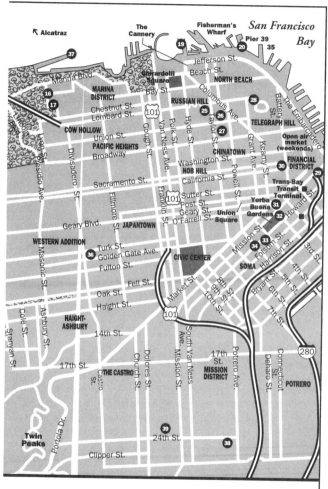

↖ Alcatraz

The Cannery

Fisherman's Wharf

Pier 39 35

San Francisco Bay

37

19

20

Jefferson St.
Beach St.

Ghirardelli Square

Marina Blvd.

Bay St.

NORTH BEACH

MARINA DISTRICT

Chestnut St.
Lombard St.

101

RUSSIAN HILL

Columbus Ave.

28

25

26

Battery St.

TELEGRAPH HILL

16

17

Lincoln Blvd.

Presidio Ave.

COW HOLLOW

Union St.

27

Taylor St.

Hyde St.

Polk St.

Van Ness Ave.

Gough St.

PACIFIC HEIGHTS

Broadway

CHINATOWN

Washington St.

Grant Ave.

Kearny St.

The Embarcadero

Open air market (weekends)

FINANCIAL DISTRICT

30

29

NOB HILL

Sacramento St.

California St.

Powell St.

Divisadero St.

Fillmore St.

Franklin St.

101

Sutter St.
Post St.
Geary St.
O'Farrell St.

Union Square

Trans-Bay Transit Terminal

Yerba Buena Gardens

31

32

Howard St.

Geary Blvd.

JAPANTOWN

Mission St.

33

Folsom St.

Harrison St.

3rd St.

WESTERN ADDITION

Turk St.

36

Golden Gate Ave.

Fulton St.

CIVIC CENTER

34

SOMA

Bryant St.

4th St.

5th St.

6th St.

7th St.

Masonic St.

Fell St.

Oak St.

Market St.

8th St.

9th St.

10th St.

Haight St.

101

South Van Ness Ave.

Mission St.

280

Cole St.

Ashbury St.

Stanyan St.

HAIGHT-ASHBURY

14th St.

17th St.

THE CASTRO

Castro St.

Church St.

Dolores St.

17th St.

MISSION DISTRICT

Potrero Ave.

Connecticut St.

De Haro St.

POTRERO

Twin Peaks

Portola Dr.

39

24th St.

38

Clipper St.

getting

4

outside

At first glance, it
might seem that
San Franciscans'
favorite outdoor
activity is loung-
ing at sidewalk
cafés—a

respectable pastime, to be sure, though hardly a hallmark of physical fitness. But very little is as it seems in this unorthodox city. A magnificent natural environment distinguishes it from most others, and even the most impassive urbanites eagerly embrace any diversion that takes place outdoors, from picnics to surfing. San Francisco may not be Montana or Wyoming, but there's still so much open space around it that cattle ranching remains a major industry in the East Bay. The Bay Area's public greenbelt—more than 860,000 acres of open land and watershed—is probably the largest of any major metropolitan center in the country, according to Greenbelt Alliance, a regional land conservation organization. Add undeveloped private land and there is easily more than a million acres of open space in and around the city, with almost a third of that set aside as public park and recreation areas, including such huge, inviting parks as Golden Gate Park and the Presidio. There's a lot of fun stuff offshore, too, in the islands that dot San Francisco Bay, some of which are just a short ferry ride from the heart of the city, and a great escape—so to speak—from the hubbub. And, of course, there is the spectacular **Golden Gate Bridge**, which you must walk across before you can truly claim to have seen San Francisco.

The Lowdown

Parks... Two dozen neighborhood parks within the city limits include facilities for baseball, basketball, barbecues, boating, bird-watching, bocce, bicycling, cricket, jogging, football, fishing, picnics, swimming, tennis, golf, soccer, volleyball, windsurfing, handball, and lawn bowling. Some even have gyms. **Golden Gate Park** covers 1,000 acres stretching from the Panhandle to the beach. Besides various major attractions covered in the Diversions chapter, it has 11 lakes, 2 waterfalls, 21 tennis courts, horseback riding stables (tel 415/668–7360, Kennedy Dr. and 36th Ave.), horseshoe pits (off Conservatory Way near Grove St.; bring your own horseshoes), a nine-hole golf course, fly-casting pools, a miniature yacht club, a five-acre Japanese tea garden, a primitive garden featuring plants from the dinosaur era, and the very same polo grounds where Allen Ginsberg and Timothy Leary ushered in the Summer of Love at the first Human Be-In in 1967. If that's not enough, there's even a resident herd of bison, at the Buffalo Paddock on John F. Kennedy Drive (parallel to 38th Avenue), adjacent to the Chain of Lakes. The breeding herd of *Bison bison* are particularly fond of stale bread tossed to them by passersby. All the animals are the progeny of two cows—Sarah Bernhardt and Princess—and a bull named Ben Harrison, who were purchased by the city in 1890 and brought down from the Montana plains. Not far from the buffalo paddock is the Model Yacht Club Boat House, where miniature yachts are prepared for racing on Spreckels Lake by the second-oldest miniature yacht club in America, founded in 1901. (One can only hope that miniature Tony Curtises and Marilyn Monroes are aboard, practicing their lines from *Some Like It Hot*.) Another goofy little wonder in the park is near the M. H. de Young Museum, off Tenth Avenue and Fulton Street: the Forgotten Works, a field of carved rocks (some hidden beneath the grass) that are actually part of the ruins of El Monasterio de Santa Maria de Avila, a monastery near Madrid, Spain, part of which was reassembled in the museum nearby. These little-known corners of the park are what make it such an incredible urban resource. Another fun spot is **Marina Green**, a bayshore strip of park where you can listen to the **Wave Organ**, a bizarre contrivance made of different lengths of pipes that extend into the bay and resonate to the motion of the waves. (To reach the green from the Golden Gate Promenade, turn off at the St. Francis Yacht Club and take a short walk east past the lighthouse and the Golden Gate Yacht Club.) Sometimes it is so quiet you can barely hear it; other times it is like a soothing liquid mantra. Just west of Marina Green, the **Presidio**—where the city was originally founded as Yerba Buena in 1776—is now a national park, with spectacular views of the Golden Gate Bridge, beautiful hiking and biking trails, a fishing stream, and other diversions, not least of which is the city's pet cemetery. At Crissy Field, at the west end of the Golden Gate Promenade in the Presidio, you can watch kite-flyers strut their stuff or windsurfers whizzing around on the bay; this is a great place to toss a Frisbee, give your dog a workout, or just bask on a sunny day. **Mountain Lake Park**, which is at the edge of the Presidio, has great running trails, four tennis courts, and fishing; **Lake Merced Park** is a beautiful park near the zoo and Fort Funston, with all the water sports you can imagine, plus two golf courses and lots of jogging trails. It's also the city's best park for bird-watching—because it's so near the Pacific Ocean, many seafaring birds fly by for a brief stopover. B.Y.O.B. (bring your own binoculars).

Stretching your legs... Some of the most beautiful—and least hilly—places to jog or walk in San Francisco are its promenades, which trace the shoreline of the bay from the Embarcadero's South Beach area to the foot of the Golden Gate Bridge at Fort Point. The 42 MUNI bus will drop you off near China Basin, a block from King Street and the Embarcadero, which is a good place to start your trek along the **South Promenade**. Heading north, you'll watch a stunning perspective change progressively as you approach and then pass directly under the Oakland–San Francisco Bay Bridge. On your left, across the street, you'll see tempting sidewalk cafés and lush palm trees. On your right, nothing but a railing separates you from the bay itself. It's the most spectacular sea-level view in the city. At Pier 24, the **Waterfront Promenade** begins with a staircase that leads down into the water, and continues to the Ferry Building. At that point, you'll have traveled approximately 1 mile. On Saturdays, you may want to stop there and wander through the outdoor farmer's market at the Ferry Plaza (across from the Embarcadero, at the end of Market St.). If you choose to continue along the Embarcadero, you'll pass Pier 39 on your left and end up at Fisherman's Wharf within $1^1/_2$ miles. **Golden Gate Promenade** starts at Aquatic Park/Fort Mason at the western edge of Fisherman's Wharf—the 28 MUNI bus route runs near the trail, so you can go one-way or round-trip, or stop anywhere along the way. The Golden Gate Promenade, which is marked by blue-and-white signs, ends at Fort Point, where steps lead up to the Golden Gate Bridge's pedestrian walkway; the entire route is less than 4 miles (not counting the walk across the bridge), and is popular with cyclists as well, because of the beautiful views, varied terrain, and decided lack of automobile traffic. Heading west, there's a $2^1/_2$-mile parcourse loop for fitness buffs who aren't satisfied with a simple walk or jog, as the trail follows the seawall along the Marina Green. Look over your left shoulder and you'll see the Marin Headlands, Mount Tamalpais, Angel Island, and

Alcatraz. When you get to the Palace of Fine Arts, you will have gone a bit more than $1^1/_2$ miles. Continue along the promenade to the St. Francis Yacht Club, where, if you want to distract yourself for a quiet moment, you can go east past the lighthouse and the Golden Gate Yacht Club to find the Wave Organ (see Parks, above). Head back out to the promenade, pass Crissy Field, and you'll have another mile to your credit. From there, it's about 1 more mile to Fort Point; on a windy day, the ocean may spray its mist onto your face as you pass. On Sundays and holidays, **Golden Gate Park** is great for jogging; John F. Kennedy Drive is closed to vehicular traffic from 19th Avenue to Kezar Stadium—about $2^1/_2$–3 miles. To get there, take the N Judah MUNI Metro streetcar or the 7 MUNI bus to Kezar, or the 5 MUNI bus to Park Presidio and Fulton Street, then walk into the park to John F. Kennedy Drive. You'll pass many potential diversions along the way—Stow Lake, the Japanese Tea Garden, the de Young Museum, the Asian Art Museum, the Conservatory of Flowers—so just pretend it's a form of interval training and stop often to indulge yourself. Neighborhood parks with running trails include the 700-acre **Lake Merced** (tel 415/753–1101) at Harding Road off Skyline Boulevard, and the 15-acre **Mountain Lake Park** (tel 415/666–7005) at Lake Street and 12th Avenue. Slightly wacky joggers and walkers—two-, four-, or many-legged—are always welcome to join the **Bay to Breakers** in May, one of America's favorite footraces, when more than 100,000 revelers in goofy costumes make their way from the Embarcadero to the ocean. If you aren't in shape to run the distance (7.5 miles), you'll have plenty of company—most people walk, trot, dance, or just sort of drift along with the crowd. It's a popular race; register well in advance (for info call 415/777–7771) to ensure getting your T-shirt at the finish line. There is no more intimate view of the city than the fantastic scenery along the route of the **San Francisco Marathon**, run in early July (register by June—call 415/3391–2123 or 800/722–3466), a time of year when the oddball weather there is generally pleasantly cool. The 26.2-mile race starts on the Golden Gate Bridge and winds past the Palace of Fine Arts and the Embarcadero, through Chinatown and Haight Ashbury, ending up at Kezar Stadium in Golden Gate Park.

Pedal pushing... There are two basic ways to ride a bicycle in San Francisco—laboring up the hills and coasting swiftly down the hills. Don't give up the idea, though. There are exceptions—most notably Golden Gate Park, the Great Highway, the Golden Gate Promenade, and the Golden Gate Bridge—which are relatively easy to ride and absolutely gorgeous to behold. The best time to ride in **Golden Gate Park** is ostensibly on Sunday, when John F. Kennedy Drive (7.5 miles) is closed to automobile traffic, but since that fact is well known to every cyclist, in-line skater, jogger, and baby stroller in the city, congestion can be a bit of a nuisance even without cars. A good alternative is to use the park during the week and steer clear of the area between Arguello Street and 19th Avenue, where most of the museums and other popular attractions are located. The **Great Highway**, from Ocean Beach (at the end of Golden Gate Park) to Lake Merced (turn right on Sloat Blvd.), is an easy 3-mile ride along the ocean on a flat sidewalk with three bike lanes. Add-ons: a 5-mile ride around Lake Merced or a 200-foot ascent on Point Lobos Avenue (near the Cliff House) on your return trip to the park. The most convenient bike rentals for these rides are at **Lincoln Cyclery** (tel 415/221–2415, 772 Stanyan St.) and **Park Cyclery** (tel 415/751–7368, 1865 Haight St.). The **Golden Gate Promenade**, from Aquatic Park/Fort Mason to Fort Point, is less than 4 miles of relatively easy riding if you don't give into the temptation of the **Presidio**'s more challenging forest trails (15 miles) or the $1^{1}/_{2}$-mile ride across the **Golden Gate Bridge**, often against heavy winds. If you do cross the bridge—and you're still optimistic about developing thighs of steel—take the bike lane (parallel to Highway 101) from the Vista Point parking lot and turn off onto Alexander Avenue for a downhill jaunt to Sausalito, another 2 miles. Just remember: What goes down, must come up. You can rent bikes for these rides at **American Bicycle Rental** (tel 415/931–0234, 2715 Hyde St.). **Angel Island** is a good place to explore on two wheels. Take a ferry (see "Islands with a past" below) to the state park, then rent a mountain bike at Ayala Cove for $12–17 per hour or $25–40 per day (helmet included). There are about 8 miles of beginning and intermediate trails and many steeper advanced trails. If you decide to get around—or out of—the city on a bicycle, BART is a good option, since it allows cyclists to board on off-peak hours. Bike route maps and information are available from the **San Francisco Recreation and Park Department** (tel 415/666–7201) and the **East Bay Regional Park District** (tel 510/635–0135).

Working up a sweat... If you're staying at any of the city's major hotels, you're probably eligible for the special $10 daily guest package (regularly $15) at the state-of-the-art **Pinnacle Fitness Club**, voted best in the Bay Area by the *San Francisco Bay Guardian*. This immaculate club with new and perfectly maintained equipment is frequented by locals as well as hotel guests; the majority tend be young (20–35), fitness-conscious professional types rather than bulky bodybuilders. The price is fantastic, but there's no pool. The list of participating hotels is far too long to give here; ask your concierge or call either of the two facilities (tel 415/195–1939, 345 Spear St., near Embarcadero BART or MUNI Metro stop; or tel 415/543–1110, 61 New Montgomery St., near Montgomery St. BART or MUNI Metro stop). **North Point Health Club** (tel 415/989–1446, 2310 Powell St., near Fisherman's Wharf), a small neighorhood gym with no pool, also welcomes drop-in visitors for $15 a day, and offers free parking at Bay and Mason Streets. If you get the urge to pump iron in the middle of the night, there's always **24 Hour Nautilus**, with four huge facilities in the city. You won't find many "gym rats" there, nor will you find many women in the middle of the night, but at other hours there's a fairly even mix of men and women, varied according to the neighborhood. Daily fee is $15 at all four locations: tel 415/776–2200, Sutter St. at Van Ness Ave.; tel 415/395–9595, 350 Bay St.; tel 415/543–7808, 2nd and Folsom Sts.; and tel 415/434–5080, 100 California St. The **Jewish Community Center** (tel 415/292–1220, 3200 California St. at Park Presidio) charges $10 a day at its facility, which has a pool and all the requisite exercise equipment—plus handball courts—but unfortunately exudes a funky chlorine-and-sweat smell. Of the city's four YMCA health clubs, the cream of the crop is the **Embarcadero YMCA** (tel 415/957–9622, 169 Stuart St., $12 a day), with a sparkling pool, state-of-the-art exercise equipment, and a spectacular view of the bay from the Lifecycle machines. During the week, the club is filled with financial district types—especially at lunchtime—but on weekends, you're likely to see locals just in from their morning espresso at a North Beach café.

Hitting the beach... Can we talk? Northern California ain't Hawaii, kids. The water is usually as cold as ice, the wind can be fierce enough to blow your tuna sandwich into the next person's picnic basket, and the summer sky is generally overcast—though it will give you a dreadful sunburn if you don't wear industrial-strength sunblock. So forget the idea of swaying palms and white-sand beaches. That's a different California. The rugged, cliffside beaches in San Francisco are some of the most spectacular in the world to look at—huge waves crash against sheer walls of rock—but a treacherous undertow and unpredictable surf conditions make them dangerous for swimming.

Ocean Beach (at the end of Golden Gate Park, near the Cliff House) is surely the most dramatic seaside vista in the city—at least the sea lions that gather on Seal Rocks seem to think so—but it is absolutely forbidden to swim there. You can enjoy sunbathing, beachcombing, hiking, sipping a drink at the **Cliff House** (tel 415/386–3330, 1090 Pt. Lobos Ave.), but don't even think about dipping your little toe in the water. Swimming is also prohibited at **Land's End Beach** (north of the Cliff House), **Kirby Beach** (below the northern end of the Golden Gate Bridge), **Rodeo Beach** (at Fort Cronkite, Marin Headlands), and **Tennessee Beach** (north of Rodeo Beach), though beachcombing can be fun if you stay a safe distance from the water. There are safe swimming beaches in the city, if you can stand the cold water: **China Beach** (28th Ave. and Sea Cliff Dr.) and **Aquatic Park** (end of Hyde St.). Both are sandy coves where lifeguards are on duty during the summer; they're open April 15–October 15, 7am–dusk. More popular with adventurous locals is **Baker Beach**, where nude sunbathing is fashionable for both gay and straight sunbathers. Officially designated clothing-optional by the city, it's easily reached by public transportation (you might want to keep your clothes on while you're riding the bus). The truly gay men's section, according to that indispensable, outrageous local guide *Betty and Pansy's Severe Queer Review*, is beyond the large rock formations, which are most easily navigated at low tide. That part of the beach is definitely a cruise scene. The rest of the beach, however, has a predominant atmosphere of comfortable indifference to the fact that many people are not wearing clothes. Swimming is not prohibited but is definitely very dangerous and should be avoided. No lifeguards are on duty; there are changing rooms, which seem rather pointless when no one's wearing clothes anyway. The beach is open April 15–October 15, 7am–9pm. If you're around in September and want to meet some real live local maniacs, get out your wetsuit and join in the **Alcatraz Shark Fest**, a 1.5-mile swim from the Rock to the city shore, at 8am. Believe it or not, it's a relatively popular event, so preregister (tel 415/868–1829). For beachcombing, tide-pool exploring, hiking, camping, or romantic bed-and-breakfast getaways, a trip to **Point Reyes National Seashore** is without equal. At 65,000 acres, it is the largest and wildest section of the Bay Area's greenbelt—32,000 acres are designated wilderness. You may even be lucky enough to spot a great white shark out in the water. Point Reyes's beaches and tiny villages are accessible by Golden Gate Transit public transportation (tel 4515/332–6600, TDD 415/257–4554), but much easier to reach by car, less than an hour from the city. A car's especially handy if you decide to linger for dinner or stay at one of the nearby inns (see Accommodations).

Poolside plunges... OK, the beaches weren't made for swimming, and not many of the hotels have pools, but if you really want to take off your summer cold-weather gear and dive in, the best poolside scene in the city is at **The Phoenix** (tel. 415/776–1380, 601 Eddy St.), where rock stars and their attendant groupies lounge, socialize, sip cocktails, and sometimes even swim—but you must be a hotel guest (or invited by one) to join in. The abstract mural on the bottom of the pool—painted by New York artist Francis Forienza—was almost outlawed by state inspectors, who insisted that it was a hazard and claimed: "People have been hurt by art before." Ultimately the governor of California enacted a bill exempting the mural from an antiquated law that requires all pool bottoms to be painted white.

Water sports... You won't have to worry about dangerous murals lurking on the bottom of the bay when you go sea kayaking, windsurfing, sailing, or fishing. Watching the windsurfers on the bay just off Crissy Field, it's easy to forget there are skyscrapers a few minutes away. On an ideal day, the waves are high and the wind is strong enough to give advanced windsurfers a ride that would make anyone forget the stress of urban life; beginners should definitely stick with calmer waters. **Lake Merced** offers lessons and rentals through the **San Francisco School of Windsurfing** (tel 415/750–0412, 40A Loyola Terrace). All-day kayaking trips (weekends only) are definitely the up-close-and-personal way to enjoy the dramatic cliffs, secluded beaches, and unbelievable views on **Angel Island**—and you don't even have to know how to paddle. All trips are led by expert naturalists and require specific advance reservations; the $110 fee includes lunch. Experienced paddlers may rent single closed-hull kayaks for $40 a half-day or $50 all day; doubles rent for $50 a half-day or $70 all day. The Angel Island Double Play, a full-day package including a half-day kayak rental, lunch, and a half-day mountain bike rental, is $60 per person for single kayaks and $50 per person for doubles. Contact **Sea Trek Ocean Kayaking Center** (tel 415/488–1000; fax 415/488–1707). Sailing is kind of a misnomer for what one does in a rented boat on **Stow Lake** in Golden Gate Park (tel 415/752–0347), but few things in life are more fun than getting in a pedal boat with someone else and simply pretending to pedal while your friend does all the work. At Stow Lake, you can also rent rowboats, which are especially suitable for afternoon trysts or for dressing up fancy and pretending you're in an Impressionist painting. If you're feeling sort of Hemingway-esque and you just have to get out on the bay in a real boat, both **Spinnaker Sailing** (tel 415/543–7333, Pier 40, South Beach Harbor) and **A Day on the Bay** (tel 415/922–0227, San Francisco Marina) offer sailing instruction and rentals. If you'd rather sip cocktails and let the captain sail the ship, there are dozens of charters, from dinner cruises to overnighters aboard yachts (see Diversions).

Reeling them in... If that Hemingway thing just won't go away, you could always pay your money and take your chances on a fishing boat—but bring the seasickness pills, lest ye be known as yet another landlubber who spent the whole day hanging over the side chumming the fish. There are dozens of charter fishing boats, but only one is owned and operated by a woman: **Wacky Jacky** (tel

415/586–9600). Skipper Jacky has been having a great time on the bay for 23 years, and her sense of humor makes even the most inexperienced angler have fun—and catch fish. A day on Jacky's sleek, fast 50-footer (board at Fisherman's Wharf at 5:30am, depart 6am, return 3pm) will cost around $75, including license, rod, tackle, and anything else you'll need to land a big fish. Here's an inside tip: When you choose a rod, ask for the Green Weenie. It has brought in so many big ones, Jacky is considering retiring it for good behavior. For tasty little trout, **Lake Merced** is a good stop. The Lake Merced Boating and Fishing Company (tel 415/753–1101) can set you up with boats, rods and reels, bait, and licenses (California requires a state fishing license that costs $8.95 a day or $24.95 annually; Lake Merced charges an additional $4 for a daily use permit). And if the swoosh-swoosh-plop of a perfect flycast is your cup of tea, bring your own rod to the **Golden Gate Park Fly Casting Pools** (tel 415/386–2630, opposite the Buffalo Paddock off John F. Kennedy Dr.), where tournament-level fly casters can be found practicing (ask them for pointers). Tuesdays, Saturdays, and Sundays are the best days; there's no fee, but then there are no fish here either—it's strictly for practice.

Par for the course... If you suddenly get the urge to sink one but you didn't bring your clubs, don't worry about a thing. The **Lincoln Park Golf Course** (tel 415/221–9911, 34th Ave. and Clement St., near the California Palace of the Legion of Honor) will rent you a set of clubs for $10 and send you out to try your luck on this 18-hole, par-68 course, where you may get distracted by the vista of the Pacific Ocean and the Golden Gate Bridge. Greens fees are $21 weekdays, $25 weekends; golf carts are $20. The **Golden Gate Park Course** (tel 415/221–9911, 47th Ave. and Fulton St.) is less challenging—9 holes, par 27, and 1,357 yards—but it is three blocks from the Pacific Ocean and is a great place to practice your swing and stay in shape without spending a fortune. Greens fees are just $8 weekdays, $11 weekends.

Lawn bowling... At the opposite end of the park, you'll find another delightfully peculiar sport—lawn bowling. Free lessons are offered at the **Golden Gate Park Bowling Green** (tel. 415/753–9298, just south of the tennis courts

GETTING OUTSIDE | SAN FRANCISCO

on Bowling Green Dr.). If you want to look the part, picture Mia Farrow's and Robert Redford's tennis whites in *The Great Gatsby*.

Islands with a past... **Alcatraz** is certainly the most commemorated of the San Francisco Bay's 14 islands—virtually every souvenir stand in the city sells a variety of tacky T-shirts proclaiming the wearer to be an inmate, escapee, or survivor of the notorious island prison, once home to folks like Al Capone and Machine Gun Kelly. But far from being a tourist trap, it's more like a set for a nightmarish Fellini movie co-authored by Stephen King—part bucolic Mediterranean island, part claustrophobic cell-block nightmare. Truly masochistic visitors can ask to be enclosed in deep six, a solitary confinement cell. After the prison was closed down, fitness guru Jack LaLanne once swam from Alcatraz to the city's shore handcuffed or blindfolded or both (who can remember?), perhaps inspiring today's Escape from Alcatraz triathlon, which originally included a bicycle ride to Marin County and a brutal Double Dip sea run over a twisted, mountainous course—better designed for billygoats—from Stinson Beach to Mill Valley and back. The race now finishes with a 12-mile run through the Golden Gate National Recreation Area, and has 500 competitors (registration deadline is June for the August race—call 415/561–1100 or 800/648–4626). Aside from morbid and/or historical fascination, however, the jagged island, 135 feet above the bay, is a surprisingly lovely spot for walking, with views of the city's skyline and the Golden Gate Bridge that are worth every penny of the $9 round-trip ferry ride (children $4.50, seniors $8; ferries operated by Red & White Fleet, tel 800/229–2784 or 415/546–2700). Admission to the island park is free. Ferry reservations are suggested at least two weeks in advance during the summer.

Angel Island—a 640-acre state park with a 360-degree view of the bay from atop Mount Livermore (781 feet)—is a favorite with locals for cycling, hiking, sea kayaking, and overnight camping, but, besides being a quarantine station and a Nike missile base, it was once a detention center for more than 175,000 Chinese and other Pacific Rim immigrants (1910–1940). It used to be nearly impossible to explore that immigration station, but now the park offers an open-air TramTour through the area, with a narrated history and aerial views that evoke audible sighs from passengers. The tram departs the Cove Café weekdays at 11, 12:30, and 2; weekends and holidays at 10:45, 11:15, noon, 12:30, 1:30, 2, 2:45, and 3:15. Fare is $9, $5 for children 5–12, $8 for seniors. Ferries to Angel Island, operated by Red & White Fleet (tel 800/229–2784, 415/546–2700), cost $9 round-trip, $5 for children, $8 for seniors. For cycling information, see "Pedal pushing"; for kayaking, see "Water sports."

Fantasy islands... It takes a little more work to get to the bay's undiscovered islets, but if you want to see a part of outdoor San Francisco rarely experienced even by locals, it's worth the effort. **Brooks Island** is tough to get to; it is accessible only at high tide, and most people sail their own boats, though boatless travelers can hook up with California Canoe and Kayak to make the trip for $70. Why bother? Because it is a rare remaining example of a bay habitat, home to more than 100 species of birds. Views from a single picnic table at the 163-foot summit easily rival those of Angel Island. And you certainly won't have to stand in line with anyone wearing a My-Mom-Went-to-Frisco-and-All-I-Got-Was-This-Lousy-T-Shirt tank top. Reservations must be made at least a week in advance; call **California Canoe and Kayak** (tel 510/562–2267). The park day fee is $5; the trip with the kayaking company is $70. The bed-and-breakfast innkeepers on **East Brother Island** ferry visitors to the island in a tiny boat, but you have to go to the San Pablo Yacht Harbor (Point Molate exit off Highway 580, east of the Richmond–San Rafael Bridge) to catch it. A defunct lighthouse station (1874–1969) has now been replaced with an automated signal, and the elegant Victorian structures that once served as the light tower and signal building have been converted into a four-bedroom bed-and-breakfast. It's a wonderfully quiet (and often sunny) retreat from the city during the summer, but be warned: from October 1 to April 1, the foghorn sounds every 30 seconds. Day visits, 11–3:30, cost just $10 (bring your own picnic lunch). Reservations should be made a month in advance for day visits and six months in advance for overnight stays (tel 510/820–9133).

Day trips... You'll need a car to get to **Mount Diablo State Park** (tel 510/837–2525), but on a clear day you can see (almost) forever from the summit. It's not that high— 3,849 feet—but because of its positioning, you can see more of the earth's surface from there than from anywhere else in North America. It's not unusual to spot Mount Lassen, an active volcano more than 200 miles north, or towering Mount Shasta toward the Oregon border. You'll almost certainly be able to pick out San Francisco landmarks and all of the bridges that cross the bay, as well as the Farallone Islands afloat in the Pacific. The weather on inland Mount Diablo is more extreme than San Francisco's temperate coastal climate; in summer temperatures often hover in the 90-degree range, and in winter the mountain almost always gets a white snowcap. Hike, picnic, or camp overnight if you want, but start off with that incredible summit view. The easiest way to get there from San Francisco is by car. Cross the Oakland–San Francisco Bay Bridge, then follow the signs to Walnut Creek (through the Caldecott Tunnel) and proceed on Highway 24 to Highway 680 north. Take the first exit—Ygnacio Valley Road—and turn right at the end of the exit onto Ygnacio Valley Road. You'll be in the middle of suburbia, but don't give up. Drive 1 ½ miles and turn right onto Walnut Avenue, which runs into North Gate Road after 1 more mile. From there on, the drive is absolutely bucolic. Follow North Gate Road 7 windy miles up the side of the mountain to the park headquarters, where you will pay a $5 day use fee. From there it is a 4$1/2$-mile drive to the summit parking lot and visitor information center. There are small telescopes on the summit tower's viewing deck.

On the other side of the bay, and only about half an hour from San Francisco, is another amazing natural wonder that shouldn't be missed—**Muir Woods National Monument** (tel 415/388–2595), an expanse of virgin redwood forest so beautiful and so quiet that you may never want to go back to the city. Some of the trees are more than 250 feet tall and many of them are 1,000 years old. When Ronald Reagan—a Southern California denizen—was governor of the state, he made redwood trees famous by declaring, "When you've seen one, you've seen 'em all." But the fact is, you'll never see even one unless you're in Northern California. They don't grow anywhere else, and they are unimaginably beautiful—

towering, majestic, and as green as green ever gets. Muir Woods is accessible by Golden Gate Transit bus (tel 415/332–6600, TDD 415/257–4554) or by car. To drive there from San Francisco, cross the Golden Gate Bridge and continue on Highway 101 north to the Stinson Beach/Highway 1 exit. Follow Highway 1 for 3 miles to Panoramic Highway, then drive 1 more mile and turn left on Muir Woods Road. The parking lot is another $1^1/2$ miles down the road.

Point Reyes National Seashore (tel 415/663–1092), one of the most pristine coastal wilderness areas in California with more than a dozen beaches in 65,000 acres, is less than an hour's drive from San Francisco. It's separated from the mainland by the famous San Andreas Fault, the primary source of San Francisco's powerful earthquakes. Don't let that scare you, though; the epicenter of the last big tremor in 1989 was about 100 miles southeast. Still, it is fascinating to take the $3/4$-mile Earthquake Walk along the fault line when you first enter the 65,000-acre park (at Bear Valley). You can also wade while you watch hundreds of species of birds at Limantour Beach; swim, hike, and picnic at Tomales Bay; canoe at Abbotts Lagoon, where you may spot a herd of tule elk; picnic at Point Reyes North and South Beaches (the undertow and hammering surf make it too dangerous to swim there); picnic, sunbathe, and wade at Drake's Beach; walk down 300 steps to the Point Reyes Lighthouse for a close-up view of seals and sea lions; and hike the many beautiful trails that traverse the area. A word to the wise: High tides, pounding surf, and treacherous rip currents can make the ocean beaches extremely dangerous; get a map and a tide table from the visitors' center before you set out. Tomales Bay is definitely the best area for swimming, a protected cove with warmer water that's often sunny when the rest of the area is overcast; Heart's Desire Beach, Pebble Beach, and Indian Beach are also great for swimming. There are about two dozen cozy inns and cottages in the area, in case you decide to stay for dinner and a moonlight walk on the Pacific; **Point Reyes Lodging** (tel 415/663–1872) can set you up in any of them.

Soothing spas and marvelous massages... After all this energetic outdoor activity, you may have a sore muscle or two. If so, you couldn't be in a better place—one

SAN FRANCISCO | GETTING OUTSIDE

of the more pleasant aspects of San Francisco's health-conscious lifestyle is an abundance of certified massage therapists (licensed by the state) whose healing hands definitely outclass those Magic Fingers motel beds. Therapeutic massage is so popular in the Bay Area that many hotels, such as the **Miyako** in Japantown, offer it as part of their service packages. If your hotel isn't one of these, get thee to a spa and find out why Californians rave about hot tubs and aromatherapy and all those other things that Europeans and Asians brought to the Left Coast. A typical therapeutic massage incorporates Swedish, Shiatsu, reflexology, and sports techniques in a half-hour or hour session. The spa that's probably most recommended by locals to their out-of-town guests—but not yet discovered by throngs of weary tourists—is **Kabuki Hot Springs Spa and Shiatsu Center** (tel 415/922–6002, 1750 Geary Blvd.) in Japantown. There are few—if any—misfortunes that a Kabuki back scrub, massage, and hot-tub soak can't cure. The ultimate San Francisco indulgence—at a very reasonable price—it has separate days for men and women (women's days are Sunday, Wednesday, and Friday; men are welcome Monday, Tuesday, Thursday, and Saturday). Their many packages range from $10 for hot-tub soaks and use of the communal spa facilities to $65 for back scrub, hot soak, sauna, steam room, 55-minute private Shiatsu massage, and full use of all spa facilities, which also include a cool plunge. If you want all of those spa services *and* one of the most beautiful urban resort settings in America, take BART just four stops across the bay to Rockridge and have a cab drop you off at the **Claremont Resort Hotel, Spa & Tennis Club** (tel 510/549–8566 for future reservations, 510/549–8555 for same-day visits; Ashby and Domingo Aves., Oakland). This spectacular Victorian landmark hotel, nestled in 22 lush acres at the foot of the Oakland/Berkeley hills, is especially lovely during the summer—when San Francisco is foggy and cold, the Claremont is sunny and warm. The full-service European spa here offers nine different types of massage, seven body-care treatment packages (wraps, masks, scrubs, massages, Swiss showers, whirlpool baths), and many varieties of facials, skin-care and salon treatments, and fitness therapies, as well as packages that include use of the health club, swimming pools (huge, outdoors), and a spa lunch at their award winning restaurant. As a bonus, tennis players who have scheduled spa treatments are allowed to use the tennis courts on an as-available basis. Reservations are a must—one to two weeks in advance for weekend visits—but midweek visits can often be arranged on the same day. The best package deal is the $79 Refresher, which includes an aroma bath, neck and shoulder massage, manicure or shampoo/blow dry, gift, lunch, and use of all facilities. On the north side of the bay, just 12 miles from the city, is **Tea Garden Springs** (tel 415/ 389–7123, 338 Miller Ave., Mill Valley), a holistic spa with a Chinese tea garden, where visitors are invited to sip a cup of calming tea or enjoy a vitalizing elixir before receiving massages or other treatments. The spa, designed in accordance with Feng Shui—the Chinese science of aesthetically and spiritually favorable architectural placement—is at the foot of Mount Tamalpais in Mill Valley, a sequoia-ringed village with more filmmakers and screenwriters per square inch than Hollywood. Even the most stressed-out movie producer would turn to putty after one of the Tea Garden Springs' 10 different types of Eastern and Western massages. What really sets this spa apart from the others is its many ancient Chinese practices and meticulous attention to aesthetic detail. Day visitors are welcome on a same-day basis, but reservations are recommended. Massages cost $35–65, depending upon the technique and duration; half-day retreats including several services and a meal are also available. If you don't want to go to a spa but would still like to experience the benefits of a therapeutic massage, don't call an escort service, where a massage generally means something quite different—instead, get a reliable referral from the American Massage Therapy Association (tel 800/696–2682).

shop

5 ping

The truly inter-

esting shopping

in San Francisco

is a matter of

combing small

neighborhood

boutiques for

their glorious hodgepodge of goodies that stretch from the merely unusual to the utterly bizarre. Vintage clothing, countercultural accoutrements, New Age paraphernalia, and all kinds of obscure books are the city's stock in trade, living up to San Francisco's reputation for the offbeat.

Then, of course, there's Union Square, where the city's conservative and classic side asserts itself with tony department stores and designer boutiques. Refined little old ladies in prim white gloves still bemoan the loss of the landmark City of Paris building, on the corner of Stockton and Geary streets, which has been replaced by the modern Nieman Marcus store, but tradition is hardly threatened in this neighborhood.

Not much can be said for San Francisco's shopping centers and malls. With few exceptions, an afternoon at the Anchorage, the Cannery, the Crocker Galleria, or Pier 39 isn't all that different from an afternoon in any other well-groomed mall. Some of the stores are housed in historic buildings—just as they are in Denver, Seattle, Sacramento, and dozens of other cities' old town areas—but the intrigue tends to end with the architecture.

Target Zones

Union Square (bordered by Kearny and Mason streets, from Market Street to Bush Street) is the stop for department stores and exclusive designer shops that rival the world's best. Even the larger stores offer courteous personal service and at least a couple of small cafes; Saks and Nieman Marcus still provide elegant lounges where female shoppers can freshen their lipstick and rest on comfy chairs when a quick trip to the toilet just isn't enough. Nearby **Maiden Lane**, a hidden 2-block alley that runs from Kearny Street to Stockton Street (between Geary and Post streets), continues to count Brooks Brothers and Chanel among its many upscale tenants.

Oh-so-prettified **Union Street** (between Van Ness Avenue and Steiner Street) has become rather old-hat and overpriced, a favorite haunt of well-heeled tourists and visiting suburbanites. Union Street's shops seem to sell stuff from everywhere but San Francisco—New York bagels, Seattle coffee, European clothes. It's also a great place to find top-quality children's clothing and toys.

Fillmore Street (between Post and Jackson streets), the nouveau chic area that proclaims itself a five-star neighborhood on obnoxious yellow banners at every street corner, is on the verge of becoming the next Union Street. A few short years ago, when there were just a handful of interesting little shops and cafes—and **D & M Wine and Liquor Co.** (2200 Fillmore St.), the best wine store in the city, bar none—some of the merchants tried desperately to establish this small patch of real estate as part of wealthy Pacific Heights rather than the notoriously slummy Fillmore District. They succeeded. Now you have to wait in line to get a cup of coffee on a Sunday morning, the bars are jammed with *GQ*-model lookalikes, and the sidewalks are congested with yuppie baby strollers. Locals looking for something truly interesting to do look elsewhere.

Chinatown is one of the most popular neighborhoods among tourists, though the bounty to be found here is often of dubious value—tacky souvenirs made in Taiwan, jade jewelry at a discount, or XXX-rated fortune cookies. Hand-painted signs swear that everybody is going out of business and must sell everything at incredibly low prices right now. Sidewalk stalls are stuffed with every plastic and rubber item ever sold for less than five dollars. Herbalists sell dragon's blood and other exotic ingredients next to vegetable stands, jewelry stores, banks, and dim sum parlors. There are some fun bazaars, though, and the smells alone are worth the visit.

The Hayes Valley (Hayes Street between Franklin and Buchanan streets) is a happy byproduct of the 1989 earthquake, which brought down a nearby freeway and let the sunshine in. It's fun, hip, eclectic, friendly, and not yet full of itself. You can find local clothing designers, bead stores, vintage clothing, African artifacts, Mexican art and knickknacks, collectible furniture, junk stores, and tarot card readers, among other things. Go there quick, before the vendors realize who they are and raise the prices.

Haight Street ain't what it used to be, but it's still quasi-psychedelic and filled with people and things you certainly won't see in Kansas. Vintage clothing stores are a big thing, but the value ranges from great deals on retro-fashions to ridiculously overpriced castoffs. Don't get caught paying $75 for a used Levi's jacket just because some guy with a mohawk cut the sleeves off it. If you're looking for avant-garde new clothing and shoes, this is the place. And if you're a man looking for a pair of shimmering red cha-cha heels in a perfect size 12, this may be the only place. Most of the shops are between Central and Stanyan streets.

North Beach will never leave you bored, with everything from beatnik bookstores and hippie poster shops to tattoo parlors and record stores. You can buy postcards, wigs, shoestrings, old clothes, new clothes, incense, bells, beads, crystals, jewelry, pasta machines, furniture, focaccia, and anything else you can imagine—even a new set of bocce balls.

The Mission District (between 16th and 24th streets) is a weird and wonderful place to shop, if you can handle being on two planets at once. Mission Street has the tightest cocktail dresses and shiniest spiked-heel shoes in town, alongside pure white confirmation and wedding dresses. Valencia Street sells used books and new vibrators, candles for Catholic and other rituals, expensive clothes that look like they've already been through the ringer, antiques, and thrift shop treasures.

Bargain Hunting

San Francisco is loaded with thrift stores and secondhand clothing stores, which may be good sources for bargains (though prices on vintage clothing, which can be very hip, can also be steep). Haight Street is a prime area for all this. (Also see "Recycled regalia" and "Cheap thrills," below.) For discounts on all kinds of new merchandise, there are more than 40 factory outlets South of Market—you really need a guide to hit them all. It's easier if you take the mall approach—start at **660 Center** (660 Third St. at Townsend St., tel 415/227–0464; 30, 42, 45 MUNI buses), two floors of factory outlets selling men's, women's, and children's clothing, shoes, and accessories; then head for **Yerba Buena Square** (899 Howard St., tel 415/974–5136; near Montgomery St. BART stop or 15, 30, 45 MUNI buses), the city's largest off-price mall, for another 100,000 square feet of bargains. (Also see "In the outlets" below.)

Trading with the Natives

San Francisco's merchants are by and large well-disposed toward out-of-towners. All major department stores will hold merchandise for a reasonable amount of time and will ship your packages home for you. (If you live out of state you won't have to pay sales tax.) Most will accept your personal check if you have proper identification, such as a driver's license with photo; it is illegal to ask for a credit card as a form of identification. Some small stores may not accept out-of-state checks, but as a rule, paying by check is not a problem in the Bay Area. It's not common practice to negotiate prices unless you're at a flea market, garage sale, or used-car lot, but it's always acceptable to point out a flaw or defect and ask for a reduction in price. (Whether you get it is up to the sales staff.) Most department stores will automatically give you 10 to 20% off for a broken zipper, missing button, or similar problem; smaller stores vary in their policies. Stores are not required to give refunds if you're not satisfied with your purchase—many stores will, though some will offer it only in the form of exchange credit. Stores cannot charge an extra fee for credit card purchases, but they may offer a discount for cash payment.

Hours of Business

Most stores tend to open around 10 or 11am (noon on Sundays) and close up at times that suit the neighborhood and clientele. Department stores, for instance, usually stay open through early evening, while many neighborhood boutiques and bookstores don't close until 10 or 11 at night. Most are open seven days a week—the Index below notes if they're not.

Sales Tax

A sales tax of 8.5% is added to every purchase unless the store ships it out of state for you. This is a state tax, with a .25% surcharge for rapid transit subsidy; some outlying areas don't include this surcharge, leaving the tax at 8.25%. To make matters more confusing, some items—including groceries—are not taxable. A few years ago California instituted a "snack tax" on foods that weren't considered principal fare, causing lots of heated debate—why should consumers pay tax on potato chips but not on potatoes, for example? The result has been that just about anything you can eat (other than dine-in restaurant food) is not taxed.

The Lowdown

Shopping bags to show off... When shopping in Union Square's exclusive stores, it's always wise to carry a shopping bag that proves you're buying—not just looking—and therefore deserve deferential treatment. Post Street is heaven for bourgeois bags; you can start small, with a cigar from **Alfred Dunhill of London** (290) or a few pieces of candy from **Saks Fifth Avenue** (384), so long as you get a nice big bag to carry it in. Then carry the bag with the logo in full view as you work your way down Post Street, visiting **Tiffany** (350), **Cartier** (231), **Louis Vuitton** (230), **Burberry's** (225), **Brooks Brothers** (201), **Gump's** (135), or **The Polo Store/Ralph Lauren** (90).

Are you being served?... The best service in town is definitely proffered by **Nordstrom**, in the San Francisco Centre. While you relax in the fitting room, sales assistants will run up and down the store's five floors to find a blouse in the exact shade of ivory that flatters your face and matches the navy skirt you're thinking about buying. They'll keep a customer card on file if you have particular needs and intend to return some other time. If that's not enough to make you feel pampered, Nordstrom's has a full-service European spa and four restaurants.

One-stop shopping... Hit the department stores. There's no shame in shopping at **Macy's**, especially now that it's got an entire building devoted strictly to men. Plus, there are almost always sales and clearance racks in every department. The other big department stores are **Emporium**, a smaller and more conservative version of Macy's; **Nieman Marcus**, the super-upscale Texas store that's sometimes bigger on price than taste (it does offer a fur salon for those who aren't afraid of being pelted by animal rights activists); **Saks Fifth Avenue**, where the sales staff can sometimes be a bit too uppity for the rather pedestrian merchandise on display; and, as mentioned above, **Nordstrom**, which is the most fun of any of them.

For foot fetishists... **Nordstrom** probably has the largest selection of women's and men's shoes in the city, in prices ranging from very reasonable to check-your-credit-limit. If expensive isn't a scary concept to you, head to **Kenneth Cole** (in the San Francisco Centre, the same mall as Nordstrom) for trendy, high-fashion shoes, or to **Stephane Kelian** (Crocker Galleria) for the most popular shoes made in Paris. If you're looking for San Francisco's hippest offbeat shoes, try **Taming of the Shoe** on Haight Street, where the latest new boots join forces with classic vintage footwear, or **Gimme Shoes** on Hayes Street, with funky new designs from Belgium and France. For women, the **Shoe Loft** and **Carole's Shoe Warehouse** offer designer shoes at a hefty discount, and **McB's Shoes** specializes in unusual large sizes, from 9 AAAAA to 14 EE (drag queen alert). **East West Leather** in North Beach has cowboy boots galore. And don't forget those sensible shoes: Get 'em at **Zebra Zone**, **Ria's**, **Birkenstock Natural Footwear**, **Shoe Palace**, and **First Step**.

If it's July, you're going to need a sweater...
Dreamweaver has fluffy American handknits to die for;
N. Peal Cashmere and **Scotch House** specialize in soft
Scottish jumpers; **395 Sutter** sells hand-loomed knits;
Tse Cashmere features rich colors and luxurious 10-ply
handknits; **House of Cashmere** is just what its name
implies; and **Irish Castle Shop** has fisherman-knit
sweaters and the claim to fame of having served Sinead
O'Connor in the past.

For men who want to look like Cary Grant... It's
tough to go wrong at **Wilkes-Bashford**, whose small line
of impeccably tailored clothing has served as a mark of
distinction in San Francisco for more than 30 years. **Sulka**
has been selling its exclusive clothes for 100 years—if you
want to out-Cary Cary, snag a pair of gorgeous Sulka
pajamas and make sure you are seen in them. **Courtoué**
features both classic and avant-garde Italian designers and
made-to-measure tailoring. If the tailoring idea appeals to
you but you're in a rush, try **Jay Briggs Clothiers**, a mostly sportswear store that offers same-day alterations.

**For men who'd rather look like Lou Reed than
Cary Grant...** **Rolo SF**, **Dinostore**, and **Daljeets** will
outfit you in off-the-rack alternative styles suitable for
clubs, cafes, or taking a little walk on the wild side.
Citizen is a bit more elegant, but still a good bet for urban
contemporary clothing that you won't find in department
stores, including a small selection of shoes.

Anything but another pair of Dockers... For special-
ly designed clothes from Michael Cronan, stop by
Cronan Artefact (south of Market), which features what
it calls threshold attire. A less pretentious description
might be "clothing for both work and play," but you're
talking capital-D designer here.

**If you can't make it to Hong Kong, but you're into
custom-made shirts...** The **California Gentleman**
by **Astanboos** makes dress and casual shirts on the premises; a staff person will come to your hotel if you prefer. They
also make suits and ties, and blouses for women. **Patrick
James** also does custom shirts and clothing, and offers tailoring and alterations for the lifetime of the garment.

If you simply can't live without a feather boa and a new tiara... You simply must go right to **Piedmont Boutique** in the Haight, where drag queens, strippers, and ultra-hip high school girls buy their velvet-and-feather bell-bottoms, sequined micro-mini-skirts, and long chartreuse gloves. When you see Piedmont's wall of earrings (more than 18,000 pairs in stock) starting at a mere $2, and racks of fishnets and other outlandish tights, you'll know why Sister Dana van Inquity, one of the drag nuns in the Sisters of Perpetual Indulgence, prays, Please, God, let only my seams be straight.

Recycled regalia... We're not talking flannel shirts and dirty hair—that's Seattle's fashion problem—we're talking the hottest street couture around. Haight Street is the used-clothing mecca of San Francisco. The best prices are at **Buffalo Exchange** (1555), where you can also sell your clothes for cash or trade. **Aardvark's Odd Ark** (1501) has a huge and fairly boring collection, but it's good for simple items like jeans and vests. **Wasteland** (1660) is staffed by inattentive young hipsters who seem truly impressed with the loud music, high prices, and each other. You can occasionally find something great, but most of the ordinary stuff here is overpriced. Upscale **La Rosa** (1711) is the Saks Fifth Avenue of the Haight Street vintage stores. Meanwhile, in other parts of the city: **American Rag Compagnie** has already sorted through the maybe rack and trimmed its stock down to the most desirable items; **Clothes Contact** sells clothing by the pound, which sounds terrific until you put an old leather jacket on the scale and see how much it weighs; **560 Hayes** sells high-end vintage clothing, much of which was bought from old stores' unsold stock and has never been worn. **Always and Forever** is the place to buy a used tuxedo and all the accessories to go with it. There are dozens of other vintage stores in the city—just look under "Clothing Used" in the yellow pages.

Cheap thrills: nonprofit thrift shops... The trouble with thrift shops is that you could spend your entire vacation combing them and never turn up a thing, or you could spend an hour in one place and come out with the outfit of the century for a couple of dollars. There's no way to predict, but if a scavenger hunt appeals to you, try these favorites: **Goodwill Stores** (nine locations);

Community Thrift Store; Repeat Performance; St. Vincent de Paul (three locations); and Thrift Town.

In the outlets... Among the city's many outlet stores, here are four of the best: **Designer's Co-op** for clothing by California designers at a serious discount; the **Esprit Outlet**, where the bargain bins are not to be missed; **North Face**, one of California's top outdoor gear manufacturers; and **Gunne Saxe**, a gem tucked away in an alley and full of frilly prom dresses and Jessica McClintock designer clothes at prices that tempt you to buy one of each.

Politically correct splurges... If you're ambling along Hayes Street and you come across a store that looks like Martha Stewart's ecologically correct attic, you're probably at **Worldware**, where you can get sheets and towels made from organically grown cotton and linen, as well as housewares made of exotic hardwoods from sustainable forests. The goods are actually very nice, but they're rather expensive, and the atmosphere is a bit contrived. **Global Exchange** is part of a national network that buys crafts from third world countries and pays the artisans roughly 40% of the retail price—far more than most importers share. Pick up that voodoo wall hanging you've always wanted, and you can sleep well knowing you've helped a Haitian artist pay the rent. **PlaNetweavers**, a UNICEF store in the Haight, also sells crafts made by indigenous people around the world and doesn't rip them off in the process. The prices can be higher than some of the large import chains, but proceeds directly benefit UNICEF's programs to fight hunger and disease among the world's children.

Crystals and other assorted New Age voodoo... What else would you expect from a city with a gigantic pyramid in the middle of its financial district? **Crystal Way** specializes in crystals, and will arrange psychic or tarot card readings for you by appointment. **Lady Luck Candle Shop** will supply you with candles and other ritual objects you might need. One of the most authentic hippie stores in the city, **Inner Dimensions Network**, sells not only crystals but also candles made by the light of particular moons for specific ritual purposes, along with other talismans and a strange variety of clothing, jewelry, and sixties concert posters.

Baubles, bangles, and beads... Be an artist for a day, or at least a wild-and-crazy jewelry maker. When you visit **The Magical Trinket**, you'll find loads of beads, as well as a staff of artisans willing to help you make your own necklaces and earrings, or even make hand-blown glass beads that are truly works of art. Call far in advance (see Index below) to register for a weekend bead-making class, limited to three students. **The Bead Store** is worth a visit to checkout the sacred statues and ethnic jewelry; **African Safari** has beads to use in hair braiding; **Gargoyle Beads** specializes in Czech beads; **General Bead** is huge—3,000 square feet—and offers many closeouts at bargain prices; and **Yone** in North Beach is hailed by locals for its unusual beads.

Goofatoriums... (or is that goofatoria?). San Franciscans pride themselves on being a bit off-center, and a handful of stores do their best to cater to that self-image. At **Forma**, you'll find absolute musts such as ant farms, Godzillas, talking goldfish, and maybe even your own celebrity-decorated toilet seat (for those of you who need Elvis with you, wherever you go). Scientific toys, gizmos, and gadgets are available at the **Exploratorium Store**, if you can still think straight after a stint in the museum's Alice-in-Wonderland-style distortion room. The window at **The Shlock Shop** is crammed with such an odd assortment of dust-covered doodads that it's tough to tell what is actually for sale. There are ornate hats small enough to fit Barbie's children and big enough for Hulk Hogan, clocks that click and whirr and rattle and roll their eyes as you walk past, old clothes, old books, posters, postcards, jewelry, jokes, junk, novelties, antiques, souvenirs—a dizzying assortment of stuff just waiting to be dusted off and taken home. Across the street, **Quantity Postcards** sells just one thing—postcards—but it has the largest, goofiest, most wonderful collection you'll ever find (more than 10,000). Don't miss the Swingin' Fifties party cards or the ridiculous dirty joke section. You should buy at least one card here, if only to get a close-up look at the funky cash register; you may take your purchases home in a hamburger bag left over from a drive-in joint that must've closed when Elvis was still King.

For that *Easy Rider* kind of feeling... If you've always wanted to be a biker or motorcycle mama—or just look like one—go to **The Outlaw** in Ghirardelli Square for licensed Harley Davidson clothing, leathers, and those formidable belt buckles that just scream, "Go ahead, make my day."

If you've got an itch for leather... North Beach Leather is probably the city's most famous manufacturer of stylish leather clothing for men and women. The quality and prices are high, but the workmanship is unbeatable, and jackets can be custom-made for hard-to-fit customers. If, however, your interests tend toward leather in its more exotic sense, head for **Stormy Leather**, which bills itself as San Francisco's premier erotic-fetish boutique. It never disappoints the whip-and-chain crowd. **A Taste of Leather** deals in adult items including leather toys and body jewelry.

Everything you ever wanted to know about sex... Don't be afraid to ask at **Good Vibrations**, an airy, comfortable bookstore/sex-toy shop owned and run by women. Their mail-order business has become one of the most successful in the country, but this flagship store in the Mission District is still small, personal, and as far from sleazy as you could possibly get. The clientele is primarily women, but the books and toys are for both sexes.

Or sexy underwear... Now that the Wonder Bra has taken the term "flat-chested" out of the popular American dictionary, you can walk into any K-Mart and buy seductive lingerie that once would've been found only at Frederick's of Hollywood. Still, there's something delicious about a small underwear boutique. Some of the city's most conventional-seeming yuppies prefer the more discreet service of **Romantasy**, where sex games, love oils, and other implements of sensual pleasure are sold along with the lace teddies and bustiers. Carol Doda, for years queen of the city's premier strip joint, the Condor, now sells all the expected sexy stuff for women at **Carol Doda's Champagne and Lace**, along with some racier inducements for both sexes, including see-through underwear and G-strings for men, stripper's accouterments, and other fun little objets d'amour. A visit to **Backseat Betty** makes lacy push-up bras seem ho-hum—this store is for people who think sex is fun, and looking sexy even more fun. Yeah,

yeah, yeah, there's all the rubber and latex stuff, but the basic mode is Cher, all the way.

Uncommon scents… **Jacqueline Perfumery** has the best selection of scents in the city, including some French perfumes that aren't available anywhere else in the United States. If you don't know what you want, ask her for a suggestion; her olfactory intuition is uncanny. Check your bag when you get back to your hotel—Jacqueline has been known to tuck in samples of expensive and exotic perfumes with customers' purchases.

Sweets to go… At **Joseph Schmidt Confections**, feast your senses on the most delectable chocolate sculptures in the western world. Buy at least a truffle or two (your taste buds will worship you for it), and do not miss the ever-changing, elaborate window displays. While you're there, step across 16th Street and peek at the outdoor mural entitled "La Madre Tonantsin," to get in the mood for a trip to the **Salvadoreno Bakery** for *pan dulce,* sugary pastries in the Central American tradition, and *bolillos,* yummy little torpedo-shaped rolls that are especially wonderful dunked in Mexican hot chocolate. **Just Desserts** is full of fabulous, fattening goodies at all its six locations, including an award-winning chocolate fudge cake that will put you on a sugar-high for hours (especially if you down it with a double cappuccino, as many locals do). For more organic types, Just Desserts also owns **Tassajara Cafe & Bakery**, featuring breads, muffins, and cakes that seem far too delicious to be good for you. A favorite takeout bakery item is the sourdough *batard,* a luscious and tangy French-style round bread.

Italian treats to go… Just about any cafe in North Beach has great pastries, but **Stella Pastry** has all that and *La Sacripantina,* too. Owner Frank Santucci will be happy to tell you about the patent he has on this puffy, sweet dessert that's one of Luciano Pavarotti's favorite confections. **Dianda's Italian American Pastry** has the best Italian cakes; **Danilo Bakery** bakes breads, *panettone,* tortes, and cookies for many of the top local restaurants; and **Italian French Baking Co.** still uses a brick oven and makes the best hand-rolled bread sticks you'll ever taste. While you're in North Beach, stop by the landmark deli **Molinari's** for a classic selection of Italian grocery and deli items; the old Italian locals shop there daily. Oddly enough, another great Italian deli is in the Mission District: **Lucca Ravioli Co.**, a traditional full-service deli with good-humored employees in white aprons. Their takeout sandwiches are superb and inexpensive.

The best deal on the best bubbly... Don't even bother shopping around. The staff at **D & M Wine and Liquor Co.** is friendly, funny, and more knowledgeable than all the wine editors in the country combined. They have the largest selection of champagne in the United States and will steer you away from overpriced status wines to lesser-known and cheaper ones that will make you think you've died and floated away to heaven. Every wine in the store has been tasted by the staff—all of whom are inveterate oenophiles—and you can be absolutely certain that any bottle they suggest will meet your expectations, and then some.

Kid stuff... You probably won't see Tom Hanks running up and down a gigantic keyboard at **FAO Schwarz** like he did in the movie *Big,* but this branch of the famous New York store is still a fantasyland for toy-lovers. Other great toy spots include **Jeffrey's Toys, Kinder Toys, Sanrio at Union Square**, and **Basic Brown Bear**, where you can see teddy bears being made and even stuff your own, if you like. If you go in for designer clothing for kids, try **Dottie Doolittle** or **Minis By Profili**. Bargain hunters should head for **Second Street Kids Outlet** for wholesale prices on clothing and gifts.

Words, words, words... A **Clean Well-Lighted Place For Books** is a favorite of author Armistead Maupin (*Tales of the City*); **The Booksmith** boasts more than 1,000 foreign and domestic magazines and newspapers; **Charlotte's Web** specializes in children's books; **City Lights Books** is Lawrence Ferlinghetti's legendary beatnik haunt; **A Different Light** is the foremost gay and lesbian bookstore in the city, as well as a resource center for gay information. **The Anonymous Place** carries 12-step recovery books; the **Buddhist Bookstore** represents many Buddhist traditions and also offers altar supplies; **Forever After Books** sells used books on spirituality, psychology, health, history, true crime, and other assorted topics. **McDonald's Bookshop** has more than a million used books and can get you a copy of *Life* published when you were born. **Dog Eared Books** is a great place to pick up some reading material—check out the Lust and Desire section before you settle in for an espresso at one of the neighboring cafes; **Argonaut Book Shop** specializes in California history. The **Sierra Club Bookstore** offers field, trail, and travel guides, as well as its collection of environmental books.

In search of 12-inch vinyl... If you are one of those people who understands the magic of a phonograph needle dropping softly into a groove, you're in luck. San Francisco has several record stores that still sell records: **Streetlight**; **Reckless Records**; **The Record Finder**; and **Medium Rare Records**.

Music meccas... Every city in America has plenty of stores that sell compact discs and cassette tapes, but not every town has a record store called **Neurotic** that also sells vintage clothes and is officially open every day until "late," or a place called **Open Mind Music**, another clothing/music emporium that features "cool collectibles and the esoteric." Avid Beatlemaniacs will love **Let It Be**, which carries Beatles memorabilia, rare and out-of-print records, collectibles, and concert items. For Latin and salsa, **Discolandia** is a good bet. **Amoeba Music** in Berkeley has more than 30,000 used CDs, plus original Fillmore and Avalon concert posters from the sixties; **Mod Lang**, also in Berkeley, features imports, indies, acid jazz, ambient, trance, and reissues; Oakland's **Saturn Records** has an eclectic collection and is in one of the most fun walking neighborhoods (Rockridge) in the East Bay; and the **Groove Yard**, also in Oakland, specializes in jazz, blues, and soul.

The Index

A Clean Well-Lighted Place For Books. This independent bookstore has a very helpful and informed staff; they will ship internationally.... *Tel 415/441–6670. 601 Van Ness Ave., Opera Plaza, Civic Center BART stop.*

A Different Light. Gay and lesbian literature, magazines, community resource information are sold here by a friendly staff.... *Tel 415/431–0891. 489 Castro St., Castro St. MUNI Metro stop (K,L,M). Open 10am–11pm, until midnight Fri and Sat.*

A Taste of Leather. The adult and custom-leather items sold here include toys and body jewelry.... *Tel 415/252–9166. 317 10th St. at Folsom St., south of Market St., 42 MUNI bus.*

Aardvark's Odd Ark. This huge store sells used clothing in current styles. It's not as eccentric as some other Haight Street shops.... *Tel 415/621–3141. 1501 Haight St., 7 MUNI bus.*

African Safari. Beads for hair braiding are sold here, wholesale and retail.... *Tel 415/922–2899. 1221 Divisidero St. between Eddy and Ellis Sts., Western Addition; 5, 38 MUNI buses. Closed Sun–Mon.*

Alfred Dunhill of London. Too bad San Francisco is so disgusted by smoking, because there's nothing like a Dunhill lighter to make you feel decadently luxurious. Unfortunately, the cigarettes don't taste quite as good as the beautiful boxes they come in.... *Tel 415/781–3368. 290 Post St., Union Square, Powell St. BART stop. Closed Sun.*

Always and Forever. This vintage-clothing store for men and women specializes in tuxedos and formal accessories. Hats,

SAN FRANCISCO | SHOPPING

ties, jewelry.... *Tel 415/285–7174. 3789 24th St., J Church MUNI Metro.*

American Rag Compagnie. The stylish, contemporary secondhand and vintage clothing sold here is very hip—and not cheap. The staff ranges from friendly to way-too-hip.... *Tel 415/475–5214. 1305 Van Ness St. between Sutter and Bush Sts., 42 MUNI bus, California St. cable car.*

Amoeba Music. This Berkeley store—voted best in the Bay Area by the *Guardian*—has a huge selection of used CDs (more than 30,000) and thousands of used videos, as well as original Fillmore and Avalon concert posters from the sixties.... *Tel 510/549–1125. 2455 Telegraph Ave., Berkeley, Berkeley BART stop.*

The Anonymous Place. The specialty here is 12-step recovery books and gifts—sold by a supportive staff, as one might well imagine.... *Tel 415/923–0248. 2030 Chestnut St. at Fillmore St.; 28, 30 MUNI buses.*

Argonaut Book Shop. Fine and rare books and manuscripts are bought and sold here, especially volumes on California history. Established in 1941.... *Tel 415/474–9067. 786 Sutter St. at Jones St., Union Square, Powell St. BART stop. Closed Sun.*

Backseat Betty. Naughty underthings and outerwear for contemporary sex kittens.... *Tel 415/431–8393. 1584 Haight St., 7 MUNI bus.*

Basic Brown Bear. Kids love this teddy bear factory, where you can buy bears off the rack or stuff your own. Discount prices.... *Tel 415/626–0781, 444 DeHaro, Potrero Hill; 2801 Leavenworth, the Cannery; 30, 42 MUNI buses or Powell/Hyde, Powell/Mason cable cars.*

The Bead Store. Come here for beads, sacred statues, ethnic jewelry.... *Tel 415/861–7332. 417 Castro St. at Market St., Castro St. MUNI Metro stop.*

Birkenstock Natural Footwear. Comfort shoes, California-style.... *Tel 415/776–5225. 1815 Polk St. at Washington St., 42 MUNI bus or Powell/Hyde cable car.*

The Booksmith. A source for lots of books and a huge selection of domestic and foreign magazines and newspapers. Knowledgeable staff.... *Tel 415/863–8688. 1644 Haight St., 7 MUNI bus.*

Brooks Brothers. In any word association game, "Brooks Brothers" would automatically be followed by "suit." They're definitely traditional, but not as stodgy as you might think. Men's, women's, and boys clothing.... *Tel 415/397–4500. 210 Post St., Union Square, Powell St. BART stop.*

The Buddhist Bookstore. As the name suggests—a source for Pure Land, Zen, Tibetan literature. Altar supplies and gifts, too.... *Tel 415/776–7877. 1710 Octavia St. between Bush and Pine Sts., near Japantown, 38 MUNI bus. Closed Sun.*

Buffalo Exchange. Come here for stylish used clothing in new condition—hip street fashions at very good prices.... *Tel 415/431–7733, 1555 Haight St., 7 MUNI bus; tel 415/346–5726, 1800 Polk St.*

Burberry's. Do you like plaid? If not, walk on. The famous Burberry plaid has found its way from the inside of raincoats to all over clothing, luggage, and other wearables....*Tel 415/ 392–2200. 225 Post St., Union Square, Powell St. BART stop. Closed Sun.*

The California Gentleman by Astanboos. This custom clothier makes dress and casual shirts and suits for men and women.... *Tel 415/781–8989 or 800/697–4478. 478 Post St., Union Square, Powell St. BART stop. Closed Sun.*

Carol Doda's Champagne and Lace Lingerie Boutique. San Francisco's No. 1 stripper sells some of the sexiest women's and men's underthings in town.... *Tel 415/776– 6900. 1850 Union St. #1, the Courtyard, 45 MUNI bus.*

Carole's Shoe Warehouse. This discount outlet sells men's and women's designer shoes from Spain and Italy, at prices up to half off retail.... *Tel 415/543–5151. 665 Third St., south of Market St.; 15, 30, 45 MUNI buses.*

Cartier. Exclusive timepieces and fine jewelry are Cartier's specialty. This is the real thing—be ready to spend at least four digits for a watch.... *Tel 415/397–3180. 231 Post St., Union Square, Powell St. BART stop. Closed Sun.*

Charlotte's Web. A delightful bookstore for children, from babies to young adults.... *Tel 415/441–4700. 2278 Union St., 45 MUNI bus.*

Citizen. The racks here are full of urban contemporary clothing for men—pricey, but worth it.... *Tel 415/558–9429. 536 Castro St., Castro St. MUNI Metro stop.*

City Lights Books. The legendary beatnik hangout and bookstore.... *Tel 415/362–8193. 261 Columbus Ave., North Beach; 15, 30 MUNI buses. Open 10am–11:45pm daily.*

Clothes Contact. Used clothing is sold here for $6 per pound. Lots of leather jackets.... *Tel 415/621–3212. 473 Valencia St., Mission District, 16th St. BART stop.*

Community Thrift Store. It's sort of junky, but there's a great book and record section here.... *Tel 415/861–4910. 625 Valencia St., Mission District, 16th St. BART stop.*

Courtoué. The line here is beautiful Italian designer clothing for men, classic to avant-garde.... *Tel 415/775–2900. 459 Geary Blvd., Union Square, Powell St. BART stop. Closed Sun.*

Cronan Artefact. This showroom features threshold attire by designer Michael Cronan..... *Tel 415/543–5222. 11 Zoe St., south of Market St., Montgomery St. BART stop or 15, 30, 45 MUNI buses. Closed weekends.*

Crystal Way. Thousands of beautiful natural crystals and New Age books are sold here.... *Tel 415/861–6511. 2335 Market St. near Castro St., Castro St. MUNI Metro stop.*

D & M Wine and Liquor Co. Come here for what is simply the best selection of champagne in the country, and discount prices to boot. The expert staff gives great advice.... *Tel 415/346–1325. 2200 Fillmore St. at Sacramento St., 6 blocks from 38 MUNI bus.*

Daljeets. This store sells super-hip men's clothing at not-totally-expensive prices.... *Tel 415/752–5610, 1744 Haight*

St., 7 MUNI bus; tel 415/431–9100, 541 Valencia St., Mission District, 16th St. BART stop. Closed Mon.

Danilo Bakery. Wonderful breads and *panettone* sold here are also featured in many local restaurants.... *Tel 415/989–1806. 516 Green St., North Beach; 15, 30 MUNI buses.*

Designer's Co-op. This factory outlet specializes in California designers, plus consignment resale.... *Tel 415/777–3570. 625 Third St., south of Market St.; 15, 30, 45 MUNI buses.*

Dianda's Italian American Pastry. Prize-winning Italian cakes have made this store's reputation.... *Tel 415/989–7745. 565 Green St., North Beach; 15, 30 MUNI buses.*

Dinostore. Alternative clothing and clubwear for men.... *Tel 415/861–3933. 1553 Haight St., 7 MUNI bus.*

Discolandia. Don't worry about finding this place—you'll hear it long before you get close enough to see the Latin/psychedelic/airbrush/jukebox storefront. The selection of Latin music is enormous, so it helps to have an idea what you're looking for.... *Tel 415/826–9446. 2964 24th St., Mission District, 24th St. BART stop.*

Dog Eared Books. A fun place for browsing and buying.... *Tel 415/282–1901. 1173 Valencia St., Mission District, 24th St. BART stop.*

Dottie Doolittle. Look here for designer clothes for infants, toddlers, girls 7–14 and boys 4–7.... *Tel 415/563–3244. 3680 Sacramento St. between Spruce and Locust Sts.*

Dreamweaver. A huge selection of fluffy, hand-knit sweaters makes this store a local favorite.... *Tel 415/383–2041. 171 Maiden Lane, Union Square, Powell St. BART stop. Also at Pier 39.*

East West Leather. The specialty here is cowboy boots galore, plus jackets and clothing.... *Tel 415/397–2886. 1400 Grant Ave., North Beach; 15, 30 MUNI buses.*

Emporium. This department store is similar to Macy's (see below) but slightly more conservative.... *Tel 415/764–2222. 835 Market St., downtown, Powell St. BART stop.*

Esprit Outlet Store. The place to buy Esprit outfits at discount prices. Don't miss the bargain bins.... *Tel 415/957–2550. 499 Illinois St., 15 MUNI bus.*

Exploratorium Store. A treasure house of gizmos and gadgets accompanies one of the goofiest science museums in the country.... *Tel 415/561–0390. Palace of Fine Arts, 3601 Lyon St., 30 MUNI bus. Closed Mon.*

FAO Schwarz. Nothing else compares to this world-class toy store. The window displays alone are worth the visit.... *Tel 415/394–8700. 48 Stockton St., Union Square, Powell St. BART stop.*

First Step. Comfortable footwear: Nike, Reebok, Rockport, etc. Great shoes, great prices, great location.... *Tel 415/989–9989. 57 and 216 Powell St., Union Square, Powell St. BART stop. Closed Sun in summer.*

560 Hayes. Upscale vintage clothing and original works by local artists are sold here. Men's shirts average $18; women's gabardine suits $180. Staff is helpful but not pushy.... *Tel 415/861–7993. 560 Hayes St., Hayes Valley, Civic Center BART stop.*

Forever After Books. Here you'll find used books on many esoteric and mainstream subjects.... *Tel 415/431–8299. 1475 Haight St., 7 MUNI bus.*

Forma. The best overall selection of wack-o-rama in the city.... *Tel 415/751–0545. 1715 Haight St., 7 MUNI bus.*

Gargoyle Beads. This store sells zillions of beads, as well as offering ear piercing and jewelry-making classes.... *Tel 415/ 552–4274. 1310 Haight St., 7 MUNI bus.*

General Bead. The biggest bead store ever—3,000 square feet. Many closeouts.... *Tel 415/621–8187. 637 Minna St. Closed Mon.*

Gimme Shoes. The eclectic, chic mix of merchandise here includes some funky, some elegant.... *Tel 415/ 864–0691. 416 Hayes St., Hayes Valley, Civic Center BART stop.*

Global Exchange. Hand-crafted items from international artisans are sold at this Fair Trade Network store.... *Tel
415/648–8068. 3900 24th St. near Sanchez St., J Church
MUNI Metro.*

Good Vibrations. This is a comfortable, clean, airy, healthy
place to shop for sex toys, sex books, and videos. Customers
are mostly women. Helpful staff.... *Tel 415/974–8980.
1210 Valencia St., Mission District, 24th St. BART stop.*

Goodwill Stores. Hit or miss secondhand shopping, but when
you hit, the price is definitely right.... *Tel 415/550–4500.
820 Clement St.; 3801 Third St.; 1700 Fillmore St.; 241
Tenth St.; 2279 Mission St.; 822 Geary Blvd.; 1700
Haight St.*

Groove Yard. If you're into jazz, blues, and soul, you'll be thrilled
with this store, where they buy, sell, and trade new, used,
and rare records and CDs. Oakland is the blues capital of
the West Coast, so get over there and groove.... *Tel 510/
655–8400. 4770 Telegraph Ave. (at 48th St.), Oakland,
Ashby BART stop. Closed Mon.*

Gump's. What used to be a grand San Francisco department
store has been scaled down, but it's still a local classic, full
of a glorious and exclusive variety of gifts. Orientalia is a particular specialty.... *Tel 415/982–1616. 135 Post St., Union
Square, Powell St. BART stop. Closed Sun.*

Gunne Sax Discount Outlet. You can get consistently good
buys here on Gunne Saxe and Jessica McClintock fashions
and fabric, including wedding dresses. It's a prom dress paradise, with the clearance section of your dreams.... *Tel
415/495–3326. 35 Stanford St. off Brannan St.; 15, 30,
42, 45 MUNI buses.*

House of Cashmere. Cashmere, wool, and angora sweaters
are the specialty of this men's and women's clothing
store.... *Tel 415/441–6925. 2764 Octavia St., off Union
St., 45 MUNI bus. Closed Sun.*

Inner Dimensions Network. A true hippie store, and a real
delight—the staff still maintains that peace-and-love attitude.... *Tel 415/885–4370. 801 Columbus Ave., North*

Beach; 15, 30 MUNI buses. Open noon–10, weekends 10–midnight.

Irish Castle Shop. Expect everything Irish, from claddagh rings to fishermen's sweaters…. *Tel 415/474–7432. 537 Geary Blvd., Union Square, Powell St. BART stop. Closed Sun.*

Italian French Baking Co. Don't miss the delectable breads baked in brick ovens and the hand-rolled bread sticks…. *Tel 415/421–3796. 1501 Grant Ave., North Beach; 15, 30 MUNI buses.*

Jacqueline Perfumery. Come here for the best selection of perfumes in the city, many not available anywhere else in America…. *Tel 415/981–0858. 310 Geary Blvd., Union Square, Powell St. BART stop. Closed Sun.*

Jay Briggs Clothiers. Featuring European clothing for men, this store has an experienced staff and offers same-day tailoring…. *Tel 415/982–1611. 61 Post St.; Union Square, Powell St. and Montgomery St. BART stops. Open daily, Sun by appointment only.*

Jeffrey's Toys. Along with toys of all kinds, you can buy books and antique toys here…. *Tel 415/546–6551. 7 Third St., Union Square, Montgomery St. BART stop.*

Joseph Schmidt Confections. A local treasure, this shop sells the most beautiful edible sculptures you'll ever see or taste…. *Tel 415/861–8682. 3489 16th St., near Church St., J Church MUNI Metro line. Closed Sun.*

Just Desserts. This mini-chain is famous for its decadent desserts…. *Tel 415/330–3600. 248 Church St.; 3 Embarcadero Center; 836 Irving St.; 3735 Buchanan.*

Kenneth Cole. A store for trendy, high fashion shoes…. *Tel 415/227–4536. 865 Market St., San Francisco Shopping Centre, Powell St. BART stop; 2078 Union St., 45 MUNI bus.*

Kinder Toys. Their motto is, "Come in and play"—and you will. The store sells classic, Old World toys, which can be personalized while you wait…. *Tel 415/673–1780. 1750 Union St., 45 MUNI bus.*

Lady Luck Candle Shop. Your basic Latino Catholic-voodoo-ritual botanica. Come on, what could it hurt to burn a little candle for good luck?... *Tel 415/621–0358. 311 Valencia St., Mission District, 16th St. BART stop.*

La Rosa. On the upscale end of the vintage clothing spectrum, especially for this neighborhood, La Rosa focuses on formal clothing.... *Tel 415/668–3744. 1711 Haight St., 7 MUNI bus.*

Let It Be. If there is a heaven for Beatlemaniacs, this may be where you buy your tickets to get there. Besides rare and out-of-print records, it has a variety of memorabilia.... *Tel 415/681–2113. 2434 Judah St., N. Judah MUNI Metro stop. Closed Sun and Mon.*

Louis Vuitton. This is the place to get that fancy luggage with the monogram that opens doors around the world. It's expensive, but every doorman in town will see you coming.... *Tel 415/391–6200. 230 Post St., Union Square, Powell St. BART stop. Closed Sun.*

Lucca Ravioli Co. Seemingly out-of-place in this Latino neighborhood, this wonderful Italian deli is always full of locals taking advantage of the good prices and friendly service.... *Tel 415/647–5581. 1100 Valencia St., Mission District, 24th St. BART stop. Closed Sun.*

Macy's. This huge store occupies two full buildings and has always been a reliable favorite for locals and visitors alike. There seems to be a sale and a clearance rack in every department, all the time.... *Tel 415/397–3333. Stockton and O'Farrell Sts., Union Square, Powell St. BART stop.*

Magical Trinket. The gorgeous selection of beads here includes hand-blown pieces by Northern California artists. Friendly, helpful staff. Classes available in beadmaking; call far in advance.... *Tel 415/626–0764. 524 Hayes St., Hayes Valley, Civic Center BART stop. Closed Mon.*

McB's Shoes. The specialty here is hard-to-find shoe sizes for women (or men who like to wear women's shoes).... *Tel 415/546–9444. 715 Market St., Montgomery St. BART stop. Closed Sun.*

SHOPPING | SAN FRANCISCO

McDonald's Bookshop. More than a million used books in stock.... *Tel 415/673–2235. 48 Turk St., Powell St. BART stop. Closed Sun.*

Medium Rare Records. This is the place to find those old vinyl LPs you haven't heard for ages, as well as all the great jazz and Latin vocalists.... *Tel 415/255–7273. 2310 Market St., Castro St. MUNI Metro stop (K,L,M).*

Minis By Profili. Local designer Christina Profili left the GAP to open her own business here. All the racks feature coordinating sportswear separates.... *Tel 415/567–9537. 2042 Union St., 45 MUNI bus.*

Mod Lang. This English Modern Rock music store caters to serious collectors, as well as curious onlookers. It's got a 24-hour fax line (510/549–1125) and features indies, imports, acid jazz, ambient music, and reissues. Many rare items.... *Tel 510/486–1850. 2136 University Ave. at Shattuck Ave., Berkeley, Berkeley BART stop.*

Molinari Delicatessen. This is the traditional North Beach deli. Brush up on your Italian here.... *Tel 415/421–2337. 373 Columbus Ave., North Beach; 15, 30 MUNI buses. Closed Sun.*

N. Peal Cashmere. The basic line here is Scottish sweaters and knits.... *Tel 415/955–8985. 110 Geary Blvd., Union Square, near Powell St. BART stop. Closed Sun.*

Neurotic Record Store. If you get tired of browsing through the music collection, you can always checkout the vintage clothing, magazines, books, and jewelry.... Tel 415/552–8069. 1100 Folsom St., 42 MUNI bus.

Nieman Marcus. This branch of the Texas-based luxury store offers the city's best shopping experience. Try the cafe on the top floor—it's a real hoot.... *Tel 415/362–3900. 150 Stockton St., Union Square, Powell St. BART stop.*

Nordstrom. Get pampered with attentive, personal service on five floors. Don't forget the eateries and the spa.... *Tel 415/243–8500. San Francisco Shopping Centre, 885 Market St., Powell St. BART stop.*

North Beach Leather. This store sells the latest fashions— some custom-made—at prices to match.... *Tel 415/441– 3208, 1365 Columbus Ave., North Beach; 15, 30 MUNI bus; tel 415/362–8300, 190 Geary Blvd., Union Square, Powell St. BART stop.*

North Face Factory Outlet. Come here for some of the best quality outdoor gear made, at discount prices.... *Tel 415/ 626–6444. 1325 Howard St., south of Market St., 42 MUNI bus.*

Open Mind Music. What else would you expect in the Haight? New and used records and CDs, in addition to assorted eso- terica and an in-store vintage clothing shop.... *Tel 415/ 621–2244. 342 Divisadero St. at Oak St., 7 MUNI bus. Closed Wed.*

The Outlaw. Harley Davidson's specialty store. Vr-r-r-r- roooom!... *Tel 415/563–8986. 900 North Point St., Ghirar- delli Square; 30 MUNI bus, Powell-Hyde or Powell-Mason cable cars.*

Patrick James. This store refers to itself as a "Purveyor to Gentlemen," if that gives you any idea.... *Tel 415/986– 1043. 216 Montgomery St., Financial District, Montgomery St. BART stop. Closed Sun.*

Piedmont Boutique. It's tough to describe a store that sells absolutely outrageous women's garments and acces- sories—mostly to men. If you've ever coveted any of the gaudy get-ups you've seen on drag queens, this is the place to find them. The proprietor commutes from her farm in Missouri.... *Tel 415/864–8075. 1452 Haight St., 7 MUNI bus.*

PlaNetweavers Treasures Store. The official UNICEF store is full of international trinkets and works of art, and all the prof- its benefit the children.... *Tel 415/864–4415. 1573 Haight St., 7 MUNI bus.*

The Polo Store/Ralph Lauren. The emphasis is on attentive service and traditional styling, for folks who affect the coun- try-squire look. Tally ho.... *Tel 415/567–7656. 90 Post St., Union Square, Powell St. BART stop. Closed Sun.*

Quantity Postcards. Here's a place you can spend less than a dollar and come out with one of the best souvenirs of your trip. A true goofatorium…. *Tel 415/986–8866. 1441 Grant Ave., North Beach; 15, 30 MUNI buses. Open 11–11.*

The Record Finder. More than 100,000 titles in stock. Good staff, too…. *Tel 415/431–4443. 258 Noe St., Castro St. MUNI Metro stop.*

Recycled Records. This is a great source for recycled CDs, vinyl, cassettes…. *Tel 415/626–4075. 1377 Haight St., 7 MUNI bus. Open 10–10.*

Repeat Performance. Some of the stuff here—used clothing, records, books, knickknacks—is great, and some of it is definitely little-old-lady material. Check it out; the proceeds go to the San Francisco Symphony…. *Tel 415/563–3123. 2223 Fillmore St. Closed Sun.*

Ria's. Birkenstocks, Timberland, Rockports, etc.—your basic sensible shoes…. *Tel 415/398–0895, 437 Sutter St.; Tel 415/834–1420, 301 Grant Ave.; tel 415/771–3140, 900 North Point St.*

Rolo SF. These four stores sell clothes for the modern urban guy, at modern urban prices (big). The one at 535 Castro—Undercover by Rolo—is a super-trendy designer store…. *Tel 415/626–7171, 450 Castro St.; tel 415/861–1999, 1301 Howard St.; tel 415/431–4545, 2351 Market St.; tel 415/864–0505, 535 Castro St.*

Romantasy. Naughty stuff for upstanding citizens, tucked in an alley between Greenwich and Lombard streets. You can get a free catalog (plain brown wrapper) by calling the store…. *Tel 415/673–3137. 199 Moulton St.; 28, 30 MUNI buses.*

Saks Fifth Avenue. This upscale department store is not always what it's cracked up to be. Not as glitzy as Nieman Marcus or as fun as Nordstrom…. *Tel 415/986–4300. 384 Post St., Union Square, Powell St. BART stop.*

Salvadoreno Bakery. One of dozens of bakeries in the Mission District, this is in the newly Bohemian part…. *Tel 415/431–6554. 535 Valencia St., Mission District, 16th St. BART stop.*

Sanrio at Union Square. Set on two floors, this store has a wide selection of international toys.... *Tel 415/981–5568. 39 Stockton St., Union Square, Powell St. BART stop.*

Saturn Records. An eclectic collection of records, tapes, CDs, and 45s makes this music store a really fun place to stop. It's in the Rockridge neighborhood, an Oakland mecca of boutiques and cafes that's extremely popular with locals but hasn't been discovered by many tourists.... *Tel 510/654–0335. 5488 College Ave., Oakland, Rockridge BART stop.*

Scotch House Sweaters from Scotland Ltd. Wonderful Scottish knits are the specialty here, including Ballantyne cashmere.... *Tel 415/392–1264. 187 Post St., Union Square, Powell St. BART stop. Closed Sun.*

Second Street Kids Outlet. Children's designer clothing at discount prices.... *Tel 415/495–6659. 625 2nd St., south of Market St.; 15, 30, 45 MUNI buses. Closed Sun.*

Shlock Shop. Bring a feather duster—you'll need it—and uncover great goodies, from funky to fabulous.... *Tel 415/781–5335. 1418 Grant Ave., North Beach; 15, 30 MUNI buses.*

Shoe Loft. Come here for women's designer shoes at cheapo-cheapo prices.... *Tel 415/956–4648. 225 Front St. at California St., Montgomery St. BART stop.*

Shoe Palace. This store offers two pluses—great service and top brand names.... *Tel 415/777–3140. 123 2nd St. at Mission St., Montgomery St. BART stop. Closed Sun.*

Sierra Club Bookstore. Heaven for walkers and hikers. If you plan to get outdoors, this is the place for maps and trail guides.... *Tel 415/923–5600. 730 Polk St., Civic Center BART stop. Closed Sun.*

St. Vincent de Paul. These classic nonprofit thrift stores can be a bit grungy, which is perfect if you're going for that Nirvana look. Cheap.... *Tel 415/626–1515. 1745 Folsom St., 1519 Haight St., and 186 West Portal.*

Stella Pastry. The specialty here is Franco's *La Sacripantina*, a puffy slice of heaven.... *Tel 415/986–2914. 446 Columbus Ave., North Beach; 15, 30 MUNI buses.*

Stephane Kelian. Très chic. One of the biggest French names in shoes.... *Tel 415/989–1412. Crocker Galleria, 50 Post St., Montgomery BART stop. Closed Sun.*

Stormy Leather. This store bills itself as the city's premier erotic-fetish boutique.... *Tel 415/626–1672. 1158 Howard St., South of Market. Civic Center BART stop.*

Streetlight Records. A major source for new and used vinyl, CDs, tapes, video, and laserdiscs.... *Tel 415/282–3550, 3979 24th St.; tel 415/282–8000, 2350 Market St., both near Castro St. MUNI Metro stop.*

Sulka. In business for over a century, this exclusive store sells exquisite clothing for gentlemen. The pajamas ("pyjamas," as they spell it) are incredible.... *Tel 415/989–0600. 255 Post St., Union Square, Powell St. BART stop. Closed Sun.*

Taming of the Shoe. Come here for oh-so-hip American and European shoes and boots for men and women.... *Tel 415/221–4453. 1736 Haight St., 7 MUNI bus.*

Tassajara Cafe & Bakery. Once owned by the locally beloved Greens restaurant, this little Cole Valley bakery/cafe is now part of the Just Desserts mini-empire, but it hasn't suffered a bit.... *Tel 415/664–8947. 1000 Cole St. at Parnassus, 7 MUNI bus or N. Judah MUNI Metro stop.*

395 Sutter. This store's exclusive hand-loomed sweaters and knits for men and women come in classic designs and natural colors.... *Tel 415/989–1288. 395 Sutter St., Union Square, Powell St. BART stop. Closed Sun.*

Thrift Town. The unique thing about this thrift store is its grab-bag section in the rear, where collections of items have been stuffed into sealed plastic bags to be sold for a dollar or two. You can see what you're getting, but you may not be able to figure out the common denominator.... *Tel 415/861–1132. 2101 Mission St. at 17th St., Mission District, 16th St. BART stop.*

Tiffany and Co. There's no breakfast here, but if there were, it would definitely cost a fortune. Jewelry and gifts, classic and very, very expensive.... *Tel 415/781–7000. 350 Post St., Union Square, Powell St. BART stop. Closed Sun.*

Tse Cashmere. This stuff is soft—really soft. Great colors, too.... *Tel 415/391–1112. 171 Post St., Union Square, Powell St. BART stop. Closed Sun.*

Victoria's Secret. It's not much of a secret anymore. There's pads in them thar bras.... *Tel 415/433–9473, 1 Embarcadero Center, Embarcadero BART stop; tel 415/882–0864, 865 Market St., Powell St. BART stop; tel 415/433–9671, 335 Powell St., Powell St. BART stop.*

Wasteland. Let the buyer beware. This is trendy secondhand clothing, for sure, but sometimes it's a little bit, you know, expensive. Especially, like, the denim, you know?... *Tel 415/863–3150. 1660 Haight St., 7 MUNI bus.*

Wilkes-Bashford. The ultimate classic men's store. Forget the trendy stuff; this is timeless. The local designers are literally top drawer.... *Tel 415/986–4380. 375 Sutter St., Union Square, Powell St. BART stop. Closed Sun.*

Worldware. Expect eco-elegant housewares and personal items, sort of like Martha Stewart meets Sierra Club.... *Tel 415/487–9030. 336 Hayes St., Hayes Valley, Civic Center BART stop.*

Yone of San Francisco. They call themselves a beehive of beads. Locals love 'em, but they're only open 12 hours a week.... *Tel 415/986–1424. 478 Union St., North Beach; 15, 30 MUNI buses. Open Thur, Fri, Sat noon–4.*

Zebra Zone. A dependable source for Timberland and Bass shoes, plus jackets and locally-made Holland bags (very durable).... *Tel 415/788–2615. 220 O'Farrell St., Union Square, Powell St. BART stop.*

SAN FRANCISCO | SHOPPING

6

tlife

San Francisco is
an exotic cocktail
of world cultures,
stirred with a
liberal splash of
wild-West flavor
that dates to the

Gold Rush. State laws and politically correct teetotalers have toned things down a bit since the notorious Barbary Coast days, but nothing can ever keep this city from being an exciting place to roam when its fabled sunsets are long extinguished.

A typical night on the town in San Francisco means grazing at a minimum of two or three restaurants, then hitting four or five clubs of whatever type you choose, which is easier than it sounds, since several neighborhoods pack at least that many clubs or other evening haunts within a few blocks of each other.

Many restaurants have food available at the bar, where seating is on a first come–first served basis, so making reservations for an informal pre-club tasting parade isn't absolutely necessary.

Liquor Laws

The drinking age is 21 in California, and bartenders can ask for a valid photo ID, no matter how old you look. Some clubs demand identification cards at the door, so it's a good idea to carry one at all times. The dreaded last call for alcohol usually rings out at around 1:30am, since state laws prohibit the sale of alcohol from 2 to 6 every morning. Don't be surprised to see crowded clubs empty just before the witching hour, as the revelers rush to buy enough six-packs to fuel them during the after-hours festivities, when some clubs stay open but stop serving alcohol. A very important word of warning: Driving under the influence of alcohol is a serious crime in California, with mandatory jail time for the first offense. You are likely to be legally intoxicated (0.08 percent blood alcohol) if you have had as little as one alcoholic drink an hour. Just don't do it. Take a taxi, as the locals do.

The Lowdown

Romantic redux—swingy supper clubs... Especially for the twenty-something crowd, some of whom are too young to even remember the heyday of the Hustle, the "in" thing these days is to dress to the nines (often in vintage clothing), rendezvous at a posh supper club, and dance all night to big-band swing and sentimental torch songs. **Club Deluxe**, on Haight Street, is a high-attitude swing-era revival house, where baggy trousers and tight skirts are de rigueur. The place is so small, though, only about two couples can get out of their seats at one time. Sunday is Frank Sinatra night.

Coconut Grove is the kind of sophisticated supper club you usually see only in old movies. A trip to this Van Ness Avenue haunt is like going to nightlife Disneyland, and costs just about as much. High ceilings, mahogany paneling, and huge, luminous palm trees create a chic backdrop for well-dressed people of all ages as they sip martinis between dances. Posh leather banquettes surround the dance floor and elevated stage, where torch singers sometimes sit in with the swing orchestra. Occasionally, headliners like Tom Jones or Charo perform. **The Starlight Room**—also a swing club—is not as glitzy as Coconut Grove, but its view from the top floor of the **Sir Francis Drake Hotel** is fantastic.

All that acid jazz... Acid jazz is a cross between modern jazz, hip-hop, rhythm and blues, funk, and even big band. It's vibrant and soulful, with big brass sections, lots of guitars, and rap-influenced vocals that all meet in an extremely danceable concoction. A leading venue for acid jazz is a supper club called **330 Ritch**, a one-time warehouse where people who come for the music mix with a more trend-conscious set who come simply because it's the fashionable thing to do. **Blondie's Bar and No Grill** is a Mission District laboratory where new musical forms regularly burst forth from the ongoing experiments in sound. Musicians flock there to jam and try out new (mostly acid jazz) riffs, and a young, artistic crowd follows because of the music, not because it's a place to be seen. Other clubs that feature jazz, including acid, are the **Up & Down Club** (South of Market), **Eleven** (also South of Market), **Blues** (Cow Hollow), and **Cafe du Nord** (north Market Street).

Get in Free

The most up-to-date guide to San Francisco after dark also includes 31 free passes and discounts (good through July 1997) to the most popular clubs in the city. The San Francisco Nightlife Guide gives detailed information about virtually every night spot in town, with neighborhood maps that make them easy to find. A single free pass is often worth more than the price of the book. The slim black volume is available at most major bookstores, Tower Records, and by mail for $12.50 including tax and postage (1182 Market St. #580, San Francisco, CA 94102).

SAN FRANCISCO | NIGHTLIFE

All that other jazz... If you're not sure about this acid jazz thing, head to North Beach. You can hear bigger-name musicians at the **Fairmont Hotel's New Orleans Room** (see "A Little Romance" below), but **North Beach** is presently enjoying a strong comeback as a major music center in the city. There are four good jazz clubs within three blocks of each other—and there's no cover charge at any of them. **Enrico's** features live jazz seven nights a week, and is the only one in the bunch that also has great food. **Jazz at Pearl's** features the most "serious" jazz of the lot. The indomitable Pearl opened her first jazz club in a Chinatown basement some 25 years ago, and usually gets the best of the local talent at her current address in North Beach. Players head to Pearl's to jam after their paying gigs are over. **The San Francisco Brewing Company** features jazz, blues, and its own brew. It has an authentic Old San Francisco feel, and the crowd is never uppity. Finally there is **Bix**, a romantic restaurant on a little alley in the only section of downtown that survived the 1906 earthquake. Bix used to be an assay office, where gold ore was evaluated and stored; it's a beautiful room, with light jazz and sometimes a vocalist.

It's only rock 'n' roll... Rock, in its various forms, dominates the music scene in San Francisco. Any night of the week you can hit a number of clubs and hear grunge, ska, post-punk, rock-a-billy, thrash, metal—in other words, just about every rock style except that acidy Jefferson Airplane/Grateful Dead thing they once called the San Francisco sound. When U2 is in town, they hang out at the **Bottom of the Hill** (South of Market), where most of the acts are locals who have landed recording contracts, but touring bands perform as well. The **Trocadero** is a South of Market hot spot for record-release parties for up-and-coming acts. It's a great venue for a concert because the dance floor is huge and the entire second floor is a balcony. On Wednesdays, a leather-clad crowd steps in for "Bondage-a-Go-Go," when spanking and chains add a little variety to the old dance routines. Hard-core thrashers checkout the Haight's **Nightbreak** and **Club Boomerang**. Both clubs allow just about anyone with guitars and drums to get on stage, and the patrons are of the black-on-black, multiple-piercings school of fashion. **The Paradise Lounge** (South of Market) is less a club and more a rock saloon, where four separate performance rooms feature two or three, acts playing simultaneously. Modern rock is the main attraction, but rock-a-billy, funk, acid jazz, and the spoken word are also on the bill. If you prefer classic-rock cover bands and oldies theme nights, **Silhouettes** can usually deliver, despite a Fisherman's Wharf location that attracts mostly tourists. On weekends, the place is packed for live oldies music, and the ample dance floor really jumps.

All-night techno parties... While modern rock dominates the city's live-music stages, techno is the music of choice for most clubs that host all-night dance parties. The clubs are known simply by their addresses because the parties—which have distinct names—float from club to club. If a promoter comes to **177 Townsend** with a party called "Colossus," for that night the location is known as "Colossus." Next week "Colossus" may be at **278 11th**. **650 Howard** and **715 Harrison** are also popular sites for floating fêtes. Each party has its own following, which can change over time. The *Bay Guardian* and *SF Weekly* are good sources for a start; parties at the legit clubs can lead you to the middle-of-the-night, deep underground scene, whose venues are even more unpredictable.

> **Even Cowgirls Hit the Booze**
> *You're in San Francisco and for some inexplicable reason you get a powerful hankering to do the Texas two-step. Trouble is, country music isn't exactly the hottest thing in the city, and the closest most people get to line dancing is late-night commercials for the Hank Williams Greatest Hits tapes "available only on TV." Not to worry— there's always the Rawhide (280 Seventh St., tel 415/621–1197). It's not exactly a traditional Western saloon—most of the regulars at the South of Market haunt are gay men—but it is a truly friendly, fun place for anyone who wants to get out there and kick up their heels, regardless of sexual orientation. Dance lessons are given Thursday through Sunday nights (7:30-9:30) for a $5.50 cover charge that includes two free cocktails. You'll learn how to do dances with names like "Ain't Goin' Down," and on a good night, you might catch a guy wearing chaps without a stitch underneath. Yee-haw!*

Disco infernal... Face it, disco is back. At first it was mostly a retro lark for people who used to dress up in their parents' platform shoes, but it gets harder and harder to distinguish the tongue-in-cheek Travolta wannabes from the real thing. If too much techno cools your dance fever, try some of these South of Market clubs, which offer a variety of sounds. **DV8** hosts up to three parties at a time, each with a different theme, a different promoter, and sometimes a different cover charge. On Saturday nights, though, you can usually dance all over the place for one admission. The music ranges from house, modern rock, and hip-hop to salsa or disco, but the sound is secondary—DV8 is a gathering place for hipsters and fashion slaves who must see and be seen. **Ten 15** (1015 Folsom St.) is another huge club (with a huge attitude) that usually has four different dance parties going at once, all for a $10 cover. House music booms in the multilevel main room; the gold room is a disco inferno, complete with a spinning, mirrored ball; in the basement are little alcoves and couches where you can take it easy and listen to acid jazz; and in the top room, anything goes. The crowd changes from night to night—Friday is a straight night, Saturday is a gay night, Tuesday is a deep underground party—but the coterie is always diverse, so don't ever feel that you have to sit the night out.

Unlike the two previously mentioned clubs, **Sound Factory** is super-friendly. The people at the door actually work to keep the lines moving. This place was built with people-watching in mind. The upstairs lobby looks out over the line outside and you can see everyone who enters. Then you can walk along a balcony and checkout the different rooms, each with its own theme. This is a high-energy Generation-X crowd.

DV8, **Ten 15**, and **Sound Factory** serve alcohol until 2am, but they all carry on after hours. There will definitely be lines outside their doors between 11:30pm and 1am.

Three babes and a bus... Get a taste of the different ingredients of San Francisco's nightlife with **Three Babes and a Bus**. About 80 percent of the bar-hoppers who take this tour are local residents, lured, perhaps, by the chauffeured ride, the pre-paid cover charges, the priority entry (no waiting in line), and, of course, the three fun-loving women who run the business. The bus will scoop you up at a downtown bar and chauffeur you to three or four more lively nightspots. Along the way, the babes introduce their passengers to one another and lay down a few house rules, the most important of which is "Never let the Three Babes buy their own drinks." Aside from that, the total cost of this party-on-wheels is about $30, which includes the clubs' cover charges.

A little romance... If you're looking for the perfect backdrop to a romantic evening, the big hotels cannot be beat. The **Fairmont** has three: **Mason's**, a beautiful dining room with large banquettes next to windows that look out on cable cars while soft jazz plays in the background; the elegant **New Orleans Room**, where some of the top jazz musicians in the country perform in a wide range of idioms; and the **Tonga Room**, which is decorated like a Polynesian village and struck nightly by simulated rainstorms, complete with lightning and thunder (but no water). The high-ceilinged **Compass Rose Room** in the **Westin Saint Francis** is the best place to dance cheek-to-cheek to a swing orchestra, and no room offers a better romantic view than the **Hilton Hotel's Cityscape**, where a retractable roof opens to the sky, and floor-to-ceiling windows offer a panorama of the whole Bay Area. For the little hideaway that has everything, **Heart and Soul** is the place. It's an intimate, sophisticated, and lively Polk Gulch supper club with cozy tables and cool, straight-ahead jazz.

Lookin' for love... Aptly named, **Johnny Love's** in Polk Gulch is the hottest singles club in town. Its horseshoe bar is designed to allow eye contact from across the room, and the diverse crowd—all ages, some locals, and some visitors—come with the idea of meeting new friends, hopefully intimate ones. Eventually, somebody always ends up dancing on the bar. On the other side of town is **Harry Denton's**, where Financial District singles gather; the suit quotient is exceptionally high, and the average age is thirty-something. Music starts in the bar at around 8pm (lively jazz or funk), but people really loosen up later on when the back dining room is cleared for dancing to a deejay's mix of Top 40 tunes.

The **Cow Hollow District** along Union and Fillmore streets has for decades attracted large crowds of singles—now mostly college students. To find the liveliest spot on any given night, just walk down either street until you hear one you like.

Drag clubs... There are two kinds of drag shows in the city—the big, famous revues like North Beach's **Finocchio** (see Entertainment), and the small neighborhood clubs that are more oriented toward drag queens who come to see and be seen by their peers. One of the most interesting neighborhood drag bars is **Esta Noche**, a small, Latino-oriented club in the Mission District where the drag queens are more likely to be at the bar or on the dance floor than on stage. (Esta Noche does host drag shows, but not on a regular basis.) The disk jockeys play mostly salsa music—with some disco thrown in—and the dance floor is always jammed. The bartenders are friendly, as are most of the customers, but this is definitely a gay club and not recommended for curious heteros wondering what drag queens do in their spare time. It is also in a kind of seedy section of 16th Street, where there have been a few isolated gay-bashing incidents in the past, so take a cab to the door. A stone's throw away is **La India Bonita**, where drag shows on Friday and Saturday nights ($3 cover) are emceed in Spanish and the queens are definitely as *bonita* as they come. The audience is predominantly Latino, but both straight and gay customers are welcome as long as they are respectful during the shows. Again, the neighborhood is best reached at night by cab. The **Motherlode**, a Polk Gulch/Tenderloin institution, is an odd combination of both straight and gay men ogling the profusion of drag queens, transvestites, and transsexuals who hang out there. Friday and Saturday night shows (11pm) include drag and strip, but the club itself is more aggressive than friendly, and the neighborhood is the pits (definitely take a cab).

Where the boys are... In practically any San Francisco neighborhood, there are too many gay bars to name, so we'll just mention a few "musts." If you are a gay man, you must go to **Twin Peaks** (Castro at Market St.), simply because it is the gateway to **the Castro** and is the first thing you see when you get out of the Castro

Street MUNI/Metro station. The huge picture windows, the wonderful old burgundy-colored sign that beacons from a block away, and the antique wooden bar make it feel like a neighborhood cafe. Much of the crowd is over 40—it's not the top cruising spot in town—but it is a wonderful place to stop by for an afternoon pick-me-up, whether you are male or female. Around the corner is another historic Castro bar, the **Elephant Walk** (Castro at 18th St.), where in 1979 police stormed in, dragged out gay men, and beat them. The bar won a famous lawsuit against the police department, and has been a landmark in gay history ever since. It is cozy and candle-lit—a great place for a date for gay men and lesbians alike. A few doors down is the youngest cruise scene in the Castro, the **Phoenix**, where a racially mixed crowd—Asian, Latin, African-American, and white—squish into a packed room to dance and sweat and pick each other up, especially on weekends. We've been told to beware of pickpockets. The **Pendulum** (around the corner on 18th St.) is frequented primarily by African-American men and those who can't resist them. Weekends are totally jammed—and jammin'. **The Mint** (upper Market St. near Guerrero) is one of the oldest gay bars in the city—open since World War II—and can be quite a hot spot during karaoke hours (9–2, Sun 4–2). If you think you may be Bette Midler trapped in a shy man's body, this is the place for you. The crowd applauds everyone who gives it a try, especially if they know it's your first time at the mike. For a full rundown on the gay scene in the city, stop by **A Different Light Bookstore** (tel 415/431–0891, 4089 Castro St.), where you can pick up any number of free gay publications that include entertainment listings. Recommended: *Bay Times*, *Odyssey*, and *The Sentinel*.

Where the girls are... Until the late 1980s, the Bay Area's homosexual population was pretty much divided into two territories—gay men in San Francisco and lesbians in Oakland. Now there is a much more active lesbian community in San Francisco—particularly in the **Mission District** and nearby **Bernal Heights**—and there are a lot of fun lesbian hangouts, including a number of gay bars with special nights for women. The longest-running Saturday night lesbian dance party in

SAN FRANCISCO | NIGHTLIFE

the city is the **Girl Spot** (at the End Up, South of Market, Sixth and Harrison streets), commonly known as the G-Spot. It is extremely popular among a wide variety of women, and when the dance floor gets crowded and sweaty, there's a big outside patio where you and whoever you've got your eye on can go get a little fresh air. They've also got go-go dancers. The G-Spot is a must, but go before 10pm to get in for a reduced cover charge (usually less than $5). **Junk** (at the Stud, South of Market, Ninth and Harrison streets) is another rent-a-club dance party for women, on Thursday nights (10–2). It was originally a sort of leather and multiple-piercings scene for stylish, freaky urban Sapphites, but it has been infiltrated by suburban girls. It's still a safe and fun place for bad girls, though, and it still has a bit of an edge to it, so give it a try. Don't get there until at least 11:30—it's a late-night kind of place. Our favorite semi-lesbian bar is **El Rio** (Mission District, Mission and Army streets), with a mixed crowd and most definitely a mixed motif. It's predominantly Latin, but it also has a big backyard that would give it that Doris Day/Rock Hudson patio party kind of feel if it weren't for the bigger-than-life Carmen Miranda paper doll out there. The music schedule varies, but there is often good live salsa. Sunday afternoons are the best. Go kind of late and stay for the transition from a mellow afternoon to a wild night.

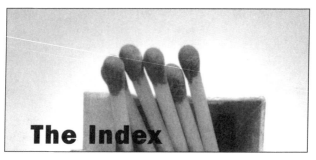

The Index

177 Townsend. An industrial-style South of Market space for floating dance parties, featuring huge columns around the dance floor, an extravagant lighting system, and a big, round bar that makes it easy to get drinks.... *Tel 415/*

974–6020. 177 Townsend St., 42 MUNI bus. Hours vary; usually includes after-hours. Cover $5–20.

278 11th. Another South of Market space for floating dance parties, this one used to be the Oasis Club, where pool parties were common. Now the pool has a plastic cover that serves as the dance floor. On nice nights, the roof is retracted and you can look down on the dancers from above.... *No phone. 278 11th St., 42 MUNI bus. Hours vary. Cover $5–20.*

330 Ritch. A modern-style supper club that features acid jazz but also hosts Latin and modern jazz. A cool crowd gathers in this industrial building, located on a little South of Market alleyway, to enjoy the tapas and listen to the latest sounds.... *Tel 415/541–9574. 330 Ritch St.; 15, 30, or 45 MUNI bus. Food 5–11 or midnight, happy hour 5–8 Tue–Fri, music in two sets: 6:30–8 & 9–1:30. Closed Mon. Cover free–$10.*

650 Howard. A three-level South of Market space for floating dance parties.... *No phone. 650 Howard St.; Powell St. BART/Muni Metro stop, 30 or 45 MUNI bus. Hours vary. Cover varies.*

715 Harrison. A high-tech dance club with an outrageous sound system. The floating parties at this, another South of Market space, are for a very young crowd; some nights, 18-year-olds are admitted. No hats, cellular phones, or athletic wear are allowed.... *Tel 415/979–8686. 715 Harrison St., 42 MUNI bus. Hours vary. Cover $10–15.*

Bix. Classy and romantic old-style San Francisco restaurant with soft jazz and a lively bar crowd. One of the four places in North Beach where jazz lovers should go.... *Tel 415/433–6300. 56 Gold St.; 15, 30 MUNI bus. Open nightly, with music most nights. No cover.*

Blondie's Bar and No Grill. A neighborhood bar in the bohemian Mission District. Musicians get together here to jam and experiment with new sounds. There's a good mix of music lovers, local regulars, and the curious.... *Tel 415/864–2419. 540 Valencia St., 16th St. BART stop. Closed Sun.*

Blues. A funky, dark saloon where blues and jazz are taken seriously. The crowd is mostly locals, with a few music lovers lucky enough to find this little place in Cow Hollow.... *Tel 415/771–2583. 2125 Lombard St. 28 MUNI bus. Closed Tue. Cover free–$5.*

Bottom of the Hill. Recently signed modern rock bands are featured in this casual club way South of Market. Two or three bands play each night. It's way off the beaten path, but worth the effort to maybe catch a new rock sensation. Burgers and such served until midnight.... *Tel 415/626–4455. 1233 17th St. Open nightly. Cover $3–6.*

Cafe du Nord. One of the hippest clubs in town is located on north Market Street in a dark, ornate, former basement speakeasy where not much has changed over the past half-century except the music. An artistic crowd comes here to hear acid jazz, jumpin' jive, salsa, and even some cabaret.... *Tel 415/861–5016. 2170 Market St. Open nightly. Cover $3–5.*

Cityscape. With floor-to-ceiling windows and a retractable roof over the dance floor, this club on the 46th floor of the Hilton Hotel offers the best views of the sky and skyline of any club in the city. Deejays play a variety of music—Frank Sinatra covers, Motown, and Top 40—and they also take requests from the touristy clientele. A romantic place to dance the night away.... *Tel 415/776–0215. 333 O'Farrell St.; Powell St. BART/Muni Metro stop, 38 MUNI bus. Open nightly most of the time. No cover.*

Club Boomerang. Loud, hard rock in a neighborhood saloon. Two or three local bands each night.... *Tel 415/387–2996. 1850 Haight St., 7 MUNI bus. Open nightly. Small cover.*

Club Deluxe. Big-band entertainment in a little bar. Most of the patrons are young hipsters who dress in 1940s garb and love to dance the boogie-woogie—which is not easy here, since there's not much room. Live music Thur–Sat; other nights, deejays keep the swing spirit alive.... *Tel 415/552–6949. 1511 Haight St., 7 MUNI bus. Open nightly. Cover free–$8.*

Coconut Grove. Clark Gable and Lana Turner would have loved this sophisticated supper club on Van Ness Avenue—luminous palm trees, leather banquets, formally dressed servers, and first class entertainment are all reminiscent of a bygone era. Most nights an orchestra plays swing music; sometimes a torch singer will sit in. To see one of the special shows—when headliners like Charo or Tom Jones perform—call ahead for reservations.... *Tel 415/776–1616. 1415 Van Ness Ave., 42 MUNI bus. Closed Sun. Cover free–$55.*

Compass Rose Room. The sort of place that gives San Francisco the reputation of being a romantic city. Its two-story ceiling, antiques, and custom-made furnishings provide a perfect setting inside the Westin Saint Francis hotel for dancing cheek-to-cheek. Classic torch songs and swing jazz keep the small dance floor crowded. Go here for dessert and romance.... *Tel 415/397–7000. 335 Powell St.; Powell St. BART/Muni Metro stop, Powell-Mason or Powell-Hyde cable cars. Open nightly. No cover.*

DV8. High-energy dance parties happen in this multi-room South of Market club, where socializing in the lines outside and gawking at the latest clubwear is all part of the fun. Special events include fashion shows and art exhibits.... *Tel 415/957–1730. 540 Howard St.; Powell St. BART/MUNI Metro stop, 30, 45 MUNI bus. Open Thur–Sun, after-hours each night. Cover $5–15.*

Elephant Walk. Made famous the night of the "White Night Riots" in 1979, this Castro bar is now a gay landmark. It is a quiet, romantic spot—perfect for a date.... *Tel 415/ 252–8441. 500 Castro St., at 18th St.; Castro St. MUNI Metro stop.*

Eleven. High ceilings and large windows lend an expansive feeling to what is really an intimate South of Market restaurant. Jazz musicians perform on a stage set high on a loft so they can be seen from both the balcony and the main floor. The food is American with an Italian influence.... *Tel 415/ 431–3337. 374 11th St., 42 MUNI bus. Closed Sun. Cover free–$5.*

Enrico's Sidewalk Cafe. (See also Dining) A North Beach sidewalk cafe with great food and great jazz. The crowd is a good mixture of locals and tourists, who all like the European feel of the place.... *Tel 415/982–6223. 504 Broadway; 15, 30 Muni bus. Open nightly. No cover.*

SAN FRANCISCO | NIGHTLIFE

Esta Noche. This Mission District bar is a friendly neighborhood hangout for drag queens, with preplanned shows scheduled on an occasional basis (call for details). Few— if any—biological women ever go here. It is lots of fun, but in a slightly seedy area, so take a cab at night.... *Tel 415/861–5757. 3079 16th St., at Valencia St.; 16th St. BART stop. No cover.*

Finocchio. This is the Queen Mother of drag clubs, known since 1936 for its glitzy female-impersonator revues. There are three shows a night—at less than a $15 cover charge—and you can often get in without reservations. You must be at least 21 years old.... *Tel 415/982–9388; after 7pm 415/362–9913. 506 Broadway, 15 or 30 MUNI bus.*

The Girl Spot. This lesbian dance party, also known as The G-Spot, is held every Saturday night at a South of Market bar called the End Up. All kinds of women stop by for the action, from suburban girls on a lark to hard-core leather types.... *Tel 415/337–4962. 401 Sixth St., at Harrison, 42 MUNI bus (cab recommended).*

Harry Denton's Bar & Grill. A popular meeting ground for thirty-something Financial District singles. Deejays spin Top-40 tunes for dancing in the back room. The San Francisco bistro fare isn't bad either.... *Tel 415/882–1333. 161 Steuart St.; Embarcadero BART/Muni Metro stop, 7 MUNI bus. Open nightly; dancing Thur–Sat only.*

Heart and Soul. Martinis and music go well together at this intimate Polk Gulch jazz supper club. The stage is set so that those in the balcony and in the long, narrow dining room below can watch the band work. A wonderful place for dinner and romance, even though there's not much room to dance.... *Tel 415/673–7100. 1695 Polk St., 42 MUNI bus and all cable cars. Dinner served until midnight. A cover charge of $4–10 will be added to the check for anyone there after 9pm.*

La India Bonita. Friday and Saturday night drag shows are extremely popular at this Mission District bar ($3 cover). They're hosted in Spanish, but you don't have to understand the language to enjoy the show (you may need to speak it to talk with the customers, however). The audience considers female impersonation to be an art form, in it's own way, and they are very respectful during shows. The neighborhood is questionable at night, so take a cab.... *Tel 415/621–9294. 3089 16th St., at Valencia St.; 16th St. BART stop.*

Jazz at Pearl's. Straightforward jazz in an old-style jazz club in North Beach. Pearl, who greets most patrons and strictly enforces her two-drink minimum, has owned a jazz club in San Francisco for decades and gets some of the best musicians in town to perform here, or jam after hours.... *Tel 415/291–8255. 256 Columbus Ave.; 15, 30 Muni bus. Closed Sun. No cover; 2-drink minimum.*

Johnny Love's. A lively Polk Gulch singles bar popular with both locals and out-of-towners. The horseshoe bar is ideal for scoping romantic prospects across the room, and the dance floor has an irresistible pull after a few drinks.... *Tel 415/ 931–8021. 1500 Broadway, Powell-Hyde cable car. Closed Sun. Cover $5–8 after 9:30.*

Junk. Every Thursday night, the Stud, a South of Market gay bar, turns into a wild party for bad-girl lesbians with a high-style attitude. Suburbanites have invaded, but even they haven't been able to take the edge off this freak-friendly dance bash.... *Tel 415/863–6623. 399 Ninth St., at Harrison, 42 MUNI bus (cab recommended).*

Mason's. A cozy, romantic hideaway, with soft jazz and a view of the cable cars. Located in the Fairmont Hotel (see also **New Orleans Room** and **Tonga Room**), this is one of the few hotel dining rooms that has good food.... *Tel 415/772– 5233. 342 Mason St., Powell-Mason cable car. Open nightly, though they close early. No cover.*

The Mint. If you haven't been to a gay karaoke bar, you haven't lived. The key to having fun at this Upper Market spot is definitely participation—the crowd loves newcomers and will be very kind to you, especially if you know any Bette Midler tunes.... *Tel 415/626–4726. 1942 Market St., near Guerrero St., Church St. MUNI Metro stop.*

The Motherlode. About half the customers at this crowded, smoky Polk Gulch bar are drag queens. The rest are transvestites, transsexuals, and assorted men (both gay and straight) who come to ogle the ostensibly 90 percent female clientele. Born-female women simply do not come here. The neighborhood can be spooky at night, so you might want to take a cab.... *Tel 415/928–6006. 1002 Post St., at Larkin St., 38 MUNI bus. No cover.*

New Orleans Room. Some of the biggest jazz musicians in the world play at this intimate, plush room at the Fairmont Hotel (see also **Mason's** and **Tonga Room**). Music can range from the blues of Charles Brown to Pete Escavedo's Latin big-band sounds.... *Tel 415/772–5259. 950 Mason St., Powell-Mason cable car. Open Wed–Sun. Show times vary. Cover $5–30.*

Nightbreak. A Haight Street bar where bands play hard rock, blues, and sometimes something unique, and deejays play the same, plus the latest imports. A hangout for artists, rock musicians, and the amply pierced.... *Tel 415/221–9008. 1821 Haight St., 7 MUNI bus. Open every day and night. Cover free–$5.*

Paradise Lounge. Up to five bands play in this unusual South of Market club every night, where modern rock, blues, funk, poetry, and occasionally even a lounge-lizard act can be heard. Sometimes three bands will play simultaneously, each on a different floor. The crowd is unpretentious, enjoys playing a little pool on the side, and is as diverse as the entertainment.... *Tel 415/861–6906. 1501 Folsom St., 42 MUNI bus. Open nightly. Cover free–$10.*

The Pendulum. This is the city's only predominantly African-American gay bar, and it is absolutely packed on weekends.... *Tel 415/863–4441. 4146 18th St., at Collingwood St., Castro St. MUNI Metro stop.*

The Phoenix. If you want loud, crowded, and sweaty—and you want it young—this is the gay bar to find it. It's a very popular Castro cruise spot, especially since the crowd is racially mixed (Asian, Latin, African-American, and white).... *Tel 415/552–6827. 482 Castro St., at 18th St., Castro St. MUNI Metro stop.*

El Rio. This eccentric Mission District dive is supposedly a Latina lesbian haunt, but it is also a friendly neighborhood bar, comfortable for men and women, gay and straight. The music can be wonderful—salsa is king, but all kinds of different dance music is played here—and the back yard is great, especially on Sunday afternoons.... *Tel 415/282–3325. 3158 Mission St., at Army St., 24th St. BART stop.*

San Francisco Brewing Company. This 1907 institution, with its plank floors and gas-lit chandeliers, looks like it could have been around since the gold rush. Brewing tanks have been added more recently, and they produce some pretty good beer. Live jazz or blues every night helps draw both locals and tourists.... *Tel 415/343–3344. 155 Columbus Ave. Open nightly. No cover.*

Silhouettes. One of the only places in town for good ol' rock 'n' roll of the Bob Seger, Eagles, or earlier vintages. It has a '50s theme decor, with those toaster-size remote juke boxes at the tables and plenty of "Happy Days" paraphernalia. It's located upstairs on Fishermen's Wharf and has a balcony, so you can take a break from the music and watch the tourists go by. It attracts a very diverse crowd of locals and visitors who like yesteryear rock. Cover bands take the stage on weekends; deejays explore bygone decades weekday nights.... *Tel 415/673–1954. 155 Jefferson St.; Powell-Hyde cable car; 15, 30, or 42 MUNI bus. Open nightly. Small cover charge on live-music nights.*

Sound Factory. The biggest dance club in town. There are six different rooms at this friendly South of Market space, and a balcony to walk along so you can check out each of them. The music is techno, with some funk, hip-hop, and disco thrown in. No athletic attire allowed.... *Tel 415/543–1300. 525 Harrison St., 42 MUNI bus. Open Fri & Sat until at least 4am. Cover $10.*

Starlight Room. The view of the city from this dance club on the top floor of the Sir Francis Drake Hotel is amazing. With the big-band sound and elegant surroundings, it's like dancing on top of the world. There is a good mix of people here of all ages who like the swing thing. A very romantic place to dance the night away.... *Tel 415/392–7755. 450 Powell St.; Powell St. BART/MUNI Metro stop, Powell-Hyde or Powell-Mason cable car. Open nightly. Cover $6–12.*

Ten 15. A South of Market dance club with multiple rooms and multiple themes: The big room is for contemporary dance music, the gold room for 1970s disco, the basement for acid jazz. And then there is the V.I.P. lounge, where anything goes. The party is straight on Friday and gay on Saturday, but most people don't pay attention to that—go any time. Just go early or you'll stand in a long line alongside plenty of attitude…. *Tel 415/431–1200. 1015 Folsom St., 42 MUNI bus. Open Fri & Sat and sometimes for special parties on other nights, always after-hours. Cover $10.*

Three Babes and a Bus. To get yourself acclimated to San Francisco's nightlife, take the bus. This is a tour of four different clubs guided by three women who have made fun their business. They pick you up in the bus, make introductions within the group, and get you into clubs without standing in line. These traveling parties happen Fridays and Saturdays unless you can get enough people together for a special party on other days. Call 415/552–2582 for details and reservations.

Tonga Room. A Fairmont Hotel room (see also **New Orleans Room** and **Mason's**) that's decorated like a Polynesian village, with a lagoon and simulated rainstorms that arrive complete with thunder and lightning. The band plays danceable Top-40 tunes, and exotic drinks are available. It's kind of campy, but can be lots of fun. Happy hour includes a great buffet for $3…. *Tel 415/772–5278. 950 Mason St., Powell/Mason cable car. Open nightly. Cover $3–8.*

Trocadero. Formerly a dance haven, this South of Market club is often now the site of record-release parties for up-and-coming rock bands. It's a good concert space since there's plenty of room to dance and a balcony from which to watch…. *Tel 415/995–4600. 520 Fourth St.; Powell St. BART/MUNI Metro stop, 30 or 45 Muni bus. Hours vary. Cover free–$15.*

Twin Peaks. This old-fashioned, picture-windowed bar sits on the corner of Castro and Market, and its burgundy and neon sign beckons you to come checkout the scene inside. The crowd is usually relatively quiet and 40-plus. It is a comfortable place to stop for one beer or stay all night and watch the crowd change.... *Tel 415/864–9470. 410 Castro St., Castro St. MUNI Metro stop.*

Up & Down Club. A fashionably quaint jazz dinner club downstairs, with a hip bar upstairs. Good food. The live music downstairs is usually acid jazz; upstairs, deejays spin a variety of dance tracks, including the latest imports, hip-hop, funk, and soul. Co-owner supermodel Christy Turlington stops in when she's in town.... *Tel 415/626–2388. 1151 Folsom St., 42 MUNI bus.* **Down** *is open Wed–Sat with dinner until 10pm.* **Up** *is open Wed–Mon. Cover is $5, free if you have dinner.*

7

inment

San Francisco
sells more theater
tickets per capita
than any major
city in America.
Most people
would be shocked

to hear that little trivia gem, given the fact that so many of the high-profile productions in town are recycled Broadway musicals that appeal mostly to out-of-towners. Sure, you can spend your money on tickets to *The Phantom of the Opera* (yawn), but your hard-earned entertainment dollar would be more wisely spent on some of the most innovative, dynamic stage productions in the country—written, produced, direct-ed, and performed by top local talent.

San Francisco leaves the monumental cost of producing mainstream shows to New York, concentrating its own money and effort on unconventional creations. The city's dozens of unusual options include the Lorraine Hansberry Theater, a small space in the downtown theater district that focuses on new and experimental works by established African-American playwrights; Theater Rhinoceros in the Mission District, the oldest gay/lesbian theater group in the country; The Marsh, another Mission District venue for avant-garde theater and dance; and Josie's Juice Joint and Cabaret, a Castro District vegetarian cafe that stages informal productions in its back room. And by all means, don't leave town without going to North Beach to see San Francisco's trademark show, *Beach Blanket Babylon*, the longest-running musical revue in history.

Here's another surprising bit of trivia—the first ballet company in the United States was the San Francisco Ballet. And its glory is not at all in the past: the *New York Times* pro-claimed the current troupe, led by artistic director Helgi Tomasson (formerly a principal dancer with the New York City Ballet), "one of the country's finest." If you're looking for more unorthodox dance performances, there are plenty of troupes to see, from the mid-size companies that perform at Theater Artaud (Potrero Hill) to the small, cutting-edge shows in the Mission District's Footwork Dance Studio and Third Wave Dance House.

The San Francisco Opera is temporarily among the homeless, at least until mid-1997, when repairs are scheduled to be completed on the opulent 1932 War Memorial Opera House. Performances continue at various sites around town, and few patrons seem to mind—especially if they have tickets to the grand ball that opens the season each September (there is a limited summer series as well). The San Francisco Symphony has its own digs—Davies Symphony Hall—and a new maestro, Michael Tilson Thomas, who left the London Symphony to become the toast of the Bay. Most other music—jazz, blues, folk, and rock—is performed primarily at the clubs you'll find in the "Nightlife" chapter.

Getting a bit too highbrow here? Not to worry. There are enough spectator sports in the Bay Area to balance out the whole culture bit—two major-league baseball teams, two NFL football teams, an NBA basketball team, an NHL hockey team, and two major horse-racing tracks. There are even two professional roller-hockey teams. The biggest news is the 1995 return of the Raiders to their rightful home in Oakland and the fact that fans paid thousands of dollars apiece for a chance in a lottery drawing in which the lucky winners were awarded the right to spend even more money on season tickets. The two words that have best described Raiders football since the first game they played at the Oakland Coliseum are "sold out," but a new policy under consideration may free up some single-game tickets.

Sources

For theater and music listings, the best mainstream source is the "Datebook" tabloid in the Sunday *Chronicle*, known to locals as "the pink section" because it's printed on pink newsprint. The *Bay Guardian* and *SF Weekly*, free alternative weeklies that can be found almost anywhere you look, are recommended for listings of more offbeat or intimate happenings. Radio stations that offer diverse programming and information on local performances and concerts include KPOO 89.5 FM, KQED 88.5 FM, and KPFA 94.1 FM.

Getting Tickets

San Franciscans are an odd lot when it comes to performing arts—they adore the opera and ballet, and snap up season

In Search of Tony Bennett's Heart

Did you ever wonder exactly where Tony Bennett left his heart? We knew his heart called to him from a spot "where little cable cars climb halfway to the stars," but we never guessed the spot was the Visitors Information Center at Hallidie Plaza, even though it is right next to the Powell Street cable car turnaround. Take the escalator from the turnaround down toward the BART entrance and go into the center, where you'll find the "I Left My Heart in San Francisco" gold record, the original song manuscript, and an earlier rough draft (be sure to read it—some of the lyrics really stink). While you're there, pick up some free walking tour leaflets and ask the multilingual staff for any information or advice you need (tel 415/391–2000). There's also a 24-hour telephone hotline—in five languages—that lists daily events and activities (English tel 415/391–2001, Spanish tel 415/391–2122, French tel 415/391–2003, German tel 415/391–2004, and Japanese tel 415/391–2101).

ENTERTAINMENT | SAN FRANCISCO

tickets so fast you barely have time to read through the season's program if you hope to get a good seat, yet the major blockbuster shows that seem to be a priority to out-of-towners are not that big of a draw for locals. (They also dine before the theater, not afterward.) Here's the moral of that story: If you want to go to an opera, symphony, or ballet performance, make arrangements before you get to town. You can call BASS (tel 800/225–BASS outside California) for one-stop ticket shopping, but if you aren't familiar with the concert halls, you may prefer to deal directly with each company's box office, where ticket representatives tend to have much more information about the best seats. If you want to see a major Broadway-type show, mention it to your hotel concierge when you secure your room reservation, or call BASS. Tickets for smaller venues and more avant-garde productions are usually available on relatively short notice, but you should check out the *Bay Guardian* and *SF Weekly* as soon as you get to town to find out what's going on and to reserve your seats.

For half-price, day-of-performance tickets to major theater, dance, and music events at selected venues, go to the **TIX** booth on the Stockton Street side of Union Square (cash only, Tue–Thur 11–6, Fri–Sat 11–7; tel 415/433–7827). Even fairly popular shows sometimes need to fill seats with the steep discount. TIX also sells full-price advance tickets (credit cards accepted). **BASS** is the primary advance-sales outlet for all major Bay Area events, including sports, and you can purchase tickets by telephone (tel 510/762–BASS, 800/225–BASS outside California). In every big city, there are scalpers on the street at sold-out events—even though the practice is against the law—but if you are not familiar with the seating chart, you can easily plunk down a bundle of cash for a "great seat" behind a pillar or up in nosebleed territory. Counterfeit tickets are also a common scam, and they are very difficult to detect—unless the nefarious scalper has neglected to wash the printer's ink off his hands. If you're willing to pay more than face value for a good seat or a sold-out event, it's probably better to go through a ticket broker. They will charge a steep price for a premium ticket, but they usually have choice seats and tickets for sold-out events. The toughest ticket to get is to an Oakland Raiders game—all of their home games have always been sold out to season-ticket holders—but **Mr. Ticket** might be able to help. Mr. T is the biggest ticket broker in the Bay Area, specializing in premium seating—at premium prices (tel 415/424–3031; 2065 Van Ness Ave.). You can also check the Yellow Pages—there are more than two dozen agencies listed under "Ticket Sales."

The Lowdown

The play's the thing... San Francisco's "theater district" is just west of picture-pretty Union Square, but like its New York counterpart, it brushes up against a less cultivated neighborhood—in this case, the Tenderloin. There is no particular danger during performance times, but you might want to take a cab at night, especially if you are dressed up and look like you might have a purse or wallet worth snatching. All of the theaters that specialize in Broadway and Broadway-bound shows are within a few blocks of each other—if Andrew Lloyd Webber turns the O.J. Simpson trial into a musical, it will eventually end up at the **Curran**, the **Golden Gate**, or the **Orpheum**. The Curran has been playing *The Phantom of the Opera* for what seems like eons; the run is open-ended, but call in advance to be sure it is still playing. The grand old Golden Gate Theater is located a little deeper into the Tenderloin than some overdressed theater-goers would prefer, but it stages lots of Broadway favorites and revivals—in 1995, Tommy Tune's new production of the fifties rock-and-roll musical *Grease* was a big favorite (the only thing missing was a young John Travolta). The Orpheum's meticulously restored Spanish baroque building is every bit as glamorous as the productions it hosts; when Carol Channing came to town with the revival of *Hello Dolly!*, she came to the Orpheum. But the theater district is not limited to Broadway blockbusters. One of the less-publicized casualties of the 1989 Loma Prieta earthquake, the Geary Theater—home of the **American Conservatory Theater** (ACT), one of the most highly regarded repertory groups in the country—is expected to reopen this year with improved production facilities. It's a company with great range—from their hilarious 1995 adaptation of *The Play's the Thing* to their riveting production of Shakespeare's *Othello* the same year. The **Marine's Memorial Theater** presents both local and off-Broadway productions; it was the San Francisco home of Tony Kushner's *Angels in America*. The ornate **Alcazar**

Theater often stages long runs of its plays; you won't see anything out of the ordinary, but classics like *The Lion in Winter* please drama lovers who can't stand the idea of another tap-dancing chorus line. The **Stage Door Theater**, which has been one of ACT's homes-away-from-home, normally presents a mixed bag of top-quality local comedy productions in its intimate space.

On the fringes... It is fitting that a city known for pioneering social change concentrates a great deal of its theatrical resources on productions that feature gay and lesbian, multicultural, and avant-garde works. Many of the most experimental companies are housed in or near San Francisco's "New Bohemia"—the Mission District—but non-mainstream theater can be found throughout the city. The current *ne plus ultra* avant-garde venue is **The Marsh**, a Mission District performance space where you pay your money (usually about $5) and take your chances, and often see remarkably talented artists right before they become trendy and famous. Aspiring actors, dancers, playwrights, and performance artists, take note: The Marsh is also the best place in town to network. The Marsh's predecessor—still among the most respected progressive art centers in the city—is another Mission District space called **Intersection for the Arts**, where Sam Shepard and Whoopi Goldberg tried out their acts before they got their 15 light-years of fame. The not-yet-discovered performers here are generally cutting-edge. Downtown, amid all the Broadway musicals and other big-money productions, the cozy little **Exit Theater** serves beer and wine and stages avant-garde "classics," from one-act comedies set in cafes to absurdist murder mysteries. You don't have to be a sullen existentialist to be experimental—this is a place to be a tad eccentric and have fun at the same time. It is always a pleasure to see a dance, theater, or multimedia production at **Theater Artaud** (Mission District), because the space itself is so well-run; this medium-sized mainstay of the experimental theater scene has been around long enough to know how to give impeccably professional stagings of the most avant-garde works. **Climate** (South of Market) is so tiny that it makes the audience feel almost intimate with the performers. Expect all kinds of experimental works here, including individual readings and performance art. The

Lorraine Hansberry Theater (downtown) provides a showcase for some of the top African-American playwrights and artists in the country, presenting both experimental and well-known works. The **Mission Cultural Center for Latino Arts** (Mission District) emphasizes works written and produced by multinational Latino artists, much of it political in nature and aimed at the neighborhood's Mexican, Central American, and Chicano population (many of the productions are in Spanish). **Theater Rhinoceros** (Mission District) was the first theater group in the United States to focus strictly on contemporary gay and lesbian issues; their productions range from bizarre, avant-garde performance pieces to traditional plays that feature gay characters. There's often a line stretching down the block in front of **Josie's Juice Joint**, a Castro District vegetarian cafe/cabaret combo where local gay performers will have you in a belly-laugh frenzy. Both gays and straights love this place, which will be obvious to you the moment you see the line full of every possible combination of couples waiting to get in. New works by local playwrights and artists are staged at the **Magic Theater** (Fort Mason)—some are stars and some are starving, but all are very, very good. The progressive **Phoenix Theater** (South of Market) also features the work of local playwrights; the productions are often mounted on a shoestring budget, but they are often powerful.

Costumes a go-go... It was a very sad day for San Francisco when Steve Silver, the mastermind behind *Beach Blanket Babylon*, died in 1995, but he left a legacy that promises to keep people laughing for years to come— the longest-running, wackiest musical revue in history. Watch reasonable facsimiles of Tina Turner, Hillary Clinton, and James Brown—all wearing huge, ridiculous headdresses—give Snow White advice on how to find a good man. (It sounds reasonable to us.) And you won't believe the hats. One of the more famous ones is a huge model of the San Francisco skyline. Reserve a few weeks in advance for the cabaret-style performances in North Beach's cozy **Club Fugazi** (to be admitted you must be at least 21 years old, with photo identification, except for Sunday matinees). There are many small bars in town where drag queens congregate and strut their stuff (see

Nightlife), but the most mainstream is **Finocchio**, a family-owned North Beach cabaret that has been presenting glitzy female-impersonator revues since 1936. It's one of the best-known drag clubs in the world, and by no means does it cater specifically to a gay clientele, as do some of the smaller neighborhood clubs around town. The cabaret atmosphere is completely comfortable for anyone who enjoys a good show, but you have to be 21—the minimum drinking age—to get in.

Men in tights... The world-class **San Francisco Ballet** normally shares its home with the opera, performing regularly at the War Memorial Opera House. Unfortunately, the opera house is in sore need of repair—some routine, some to fix damage from the 1989 earthquake—so the company is performing in a number of locations around the Bay Area until mid-1997. Artistic director Helgi Tomasson is a darling of dance critics, especially in New York, where he was considered a premiere danseur, and worked closely with Balanchine. His production of *Romeo and Juliet* was hailed as one of the most inventive ever staged. The ballet's primary seasons are spring and fall, but there are special Christmas performances, including, of course, *The Nutcracker*. If you're inclined to take BART across the bay, you can see the **Oakland Ballet** perform at the beautiful art-deco Paramount Theater, a perfectly restored landmark Art Deco movie palace that alone is worth the trip. This exuberant, multiracial company is not as developed as its San Francisco counterpart, but some of the pieces are actually more interesting, in part because they feature a number of brilliant young dancers who are obviously delighted to be performing. Their enthusiasm is refreshing; the dancing isn't always perfect, but they are a lot of fun to watch. Their 1995 *Romeo and Juliet* may not have caught the attention of the big-time national critics, but it was beautifully staged and featured a black Romeo, quite a departure for the conservative ballet world.

Dancing with the avant-garde... The city's unconventional dance companies gather where the rest of the avant-garde performing artists do—in the Mission District. Small, funky groups and extreme, cutting-edge choreographers showcase their work at **Footwork Dance**

Studio, a small Mission District studio where local choreographers are having a creative field day and neighborhood audiences are eating it up. The best part is that the
Attitude Factor is minor. Some very innovative productions are staged at **Third Wave Dance House**, which
concentrates on local choreographers and ethnic traditions (a natural for the Mission District). Like Footwork,
The Third Wave is very popular in the neighborhood, but
neither is so utterly "discovered" that you can't get in. A
few blocks away, experimental, mid-sized touring and
local companies perform at **Theater Artaud**. Can't
decide? Try them all. Most of these performances are very
well suited for limited budgets.

Grand opera... The **San Francisco Opera** is an experience,
not just for the thrilling performances by top international
stars, but also for the little risks the company takes just
because, after all, this is San Francisco. There were, for
example, the nuns (played by "supernumeraries," opera's
version of extras) who stripped totally naked and physical-
ly climbed the walls to illustrate their possession by the
devil, and an opera composed by jazz/pop vocalist Bobby
McFerrin with progressive novelist Ishmael Reed as the
librettist. Then there is the audience, half of whom are
dressed to the nines while the other half arrives in jeans
and sneakers. The grand old War Memorial Opera House
(which, as we've mentioned, is under repair until mid-
1997), is a wonderfully comfortable concert hall despite its
opulence; the boxes are fabulous, with elegant brocade
chairs and heavy velvet curtains. With or without its accus-
tomed abode, the opera season starts in September and
runs through mid-December, with a short summer season
as well. Tickets are not easy to come by, so plan in advance.
If you arrive without tickets, your only alternative may be
standing-room tickets, available for every performance for
$8—line up at the box office at 10:30 that morning and
hope they don't sell out before you get to the window.

Take me out to the ballgame... If you love sports, you
came to the right place. From April to October, there is
major-league baseball—the **San Francisco Giants** play at
3Com Park (formerly Candlestick Park), which can get
so cold at nights that the Giants used to give out a little
orange pin—a badge of courage called a *Croix de Candle-*

stick—to every fan who stayed until the end of an extra-inning night game. (The pin bore a motto that was Latin for "I came, I saw, I froze.") It's fine during the day, though, and wonderfully balmy throughout 49er football season. The **Oakland A's** play across the bay at the **Oakland Coliseum**, a sunny, warm, and much smaller ballpark (20,000 fewer seats, A's fans happily brag) with wide-open bleachers, old-fashioned manual scoreboard, fantastic food, and imported beers. Tickets to see either team have been plentiful since the strike that cancelled the 1994 World Series and made fans mad as hell. Come the end of summer, football teams start filling the stadiums—the **San Francisco 49ers** play on Sundays at Candlestick, and the **Oakland Raiders**, who have just returned to Oakland after a 13-year fiasco in Los Angeles, move into the Coliseum. With the Raiders' return, "improvements" will eventually add 10,000 seats and probably turn the Coliseum into just another bowl-style stadium. Bay Area football fans are often characterized as falling into two distinct molds—the wine-and-brie set at Candlestick and the Bud-and-burgers bunch at the Coliseum. Either way, tickets are hard to come by, but if you're willing to spend enough money, you can usually snag one from a ticket broker. Just about the time you get used to football, hockey and basketball start (October and November, respectively). The **San Jose Sharks**—whose logo of a shark devouring a hockey stick made their licensed hats and clothing into best-sellers before the team played its first game—skate at the **San Jose Arena**, about an hour south of San Francisco. The **Golden State Warriors** play at the Oakland Coliseum arena, at least for now. There is talk of a possible move, but nothing has been established yet. The newest pro sport in the Bay Area is roller hockey, played June through August; the **Oakland Skates** play at the Coliseum arena, and the **San Jose Rhinos** play at the San Jose Arena. (Frankly, we preferred Roller Derby.) Finally, if you like to play the ponies (we love to), you have two choices for a sunny day at the races: **Bay Meadows** in San Mateo or **Golden Gate Fields** near Berkeley. Bay Meadows seems to be preferred by San Franciscans, who are loathe to cross the Bay Bridge for any reason, but Golden Gate Fields is a real salt-of-the-earth racetrack.

The Index

Alcazar Theater. A variety of top-quality, if not exactly new, plays are produced here, often for long runs.... *Tel 415/ 441–4042. 650 Geary St., 19 or 38 MUNI bus.*

American Conservatory Theater (ACT). Until the earthquake damage to its home at the Geary Theater (415 Geary St.) is completely repaired—hopefully by mid-1996—ACT will continue to stage its productions at other theaters in the theater district, including the Stage Door (420 Mason St.), Marine's Memorial (609 Sutter St.), and the Orpheum (1192 Market St.). For information about the renowned repertory company's schedule, call the ACT administration office at the Geary Theater.... *Tel 415/ 834–3200.*

Bay Meadows. This is a beautiful place for thoroughbred horse racing, with picnic facilities and a playground for children.... *Tel 415/574–7223. 2600 S. Delaware St., San Mateo. Take CalTrain directly to Bay Meadows. To drive: Take Hwy. 101 South to the Hillsborough exit, head west, and follow the signs to the track. Season runs from late Aug through Jan. Post time 1:15, 6 on Fri.*

Beach Blanket Babylon. It wouldn't be San Francisco without this totally wacky musical revue—and the gigantic, ridiculous headdresses that made it famous—at Club Fugazi, a cozy cabaret in North Beach. It's been the goofiest show in town for more than two decades, and shows no signs of slowing down. Reserve well in advance, or purchase your tickets by telephone before you get to town.... *Tel 415/421–4222. Club Fugazi, 678 Green St.; 15, 30, or 45 MUNI bus. Shows Wed, Thur at 8, Fri, Sat at 7 & 10, Sun 3 & 7.*

Climate. This South of Market theater features monologues, plays, political satires, and performance art.... *Tel 415/ 626–9196. 252 Ninth St. (near Folsom); 10, 12, 20, 50, 60, 70, or 80 MUNI bus.*

Curran Theater. The Curran presents both warmed-over Broadway hits and Broadway-bound musicals.... *Tel 415/ 474–3800. 445 Geary St., 19 or 38 MUNI bus.*

Exit Theater. Closer to the mainstream than many of the neighborhood theaters, this small theater district house is gaining a national reputation for avant-garde "classics".... *Tel 415/673–3847. 156 Eddy St., Civic Center BART/MUNI Metro stop, 19 or 31 MUNI bus.*

Finocchio. The Queen Mother of drag clubs, crossing over to an audience of straights as well as gays. There are three shows a night—for a cover charge of less than $15—and you can often get in without reservations. But you must be at least 21 years old.... *Tel 415/982–9388; after 7pm 415/362–9913. 506 Broadway, 15 or 30 MUNI bus. Open Wed–Sat 8:30, 10 & 11:30.*

Footwork Dance Studio. Most dance buffs are really excited about this small Mission District studio.... *Tel 415/824–5044. 3221 22nd St., 24th St. BART stop.*

Geary Theater. The home of the American Conservatory Theater sustained heavy damage during the 1989 Loma Prieta earthquake, but is expected to open in 1996 with improved production facilities. The show schedule is uncertain. Call for specifics.... *Tel 415/834–3200. 415 Geary St., 5 MUNI bus.*

Golden Gate Fields. Across the bay in Albany (next to Berkeley), Golden Gate Fields offers thoroughbred horse racing and a view of the bay—but not at the same time: The track faces Interstate 80.... *Tel 510/526–3020. Season runs from late Jan through June. Take shuttle or cab from N. Berkeley BART station. AC Transit (Tel 800/559–4636) runs buses direct from Transbay Terminal. To reach the track by car, cross the Oakland–San Francisco Bay Bridge and take Interstate 80 east (toward Berkeley/Sacramento) to the Gilman St. exit; turn left to get to the track.*

Golden Gate Theater. This grand old theater offers Broadway touring shows and revivals.... *Tel 415/474–3800. 1 Taylor St. (near Sixth and Market Sts.); Powell St. BART/MUNI Metro stop; 6, 7, 8, 9, 21, or 66 MUNI bus.*

Intersection for the Arts. This Mission District institution, the oldest experimental arts center in the city, features plays, visual arts, dance performances, and readings.... *Tel 415/ 626–2787. 446 Valencia St., 16th St. BART/MUNI Metro stop, 26 MUNI bus.*

Josie's Juice Joint. Local gay performers wow an eclectic crowd at this Castro District cabaret. There's virtually no parking, so take public transportation. Reservations are recommended, but get there early, because there's always a line to fill in for last-minute no-shows.... *Tel 415/861–7933. 3583 16th St. (near Market), Castro St. MUNI Metro stop.*

Lorraine Hansberry Theater. Some of the most prominent African-American playwrights and performers are featured at this downtown theater. The emphasis is usually on new approaches or pieces with social significance.... *Tel 415/ 288–0320. 500 Sutter St. (at Powell); Powell-Mason cable car; 2, 3, 4, or 76 MUNI bus.*

Magic Theater. Works by Bay Area playwrights are the main attraction at this Fort Mason theater.... *Tel 415/441–8822. Building D, Fort Mason, Marina Blvd. at Buchanan St., 28 MUNI bus.*

Marine's Memorial Theater. Recently hosting productions of the homeless American Conservatory Theater, this theater also held the San Francisco run of Tony Kushner's *Angels in America*.... *Tel 415/771–6900. 609 Sutter St.; 2, 3, 4, or 76 MUNI bus.*

The Marsh. *The* place to see the latest avant-garde productions, it's hip, it's fun, it's good, and it's cheap (usually about $5).... *Tel 415/641–0235. 1062 Valencia St., 24th St. BART/MUNI Metro stop, 26 MUNI bus.*

Mission Cultural Center for Latino Arts. Latino artists from many different cultures are featured at this Mission District showcase.... *Tel 415/821–1155. 2868 Mission St., 24th St. BART stop.*

SAN FRANCISCO | ENTERTAINMENT

Oakland Ballet. This lively young company is made up of brilliant young dancers from several countries. Their performance hall, the landmark art-deco Paramount Theater, is breathtaking.... *Tel 510/465–6400. 2025 Broadway, Oakland, 19th St. BART stop (3 stops from San Francisco's Embarcadero station).*

Oakland Coliseum. The Oakland A's and, once again, the Oakland Raiders play across the bay here.... *For tickets to A's games, call BASS (tel 510/762–BASS, 800/225–BASS outside California); for Raiders tickets, light a candle, do some voodoo, take all your money out of savings, and call a ticket broker. Coliseum BART stop.*

Orpheum Theater. Fans of big Broadway musicals love this restored Spanish baroque theater, in the theater district.... *Tel 415/474–3800. 1192 Market St., Civic Center BART/ MUNI Metro stop.*

Phoenix Theater. A progressive South of Market theater, the Phoenix presents works by local as well as world-famous playwrights. Check reviews in the alternative weekly newspapers (the *Bay Guardian* and *SF Weekly*) to get an idea of the merits of a particular production before you buy tickets.... *Tel 415/621–4423. 301 Eighth St., 19 or 26 MUNI bus.*

San Francisco Ballet. The San Francisco Ballet is among the city's cultural treasures. The ticket situation is a bit unpredictable because the company performs in so many different locations while the opera house is being repaired (until mid-1997), so it's best to call far in advance to determine your strategy. Ordinarily, there are some balcony seats available for most performances, even without advance purchase.... *Tel 415/703–9400.*

San Francisco Opera. San Franciscans have had an unconditional love affair with opera since the gold rush, so most of them don't mind hopping around to substitute locations while the opera house is being repaired (until mid-1997). You can go in a tuxedo or in blue jeans—nobody cares. The season runs from September to mid-December, plus a short summer season. Get tickets far in advance.... *Tel 415/864–3330. The box office is still at the opera house, 301 Van Ness Ave., Civic Center BART/MUNI Metro stop.*

San Jose Arena. Well, the Sharks haven't exactly brought home a Stanley Cup yet, but their fans don't care. They packed the arena just to watch them on television when they were in the playoffs. You probably will want to drive to the arena, which is about an hour south of San Francisco.... *For tickets call BASS (tel 510/762–BASS, 800/225–BASS outside CA); for other information, call the arena (tel 408/287–4275). Take CalTrain from Fourth St. & Townsend St. depot to 65 Cahill station; free shuttle from station to arena. To drive: Take Hwy. 101 S. to Guadalupe Pkwy.; exit at Julian St.; take right. Follow Julian St. to Burns Ave. S., then turn left and follow signs to stadium. Free shuttle from parking lot.*

Stage Door Theater. When the temporarily dispossessed ACT goes back to its own home at the Geary Theater in 1996, the Stage Door will most likely go back to specializing in comedies, with local casts.... *Tel 415/749–2228. 420 Mason St. Powell St., BART/MUNI Metro stop.*

Theater Artaud. Dance, theater, or multimedia productions appear at this well-run Mission District experimental theater.... *Tel 415/621–7797. 460 Florida St. (near 16th St.), 16th St. BART/MUNI Metro stop, 12 or 33 MUNI bus.*

Theater Rhinoceros. This Mission District company focuses strictly on contemporary gay and lesbian issues.... *Tel 415/861–5079. 2926 16th St., 16th St. BART/MUNI Metro stop.*

Third Wave Dance House. The ethnic diversity of the Mission District makes it an ideal spot for this dance studio, which showcases local choreographers and ethnic traditions.... *Tel 415/282–4020. 3316 24th St., 24th St. BART stop.*

3Com Park. Home to the Giants for baseball and the 49ers for football, it's pretty cold on summer nights—you'll need a down parka—but it's fine during the day, and wonderfully balmy throughout football season.... *For tickets, call BASS (tel 510/762–BASS, 800/225–BASS outside CA) or a ticket broker. Express bus service is available through MUNI (tel 415/673–MUNI). If you must drive (we don't recommend it), take Hwy. 101 S. to the stadium exit.*

SAN FRANCISCO | ENTERTAINMENT

hotlines & other basics

Airports... Two major airports serve the city—**San Francisco International Airport (SFO)** *(tel 415/761–0800)* and **Oakland International Airport (OAK)** *(tel 510/577–4000)*. Most travelers will use SFO, which is served by 46 major airlines and is located 15 miles south of downtown San Francisco (Highway 101 or 280*)*. Fares to either airport are usually identical, so if a flight to SFO is sold out, there may still be available seats on flights to the lesser-known stepsister, OAK, situated within a few minutes of the Coliseum BART stop (four stops from San Francisco's Financial District).

Airport transportation to the city... Super-cheap public transport is available from the airport to downtown via **SamTrans** *(tel 800/660–4287)*; from the International terminal on the upper level or the United Airlines terminal, catch the 7F express bus for just $1 (you are allowed only one carry-on bag) or the 7B bus for $2 (bring as much baggage as you like). The 7F express takes about 30 minutes; the 7B takes about an hour. A taxi ride to the city center costs about $30 including tip and usually takes about 20–30 minutes, depending on traffic. Shuttle vans that carry up to six passengers offer door-to-door service for around $10 and take 20–30 minutes; they're easy to catch at the airport, but reservations are recommended for your return trip from the city to the airport. Some of the most popular shuttles are **Super Shuttle** *(tel 415/558–8500)*; **American Airporter** *(tel 415/546–6689)*; **Bay Shuttle** *(tel 415/564–3400)*; and **Quake City Shuttle** *(tel 415/255–4899)*. The **SFO Airporter** *(tel 415/673–2432)* is an express bus that offers door-to-door service to most major hotels for $9 ($15 round-trip); no reservations are required.

All-night pharmacies... Got that itchy, sneezy, whatever-else-it-is, can't-sleep thing happening? Worse yet, did you just drop your last estrogen pill down the drain? Not to worry. **Walgreens 24-Hour Prescription Service** *(tel 415/861–3136, 498 Castro St.; tel 415/931–6417, 3201 Divisadero St.)* is there to help you.

Babysitters... First ask the concierge if your hotel offers child care service. Otherwise, try these agencies (all members of the San Francisco Convention and Visitors Bureau): **American Childcare Service** *(tel 415/285–2300)*, private in-room service at your hotel, excursions arranged for children 12 and older, fully licensed, bonded, and insured; **Starr Belly Child Care Services** *(tel 415/642–1950; pager tel 415/207–2558)*, 24-hour on-call child care at your hotel, seven days a week, all providers trained in CPR, licensed, bonded, insured.

BART... Bay Area Rapid Transit—BART—is essentially a commuter railway that links neighboring communities with San Francisco. There are eight stations in the city itself. Fares depend on the distance of the ride, but for a special $2.60 excursion fare, you can ride the entire system as far as you want, any direction you want, as long as you exit the system at the exact same station you entered. All tickets are dispensed from machines at the stations.

Buses... San Francisco Municipal Railway (MUNI) buses are marked on the front with the number of the line and the destination. Fare is $1 for adults, 35¢ for children and seniors. To find out which bus to take to get where you want to go, call 415/673–MUNI. Official MUNI route maps are available throughout the city at newsstands and many other stores for $2.

Cable cars... There are three cable car routes—the Powell-Hyde line begins at Powell and Market streets and ends at Victorian Park near the Maritime Museum and Aquatic Park; the Powell-Mason line also begins at Powell and Market, but it ends at Bay and Taylor streets near Fisherman's Wharf; the California Street line starts at California and Market streets, and ends at Van Ness Avenue. Fare is $2.

Car rentals... Suit yourself—pick up a tiny little bread box on wheels from Enterprise Rent-A-Car at the airport for less than $20 a day, with unlimited free mileage; or cruise through your vacation in a Ferrari 348 Spyder convertible from Sunbelt Sports Cars for $850 a day and $2 a mile. Or settle for something in between—economy cars with unlimited mileage tend to rent for around $30–$40 a day, while a zippy convertible like a Mazda Miata will set you back about $80 a day. Here are several San Francisco rental companies (most have more than one location): **A-One Rent-A-Car** *(tel 415/771–3977, 434 O'Farrell St.)*; **Alamo Rent-A-Car** *(tel 415/882–9440, 687 Folsom St.)*; **Avis Rent-A-Car** *(tel 800/331–1212 or 415/885–5011, 675 Post St.)*; **Bay Area Rentals, Cars, Trucks and Vans** *(tel 415/621–8989, 229 Seventh St.)*; **Budget Rent-A-Car** *(tel. 800/527–0700 or 415/875–6850, 321 Mason St.)*; **California Compacts Rent-A-Car** *(tel 800/954–7368 or 415/871–4421, 245 S. Airport Blvd.)*; **Dollar Rent-A-Car** *(tel 800/800–4000 or 415/244–4130, San Francisco International Airport)*; **Enterprise Rent-A-Car** *(tel 800/325–8007 or 415/441–3369, 1133 Van Ness Ave.)*; **Hertz Rent-A-Car** *(tel 800/654–3131 or 415/771–2200, ext. 518, 433 Mason St.)*; **Reliable Rent-A-Car** *(tel 415/928–4414, 349 Mason St.)*; **Sunbelt Sports Cars** *(tel 415/771–9191, 320 O'Farrell St.)*; **Thrifty Car Rental** *(tel 800/367–2277 or 415/788–8111, 520 Mason St.)*.

Cash advances, check cashing, and ATM cards... If you aren't having any luck at Automated Teller Machines and want to ask a human teller for a cash advance against your credit card, try calling **Bank of America** *(tel 415/622–3546)* or **First Interstate Bank** *(tel 415/765–4511)*. **American Express** has four offices with full financial services including personal check cashing: Downtown *(tel 415/981–5533, 237 Post St.)*; Financial District *(tel 415/788–4367, 295 California St., or tel 415/512–8250, 455 Market St.)*; and Fisherman's Wharf *(tel 415/788–3025, 2500 Mason St.)*. To find out the nearest ATM that will accept your **Cirrus Network** card, call 800/424–7787; for **Plus System**, call 800/843–7587.

Chauffeurs... Can't resist a man in uniform? Sometimes you've just got to lounge in the back of a long, black limousine with a chauffeur at the wheel. If the need arises while you're in San Francisco, call **Drivers Exclusive** *(tel 800/288–6261)* for 24-hour service, or **We Drive U, Inc.** *(tel 800/773–7483 or 415/579–5800)*. The company names may be a bit tacky, but what do you want for borrowed luxury?

Climate... Everybody knows that Mark Twain supposedly said the coldest winter he ever spent was summer in San Francisco. It's true that July can be downright chilly, but the truth is that the city is rarely—if ever—what a New England Yankee would call cold, or what a New Orleans belle would call hot. In fact, the weather is predictably unpredictable. A sunny morning can turn into a chilly afternoon, just as a thick morning fog often gives way to a gorgeous sun-drenched day. The standard pitch is that temperatures don't drop below 40°F (5°C) or rise above 70°F (21°C), but don't believe it. Every year there are many 80° days that are sworn to be the exception; there's just no predicting when they might occur. In general, September and October are the warmest months, and May through September are the driest. No matter when you visit, be sure to dress in layers. Whatever you expect the weather to be, it will almost certainly be otherwise—at least part of the time.

Concierges... For personalized travel planning, shopping excursions, entertainment, ticket purchasing, or anything else you'd like someone else to handle for you, enlist your own private concierge—after you arrive or while you're still planning your vacation. Try **Ideas Unlimited/ Unlimited Ideas** *(tel 800/900–4884 or 415/668–7089)* or **Instead of You, Inc.** *(tel 415/567–1985)*.

Convention center... The elegant—and extremely popular—**Moscone Center** *(tel 415/974–4000, 747 Howard St.)* was named in memory of San Francisco's well-liked mayor who was slain—along with the city's first openly gay elected official, Harvey Milk—by a man who convinced a jury he could not be held responsible because he had eaten too many Twinkies and it made him insane. It was a bitter tragedy for San Franciscans, but the Moscone Center is a fitting tribute in its unparalleled success—it is one of the most popular convention sites in the country, despite all the bad press about the city's earthquakes and frigid summer weather.

Dentists... The San Francisco Convention and Visitors Bureau recommends **San Francisco Dental Office** *(tel 415/777–5115, 132 The Embarcadero, between Mission* *and Howard Sts.; non-emergency hours: Mon and Fri 8–4:30; Tue–Thur 10:30–7; closed Sat and Sun)* for 24-hour emergency service.

Doctors... If you have a serious emergency, you should go directly to a hospital emergency room, but for other medical needs, try **Traveler Medical Group** *(tel 415/981–1102)*, a 24-hour, multilingual medical staff of internal medicine physicians who will make "house calls" to your hotel. No appointments are necessary at **Physician Access Medical Center** *(tel 415/397–2881, 26 California St.)*. Same-day appointments can be made at **Downtown Medical** *(tel 415/362–7177, 450 Sutter St.)*, whose doctors are familiar with all travel-related medical conditions.

Driving around... Lots of people drive in the city, and as a rule they're much more courteous than in New York or Paris or Rome. The city is compact, but can be a bit confusing, so if you're going to drive be sure to get a map. Your driver's license from any other state (and most Western nations) is valid in California for a year, but there are a few things you should know about local safety precautions and laws. Remember, San Francisco is a city of hills (43, to be exact), and since you probably don't want your car to roll down one while you're not in it, there's only one sure bet: **Curb your wheels**. Turn the front tires toward the street when you're parked facing uphill, and toward the curb when you're parked facing downhill. This is not just a good idea, it's the law in San Francisco. **Know what the curb colors mean: Red** means no stopping or parking; **yellow** means all commercial vehicles may stop for up to a half-hour; **yellow-and-black** means only commercial trucks may stop for up to a half-hour; **green-yellow-and-black** is a taxi zone; **blue** is for cars with California disabled placards; **green** means all vehicles may stop for up to 10 minutes; **white** means all vehicles are limited to a 5-minute stop while the adjacent business is still open. **Towaway zones**: Nobody loves to tow cars more than San Francisco's finest. It's big money for the city (almost 30% of all parking tickets issued in the state are issued in San Francisco), and the odds are always against you if you park illegally. You'll shell out a minimum of $20 for the most minor parking violation, plus another $100 for towing, plus storage fees. If you park in a disabled zone, the violation alone will cost $250–275, not to mention the towing fees and hassle of getting the car back.

Emergencies... Like anywhere else, **call 911**, but don't be surprised if you get put on hold. It's always best to try to stay out of dangerous areas and situations to begin with. Other emergency/information numbers: **Ambulance** *(tel 415/931–3900)*; **Poison Control Center** *(tel 415/476–6600)*; **Suicide Prevention** *(tel 415/221–1424)*; **Traveler's Aid** *(tel 415/255–2252)*.

Events hotline... Call the **Visitor Information Center** 24 hours a day for a recorded message listing San Francisco's events and activities—in five different languages: English *(tel 415/391–2001)*; French *(tel 415/391–2001)*; Spanish *(tel 415/391–2122)*; Japanese *(tel 415/391–2101)*; German *(tel 415/391–2004)*.

Ferries... Several ferries connect San Francisco with communities around the bay. Be sure to call for schedule information. The **Blue & Gold Fleet** *(tel 415/705–5444)* provides daily round-trip service from the Ferry Building and Pier 39 to Oakland, Alameda, and Vallejo. Fare to Oakland or Alameda is $3.50, $1.50 for children, $2.50 for seniors; to Vallejo, $7.50, $4 for children, $6 for seniors. Package fare to Marine World/Africa USA (Vallejo), including round-trip ferry, bus shuttle, and park admission is $36, $20.50 for children 5–12 (under 5 free), $30 for seniors. **Golden Gate Ferries** *(tel 415/332–6600, TDD 415/257–4554)* serve Sausalito and Larkspur from the Ferry Building. Fare is $4.25, $3.20 for children, $2.10 for seniors; weekdays to Larkspur, $2.50, $1.90 for children, $1.25 for seniors. **Harbor Maritime Ferry** *(tel 415/769–5500)* goes to Harbor Bay Island in Alameda from the Ferry Building. Fare is $4, $2 for children, $3 for seniors. The **Red & White Fleet** *(tel 800/229–2784, 415/546–2700)* serves Sausalito, Tiburon, Angel Island, and Alcatraz. Fare to Angel Island or Alcatraz (Alcatraz includes audiocassette rental) is $9, $4.50 for children, $8 for seniors; to Sausalito/Tiburon, $5.50, $2.74 for children, $5.50 for seniors.

Festivals and special events... From the crowning of Japantown's Cherry Blossom Queen and the Gay Pride Parade of self-styled queens to Chinese New Year and *Dia de los Muertos* (Day of the Dead), San Francisco's extraordinary diversity is celebrated year-round in one festival after another. A complete monthly listing is published in the ***Bay City Guide***, free at information racks in the airports and at most hotels. Here is a brief sample of some of the major events:

January: **International Boat Show** *(tel 415/469–6065)*, Moscone Center; nine days. **Tet Festival** *(tel 415/885–2743)*, Vietnamese New Year, held at Larkin and O'Farrell streets.

February: **Chinese New Year** *(tel 415/982–3000)* can be in late January or early February, depending on the lunar calendar; climaxes with giant parade down Chinatown's Grant Avenue. **Russian Festival** *(tel 415/921–76.31)*, three-day celebration around Sutter and Divisadero streets.

March: **St. Patrick's Day Parade** *(tel 415/391–2000)* starts at Market and 2nd streets and goes past City Hall.

April: **International Film Festival**, one of the most popular film festivals in America *(schedule information tel 415/932–FILM; tickets tel 415/931–FILM; Kabuki 8 Cinemas, Fillmore and Post Sts.)*. **Cherry Blossom Festival** *(tel 415/563–2313)*, held in Japantown and Golden Gate Park's Japanese Tea Garden, traditional arts, music, theater, and food booths.

May: **Bay to Breakers** *(tel 415/777–7771)*, a kooky-costume foot race across town from the Embarcadero (on the bay) to the ocean. **Black and White Ball** *(tel 415/431–5400)*, flashy fundraiser held in odd-numbered years to benefit the San Francisco Symphony; Civic Center is closed off for this all-night party-hop that attracts the city's biggest celebrities and those who are willing to pay $150 apiece to rub shoulders with them. **Carnaval** *(tel 415/826–1401)*, a week-long fiesta in the Mission District, leading up to a parade that ends up on 14th Street (near Harrison Street) with a huge samba party. **Cinco de Mayo** *(tel 415/826–1401)*, two-day fiesta; parade runs from 24th and Mission streets to Civic Center Plaza.

June: **Lesbian and Gay Freedom Day Parade** *(tel 415/864–3733)*, a celebration of gay pride with floats and groups from the Sisters of Perpetual Indulgence to Dykes on Bikes. **Stern Grove Midsummer Music Festival** *(tel 415/252–6252)*, a series of free 2pm Sunday concerts held at 19th Avenue and Sloat Boulevard, featuring local performers, from the opera and symphony to jazz and ballet.

July: **San Francisco Marathon** *(tel 415/391–2123)*, mid-month. **Jewish Film Festival** *(tel 510/548–0556 held at Castro Theater and the U.C. Theater, Berkeley)*, the world's largest Jewish film festival; two weeks.

August: **San Francisco Shakespeare Festival** *(tel 415/666–2221)*, free performances in Golden Gate Park run through October.

SAN FRANCISCO | HOTLINES & OTHER BASICS

September: **Blues Festival** *(schedule tel 415/826–6837; tickets tel 415/835–3849)*, outdoors at Fort Mason; two days. **San Francisco Fair** *(tel 415/391–2000)*, sophisticated county fair (the city and county are one and the same) in Fort Mason, with vintage wines and California cuisine instead of corn dogs and carnival rides. **Opera in the Park** *(tel 415/861–4008)*, free opera in Golden Gate Park kicks off the San Francisco Opera's fall season.

November: ***Dia de los Muertos* (Day of the Dead)** *(tel 415/826–8009)*, a Mexican fiesta and parade in the Mission District designed to honor the dead and to be so much fun it entices their spirits to return for the party. ***The Nutcracker*** *(tel 415/776–1999, San Francisco Ballet box office)* and **Sing-It-Yourself Messiah** *(tel 415/431–5400, Louise M. Davies Symphony Hall box office)* are extremely popular holiday traditions that are sold out far in advance.

Gay and lesbian resources... The lesbian and gay communities in the Bay Area are very well organized, and have countless resources at their disposal. The *San Francisco Sentinel* (free, weekly) and the *Bay Area Reporter* (free, weekly) are the best-known gay publications with complete listings of organizations and events; the latest addition is *On-Q* (free, every two weeks). All are distributed at bars, bookstores, cafes, and stores around the city. The **Gay/Lesbian/Bisexual/Transgendered Switchboard** *(tel 510/841–6224)* is in Berkeley. **Electric City Network** is a gay television show on cable channel 53, Fri 10:30pm. **Lavender Lounge** is a gay variety show, Tue 10pm, cable channel 47. **Fruit Punch** is a long-running gay radio show (since 1973), Wed 7pm, KPFA 94.1 FM and KPFB 89.3 FM; **Hibernia Beach** is a gay radio talk show, Sun 7am, KITS 105.3 FM. The **Gay and Lesbian Historical Society** *(tel 415/626–0890, archive open weekends 2–5 by appointment)* collects and preserves historically significant materials. The **Deaf Gay and Lesbian Center** *(tel 415/266–9944 TDD or 800/735–2922 for Cal Relay voice callers)* provides news and updates on community events. **Dial-A-Dyke** *(tel 415/241–1564)* is a free 24-hour bulletin board for lesbians. The **Names Project** *(tel 415/882–5500)* AIDS memorial quilt consists of more than 26,000 panels.

Liquor laws... Packaged alcoholic beverages are sold at liquor, grocery, and some drug stores 6am–2pm daily. Most bars and restaurants are licensed to sell all alcoholic beverages during those same hours, but some have only beer-and-wine licenses. No alcohol may be sold 2am–6am. Legal drinking age is 21; proof of age is required.

MUNI Metro streetcars... There are five streetcar lines, which operate underground downtown and on the streets in the neighborhoods. Fares are the same as for buses—$1 adults, 35¢ for children and senior citizens.

Newspapers... There are more than 30 foreign language publications in the Bay Area, not to mention the sex tabloids, business and professional journals, entertainment publications, and dozens of others. The two major English-language dailies are the ***Chronicle*** and the ***Examiner***, which combine for a single paper on Sunday. Local weekly newspapers, such as the ***Bay Guardian***, ***SF Weekly***, and the ***Sentinel*** are free, and have better entertainment listings than the dailies.

Parking garages... You can spend a fortune to leave your car for a half-hour, or a pittance to park it overnight, depending upon the garage. City-run garages tend to be cheaper than those that are privately owned, but you should call in advance to check rates and availability, if possible. The best deals in town are the **Sutter-Stockton and Ellis-O'Farrell garages**, where you can leave your car overnight for just $3. A partial list of garages: **Chinatown** *(tel 415/956–8106, 433 Kearny St.; tel 415/982–6353, 733 Kearny St.)*; **Civic Center** *(tel 415/863–3187, 355 McAllister St.; tel 415/626–4484, 370 Grove St.)*; **Downtown** *(tel 415/982–8522, 833 Mission St.; tel 415/ 771–1400 ask for garage, Mason and Ellis Sts.; tel 415/986– 4800, Ellis-O'Farrell, 123 O'Farrell St.; tel 415/982–8370, Sutter-Stockton; tel 415/397–0631, 333 Post St.)*; **Embarcadero Center** *(tel 415/433–4722, 250 Clay St.; tel 415/ 398–1878, Embarcadero Center Garage)*; **Fisherman's Wharf** *(tel 415/673–5197, 665 Beach St. at Hyde St.)*; **Japan Center** *(tel 415/567–4573, 1660 Geary Blvd.)*; **Mission District** *(tel 415/567–7357, 90 Bartlett St., near 21st St.)*; **Moscone Center/South of Market** *(tel 415/ 777–2782, 255 3rd St.; tel 415/543–4533, Museum Center Parc, 3rd and Folsom Sts.)*; **North Beach** *(tel 415/558– 9147, 766 Vallejo St.)*; **Union Street** *(tel 415/563–9820, 1910 Laguna St.; tel 415/495–3772, 2055 Lombard St.)*; **Van Ness** *(tel 415/567–9147, 1230 Polk St.)*.

Phone facts... The area code for San Francisco is 415. To call the East Bay (Berkeley, Oakland, or anywhere else in Alameda or Contra Costa County), dial 1, then area code 510, then the seven-digit telephone number. Local calls are free on private phones, 20¢ in a pay phone. For directory assistance, dial 411. **TDD users**: For operator assistance, TDD users call 800/855–1155. California Relay Service relays calls between a TDD caller and any other phone in the United States and allows people without TDD to call TDD users. It is a free, 24-hour service, 365 days a year. All calls placed through California Relay are billed at discounted Sprint rates. To use the service, call 800/735–2929 if you have a TDD, or 800/735–2922 if you don't have a TDD.

Taxis... It's fairly easy to hail a cab on major thoroughfares, especially in tourist areas, but if you are on a tight schedule, it's best to phone in advance for door-to-door service (the wait is usually 5–15 minutes during the day, occasionally up to a half-hour during rush hour or on busy weekend nights). There are more than 40 taxi companies listed in the Yellow Pages, but the most commonly used are: **Yellow Cab** *(tel 415/626–2345)*, **City Cab** *(tel 415/468–7200)*, **De Soto** *(tel 415/673–1414)*, **Luxor** *(tel 415/282–4141)*, and **Veteran's** *(tel 415/552–1300)*. The fare is the same in every cab (regulated by the city): $1.70 when the meter is turned on plus $.30 for every $1/6$ mile (about 2 blocks) thereafter. Since the city is no more than 7 miles in any given direction, most cab rides are around $5–7 plus tip (15% is customary).

Time... For the correct time, call 767–8900 from either the 415 or 510 area codes.

Tipping... Gratuities are not included in restaurant or bar checks. Most guides suggest 15% of the total amount as a decent tip, but 20% has become more commonly accepted at restaurants. Taxi drivers should be tipped around 15%; skycaps and bellpersons should get at least $1 per bag each time they carry it.

Visitor information center... The **San Francisco Visitor Information Center** *(tel 415/391–2000; open 9–5:30, Sat until 3, Sun 10–2)* is located at Benjamin Swig Pavilion on the lower level of Hallidie Plaza at Market and Powell streets. The center's neighborhood-walking-tour leaflets are really unbeatable. When you arrive, it's definitely worth a stop here to help plan your adventures.

FROMMER'S COMPLETE TRAVEL GUIDES

*(Comprehensive guides to sightseeing, dining and accommodations,
with selections in all price ranges—from deluxe to budget)*

Acapulco/Ixtapa/Taxco,		Italy '96 (avail. 11/95)	C183
2nd Ed.	C157	Jamaica/Barbados, 2nd Ed.	C149
Alaska '94-'95	C131	Japan '94-'95	C144
Arizona '95	C166	Maui, 1st Ed.	C153
Australia '94-'95	C147	Nepal, 3rd Ed. (avail. 11/95)	C184
Austria, 6th Ed.	C162	New England '95	C165
Bahamas '96 (avail. 8/95)	C172	New Mexico, 3rd Ed.	C167
Belgium/Holland/Luxembourg,		New York State, 4th Ed.	C133
4th Ed.	C170	Northwest, 5th Ed.	C140
Bermuda '96 (avail. 8/95)	C174	Portugal '94-'95	C141
California '95	C164	Puerto Rico '95-'96	C151
Canada '94-'95	C145	Puerto Vallarta/Manzanillo/	
Caribbean '96 (avail. 9/95)	C173	Guadalajara, 2nd Ed.	C135
Carolinas/Georgia, 2nd Ed.	C128	Scandinavia, 16th Ed.	C169
Colorado '96 (avail. 11/95)	C179	Scotland '94-'95	C146
Costa Rica, 1st Ed.	C161	South Pacific '94-'95	C138
Cruises '95-'96	C150	Spain, 16th Ed.	C163
Delaware/Maryland '94-'95	C136	Switzerland, 7th Ed.	
England '96 (avail. 10/95)	C180	(avail. 9/95)	C177
Florida '96 (avail. 9/95)	C181	Thailand, 2nd Ed.	C154
France '96 (avail. 11/95)	C182	U.S.A., 4th Ed.	C156
Germany '96 (avail. 9/95)	C176	Virgin Islands, 3rd Ed.	
Honolulu/Waikiki/Oahu,		(avail. 8/95)	C175
4th Ed. (avail. 10/95)	C178	Virginia '94-'95	C142
Ireland, 1st Ed.	C168	Yucatán '95-'96	C155

FROMMER'S $-A-DAY GUIDES

(Dream Vacations at Down-to-Earth Prices)

Australia on $45 '95-'96	D122	Ireland on $45 '94-'95	D118
Berlin from $50, 3rd Ed.		Israel on $45, 15th Ed.	D130
(avail. 10/95)	D137	London from $55 '96	
Caribbean from $60, 1st Ed.		(avail. 11/95)	D136
(avail. 9/95)	D133	Madrid on $50 '94-'95	D119
Costa Rica/Guatemala/Belize		Mexico from $35 '96	
on $35, 3rd Ed.	D126	(avail. 10/95)	D135
Eastern Europe on $30,		New York on $70 '94-'95	D121
5th Ed.	D129	New Zealand from $45,	
England from $50 '96		6th Ed.	D132
(avail. 11/95)	D138	Paris on $45 '94-'95	D117
Europe from $50 '96		South America on $40,	
(avail. 10/95)	D139	16th Ed.	D123
Greece from $45, 6th Ed.	D131	Washington, D.C. on	
Hawaii from $60 '96		$50 '94-'95	D120
(avail. 9/95)	D134		

FROMMER'S SPECIAL-INTEREST TITLES

FROMMER'S BEST BEACH VACATIONS

(The top places to sun, stroll, shop, stay, play, party, and swim—with each beach rated for beauty, swimming, sand, and amenities)

FROMMER'S BED & BREAKFAST GUIDES

(Selective guides with four-color photos and full descriptions of the best inns in each region)

FROMMER'S IRREVERENT GUIDES

(Wickedly honest guides for sophisticated travelers and those who want to be)

FROMMER'S DRIVING TOURS

(Four-color photos and detailed maps outlining spectacular scenic driving routes)

FROMMER'S BORN TO SHOP

(The ultimate travel guides for discriminating shoppers—from cut-rate to couture)

irreverent notes

irreverent notes

irreverent notes

irreverent notes

irreverent notes